Beginning Java Game Development with LibGDX

Lee Stemkoski

Lee Stemkoski

Apress®

Beginning Java Game Development with LibGDX

ISBN-13 (pbk): 978-1-4842-1501-2

ISBN-13 (electronic): 978-1-4842-1500-5

Trademarked names, logos, and images may appear in this book. Rather than use a trademark symbol with every occurrence of a trademarked name, logo, or image we use the names, logos, and images only in an editorial fashion and to the benefit of the trademark owner, with no intention of infringement of the trademark.

The use in this publication of trade names, trademarks, service marks, and similar terms, even if they are not identified as such, is not to be taken as an expression of opinion as to whether or not they are subject to proprietary rights.

While the advice and information in this book are believed to be true and accurate at the date of publication, neither the authors nor the editors nor the publisher can accept any legal responsibility for any errors or omissions that may be made. The publisher makes no warranty, express or implied, with respect to the material contained herein.

Managing Director: Welmoed Spahr
Lead Editor: Ben Renow-Clarke
Technical Reviewer: Garry Patchett
Editorial Board: Steve Anglin, Pramila Balan, Louise Corrigan, Jonathan Gennick, Robert Hutchinson,
    Celestin Suresh John, Michelle Lowman, James Markham, Susan McDermott, Matthew Moodie,
    Jeffrey Pepper, Douglas Pundick, Ben Renow-Clarke, Gwenan Spearing
Coordinating Editor: Mark Powers
Copy Editor: Sharon Wilkey
Compositor: SPi Global
Indexer: SPi Global
Artist: SPi Global

Distributed to the book trade worldwide by Springer Science+Business Media New York, 233 Spring Street, 6th Floor, New York, NY 10013. Phone 1-800-SPRINGER, fax (201) 348-4505, e-mail orders-ny@springer-sbm.com, or visit www.springeronline.com. Apress Media, LLC is a California LLC and the sole member (owner) is Springer Science + Business Media Finance Inc (SSBM Finance Inc). SSBM Finance Inc is a Delaware corporation.

For information on translations, please e-mail rights@apress.com, or visit www.apress.com.

Apress and friends of ED books may be purchased in bulk for academic, corporate, or promotional use. eBook versions and licenses are also available for most titles. For more information, reference our Special Bulk Sales–eBook Licensing web page at www.apress.com/bulk-sales.

Any source code or other supplementary materials referenced by the author in this text is available to readers at www.apress.com/9781484215012. For detailed information about how to locate your book's source code, go to www.apress.com/source-code/. Readers can also access source code at SpringerLink in the Supplementary Material section for each chapter.

Contents at a Glance

Contents

About the Author

Lee Stemkoski is a professor of computer science and mathematics. He has been teaching for ten years, with a focus on video game programming and related courses for the past five years. He has authored many scholarly articles as well as game development tutorials.

About the Technical Reviewer

Garry Patchett has worked in IT and engineering for more than 20 years designing products, creating software, and administering and documenting systems. With a Masters Degree in Project Management he is a dedicated 'systems nerd' whose interests vary from the technological to the philosophical. Garry is currently working freelance and is involved in various Open Source projects.

Acknowledgments

I would like to acknowledge the amazing editorial and support staff at Apress, for without their talent and dedication, this book you are reading would not exist. In particular, I'd like to thank Ben Renow-Clarke, for believing in this book from the very beginning, and Mark Powers, for his constant words of support and encouragement.

I'd also like to thank the technical reviewer, Garry Patchett, for his attention to both the programming and the pedagogical aspects of this book. From the very beginning, he intuitively understood who the target audience was and the level of detail and guidance they needed. Garry's many insightful comments and suggestions greatly improved the clarity of this book, and I am grateful for all the time and energy he put into helping to make this book the best that it could be.

Finally, a special thanks to my students, past and present, for their continuous and infectious enthusiasm. Your drive and devotion to game development is what inspired me to write this book.

Introduction

Welcome to Beginning Game Development with LibGDX!

In this book, you'll learn how to program games in Java using the LibGDX game development framework. The LibGDX libraries are both powerful and easy to use, and they will enable you to create a great variety of games quickly and efficiently. LibGDX is free and open-source, can be used to make 2D and 3D games, and integrates easily with third-party libraries to support additional features. Applications created in LibGDX are truly cross-platform; supported systems include Windows, Mac OS X, Linux, Android, iOS, and HTML5/WebGL.

I have taught courses in Java programming and video game development for many years, and I've often struggled to find game programming books that I can recommend to my students without reservation, which lead me to write this book you are currently reading. In particular, you will find that this book contains the following unique combination of features, chosen with the aspiring game developer (that's you!) in mind:

- This book recommends and explains how to use a simple Java development environment so that you can move on to programming games more quickly.

- By using the LibGDX framework, you won't have to "reinvent the wheel" for common programming tasks such as rendering graphics and playing audio. (An explanation of how to write such code from scratch could easily require fifty or more additional pages of reading.) LibGDX streamlines the development process and allows you to focus on game mechanics and design.

- This book contains *many* examples of video games that can be developed with LibGDX. The first few example projects will introduce you to the basic features provided by the framework; these starter projects will be extended in the chapters that follow to illustrate how to add visual polish and advanced functionality. Later projects will focus on implementing game mechanics from a variety of genres: shoot-'em-ups, infinite side scrollers, drag-and-drop games, platform games, adventure games with a top-down perspective, and 2.5D games. I believe that working through many examples is fundamental in the learning process; you will observe programming patterns common to many games, you will see the benefits of writing reusable code in practice, you will have the opportunity to compare and contrast code from different projects, and you will gain experience by implementing additional features on your own.

- At the beginning of this book, I am only assuming that you have a basic familiarity with Java programming. (For more details about what background knowledge you need, please consult the appendix.) Throughout the first few chapters of this book, advanced programming concepts will be introduced and explained as they arise naturally and are needed in the context of game programming. By the time you reach the end of this book, you will have learned about many advanced Java programming topics that are also useful for software development in general.

Thank you for allowing me to be your guide as you begin your journey as a game programmer. I hope that you find this book both informative and enjoyable, and that it enables and inspires you to create your own video games to share with the world.

CHAPTER 1

■ ■ ■

Getting Started with Java and LibGDX

This chapter explains how to set up a Java development environment and configure it to run with the LibGDX game development framework. You'll see a simple example of a "Hello, World!" program, and explore it in enough detail to understand the different parts. Finally, you'll learn some of the advantages to be gained by working with the LibGDX library.

Choosing a Development Environment

Before diving into Java programming, you need to set up an integrated development environment (IDE): the software you will use for writing, debugging, and compiling code. There are many editors for writing your Java programs, each customized for different skill levels. BlueJ (www.bluej.org) and DrJava (www.drjava.org) are designed for beginners and educational use, and are frequently used in introductory programming courses in schools and colleges. IntelliJ IDEA (www.jetbrains.com/idea/), NetBeans (netbeans.org), and Eclipse (eclipse.org) are advanced editors, preferred by practicing professionals. For compiling and running Java code, you'll need the Java Development Kit (JDK), which is available directly from the Oracle Corporation, or bundled directly with some of the editors listed.

Each editor has advantages and disadvantages. BlueJ and DrJava are user-friendly and have a simple, minimal user interface, but lack some of the advanced editors' features, such as autocompletion of fields, methods, and import statements. The advanced editors are faster, feature-packed, more powerful and customizable, and have various plug-ins available, but they also have a steep learning curve and user interfaces that may be more daunting to beginners. Figure 1-1 illustrates this point with a side-by-side comparison of the Eclipse and BlueJ interfaces.

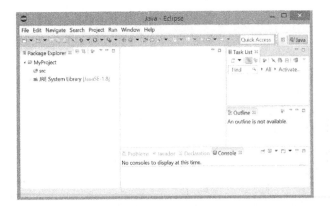 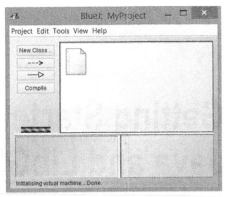

Figure 1-1. *User interfaces for Eclipse (left) and BlueJ (right)*

This chapter covers how to set up BlueJ. I've selected this particular IDE because it is quick and easy to set up and configure, which will enable you to start programming games even faster. However, if you are already familiar and comfortable with one of the more advanced editors, of course you should feel free to use it rather than BlueJ. A wealth of informational material is available for setting up Eclipse, NetBeans, and IntelliJ IDEA with LibGDX, available online at the LibGDX wiki (`https://github.com/libgdx/libgdx/wiki`). If you choose to use one of these programs, then after your IDE is set up, skip ahead to the upcoming section "Creating a 'Hello, World!' Program for LibGDX."

Setting Up BlueJ

This section covers how to set up the BlueJ IDE. Since it was designed for beginners, the number of steps is small and the process is straightforward, as you will see.

Downloading and Installing

BlueJ can be downloaded from `www.bluej.org`.

There are two download options: one bundled with the JDK, and one without. The JDK includes tools for developing and debugging Java applications; in particular, it is necessary for compiling your code. If you have used your computer to develop Java applications before, you likely already have the JDK installed and can just select the stand-alone BlueJ installer. If you aren't sure, you should download and run the BlueJ combined installer.

Using BlueJ

When learning a new programming language or library, it is a well-established tradition in computer science to write a "Hello, World!" application as a first program. This section covers the basics of using BlueJ in the process of writing this program:

1. Start up the BlueJ software. (The first time you run it, it may prompt you for the location of the directory where the JDK is stored.)

2. When the main window appears, in the menu bar, select Project ➤ New Project. BlueJ organizes your work into projects, which are stored as directories; all Java source code and compiled class files are stored in the project directory.

3. When prompted for a project name, navigate to your Desktop folder, enter **MyProject**, and click the OK button. This creates a directory in the Desktop folder with the same name.

   After step 3, your screen should look similar to Figure 1-2.

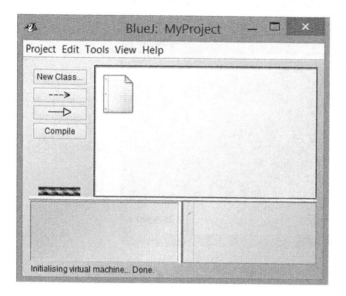

Figure 1-2. *The BlueJ project window*

4. Create a new class, either by clicking the New Class button or by choosing Edit ➤ New Class from the menu bar.

5. When you are prompted to enter a name for the class, type **HelloWorld** and press the Enter key or click the OK button. An orange rectangle appears with the name of your class at its top. The gray diagonal lines indicate that the code has not yet been compiled.

6. Either double-click the rectangle or right-click and select Open Editor to edit the file. You will see that some template code has been added; delete all of this code, and enter the following code in its place:

```java
public class HelloWorld
{
    public static void main()
    {
        System.out.print("Hello, World!");
    }
}
```

After entering this code into BlueJ, it should appear similar to the screenshot in Figure 1-3.

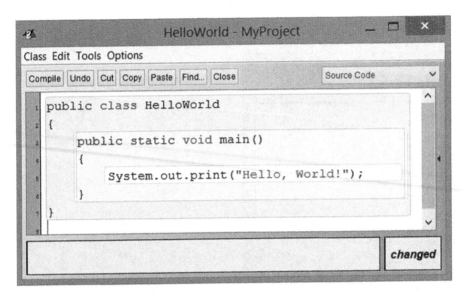

Figure 1-3. *A "Hello, World!" program displayed in the BlueJ code editor*

7. Click the Compile button to compile your code. (This action also automatically saves your code.) You should see the message "Class compiled – no syntax errors" in the status bar at the bottom of the window.

8. Right-click the orange rectangle for the class, and select the method void main() from the list that appears. This runs the method that you have just written. A terminal window appears, containing the text *Hello, World!*, as shown in Figure 1-4.

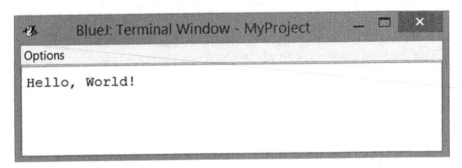

Figure 1-4. *Text displayed by the "Hello, World!" program*

Congratulations on running your first program using BlueJ!

BlueJ has a number of features that make programming easier. While entering the preceding code, you may have noticed the syntax highlighting (Java keywords and strings appear in different colors), and also that classes and methods appear surrounded by different background colors, to make it easier to visually inspect your code. (Later, you'll notice that conditional statements and loops are similarly distinguished with background colors.) BlueJ contains additional features that you may find useful, such as these:

- Automatic code formatting. Selecting Auto-Layout from the Edit menu will adjust the whitespace in your code so that nested statements are aligned consistently.

- Listing available method names. After typing the name of a class or object, followed by a period, pressing Ctrl+Space will display a list of available method names.

- Shortcut keys for indenting/un-indenting and commenting/uncommenting blocks of code. These are listed in the Edit menu.

- A simple interface for adding breakpoints, which activates a debugger that allows you to step through code line by line and easily inspect objects.

For complete information on these and other features, see the BlueJ reference manual at `www.bluej.org/doc/bluej-ref-manual.pdf`.

Setting Up LibGDX

In this section, you'll configure BlueJ so that it can use the LibGDX software library. *Software libraries* are collections of prewritten code and methods that can be used by other programs. Their value lies in their reusability—they accelerate and simplify the development process when they implement frequently needed processes, saving programmers from needing to "reinvent the wheel" every time they write a program. The LibGDX libraries, for example, contain methods for displaying graphics, playing sounds, and getting input from the user. (Advanced functions are available as well, which are discussed later in this chapter.)

In Java, libraries are stored in Java Archive (JAR) files. A JAR file contains many files (similar to a ZIP file)—compiled Java files, stored in a standardized directory structure that the JDK can navigate. Your first step is to download the LibGDX JAR files that you will need for our project. There are two online sources to obtain these files:

- From the web site `https://libgdx.badlogicgames.com/releases/`, download the latest version of the file with a file name of the form `libgdx-x.y.z.zip`. This is an archive file that contains all the various LibGDX JAR files. Extract the following files to your Desktop directory: `gdx.jar`, `gdx-natives.jar`, `gdx-backend-lwjgl.jar`, and `gdx-backend-lwjgl-natives.jar`. These files contain the core code for the LibGDX library.

- Alternatively, the most up-to-date versions of these four JAR files can be obtained from the web site `https://libgdx.badlogicgames.com/nightlies/dist/`. These are the *nightly builds* of the LibGDX libraries (in contrast to the previous link, which points to the most recent stable version of the software). These files are the most up-to-date, but they are also under development and thus may contain a few bugs or glitches.

Once these four JAR files have been obtained, BlueJ needs to be configured so that it recognizes and can use the contents of these files. There are two main ways to do so:

- The easiest way to make BlueJ aware of JAR files is to create a directory named +libs within the project directory, then copy the JAR files into this directory, and restart the BlueJ software. By default, when a project is opened in BlueJ, it automatically scans for the presence of a folder named +libs and takes its contents into account when compiling new code.

- When there are JAR files that may be used in multiple projects, rather than creating redundant copies of these files in +libs directories for each of these projects, they can be copied to a special subdirectory, named userlib, in the folder where the BlueJ software is installed. The full path to the directory should be something similar to C:\Program Files\BlueJ\lib\userlib\; the exact name can be checked by selecting the menu option Tools ➤ Preferences in Windows, or BlueJ ➤ Preferences in OS X, and clicking the Libraries tab.

Once these steps are complete, BlueJ needs to be restarted, and then you'll be ready to write your first program in LibGDX.

Creating a "Hello, World!" Program with LibGDX

Traditionally, a "Hello, World!" program displays a text message on the screen. Since our ultimate goal is to create video games—primarily visual programs—your first LibGDX program will draw a picture of the world in a window, as shown in Figure 1-5.

Figure 1-5. A "Hello, World!" program created using LibGDX

Here, you will begin to see some of the advantages and start to understand what I mean by *building upon* the classes provided by the LibGDX libraries. Our first project contains two classes. The first class, called HelloWorldImage, makes use of the functionality of a LibGDX class, called Game, by extending it.

EXTENDING A CLASS

One of the central principles of software engineering is to design programs that avoid redundancy by creating reusable code. One way to accomplish this is by the object-oriented concept of inheritance: the creation of a new class based on an existing class.

For example, if we were designing a role-playing game, it would probably have many types of playable characters, such as warriors, ninjas, thieves, and wizards. If we were to design classes to represent each of these characters, they would have certain features in common: they each have a name, a certain number of health points (HP), and perhaps a method named attack that can be used when simulating combat.

Some features also may be unique to each character; for example, perhaps wizards also have a certain number of magic points (MP), and a method named castSpell that is called when they use magic. Because of the differences between these characters, we can't create a single class that represents all of them; at the same time, it feels redundant to keep entering the same fields over and over again in each of their separate classes. An elegant approach to this type of scenario is to create a base class that contains all the features common to these characters, and other classes will extend this base class. The extending class has access to all the fields and methods of the base class, and can also contain its own fields and methods as usual. We could implement this scenario with the following code:

```java
public class Person
{
        String name;
        int HP;
        public void attack(Person other)
        {
                // insert code here…
        }
}
```

And then we can extend the Person class as follows:

```java
public class Wizard extends Person
{
        int MP;
        public void castSpell( String spellName )
        {
                // insert code here…
        }
}
```

Then, if we were to create instances of these classes:

```
Person percy = new Person();
Wizard merlin = new Wizard();
```

Then commands such as merlin.MP += 10 and merlin.castSpell("fireball") are valid, as well as commands involving fields and methods of the base class, such as merlin.HP -= 3 and merlin. attack(percy). However, the object called percy can use only the fields and methods of the Person class; code such as percy.HP += 5 will compile, but percy.castSpell("lightning") will result in an error when the file is compiled.

The concept of extending a class is not only useful for in-game entities, but also for framework-like elements. For example, it would be useful to have a Menu class that contains functionality common to all types of menus, such as opening and closing the menu. It might then be useful to create other classes that extend this one: for example, a class named SelectionMenu could be created, which is a Menu that specializes in displaying some sort of information and asks the player to make a selection from a set of options. An InformationMenu class might be a menu that displays some text-based information and simply closes when the player is finished reading it.

Create a new class in your project, called HelloWorldImage, and enter the source code that follows. Note that before the class itself, there are a number of import statements that indicate which of the LibGDX classes you'll be using in this program. Also note that this program uses an image with the file name world. png; this image is included in the source code for this chapter, in the folder MyProject (the source code is available from apress.com). You should copy this image into your MyProject folder. Alternatively, you could use an image of your own choosing instead; a size of 256 by 256 pixels is recommended for this program, and don't forget to change the file name in the following code accordingly if you do.

```
import com.badlogic.gdx.Game;
import com.badlogic.gdx.Gdx;
import com.badlogic.gdx.files.FileHandle;
import com.badlogic.gdx.graphics.GL20;
import com.badlogic.gdx.graphics.g2d.SpriteBatch;
import com.badlogic.gdx.graphics.Texture;

public class HelloWorldImage extends Game
{
    private Texture texture;
    private SpriteBatch batch;


    public void create()
    {
        FileHandle worldFile = Gdx.files.internal("world.png");
        texture = new Texture(worldFile);
        batch = new SpriteBatch();
    }
```

```java
public void render()
{
    Gdx.gl.glClearColor(1, 1, 1, 1);
    Gdx.gl.glClear(GL20.GL_COLOR_BUFFER_BIT);

    batch.begin();
    batch.draw( texture, 192, 112 );
    batch.end();
}
}
```

The HelloWorldImage class contains two objects: a Texture and a SpriteBatch. A Texture is an object that stores image-related data: the dimensions (width and height) of an image, and the color of each pixel. A SpriteBatch is an object that draws images to the screen.

The HelloWorldImage class also contains two methods: create and render.

The create method initializes the Texture and SpriteBatch objects. In particular, the Texture object requires an image file from which it will get its image data. For this purpose, you create a FileHandle: a LibGDX object that is used to access files stored on the computer. The Gdx class contains many useful static objects and methods (similar to Java's Math class); here, you use a method named internal to generate a FileHandle object that will be used by the Texture object. The internal method will search for the file in the BlueJ project directory, the same location where the compiled class files are stored.

After the create method is finished, the render method will be called by LibGDX approximately 60 times per second.[1] This method contains a pair of static method calls: one to select a particular background color, and another to use that color to clear the window.

Next, you'll create a second class that creates an instance of the HelloWorldImage class and activates its methods; such a class is often called a *driver class*, and requires you to write a static method.

STATIC METHODS AND DRIVER CLASSES

By default, the methods of a class are called by instances of that class. However, a method can also be declared to be *static*, meaning that it is called from the class directly (rather than an instance). Whether a method should be instance-based or class-based (static) depends on how the method is used and what data it requires.

An instance-based method usually depends on the internal data specific to that instance. For example, every String object has a method called charAt, which takes an integer as input, and returns the character stored at that position in the String. If we create two String objects as follows:

```java
String player1 = "Lee";
String player2 = "Dan";
```

then the expression player1.charAt(1) returns the character e, while player2.charAt(1) returns a. The value returned by this method depends on the data stored in that instance, and thus charAt is most assuredly an instance-based method.

---

[1]Since neither the texture nor the coordinates are changing in this example, the fact that the render method is called repeatedly is irrelevant here. However, if you were to periodically change the image, you could generate an animation; if you were to gradually change the coordinates, you could simulate motion. You will see how to accomplish both of these variations in the following chapter.

In object-oriented programming languages, most of the methods of a class will be instance-based because they either depend upon or potentially change the values of an instance's variables. There are, of course, situations where static methods are more natural. In general, any method that does not involve the internal state of an object could be declared as static (such as mathematical formulas—all the methods of Java's Math class are static).

A *driver class* (also sometimes referred to as a *main, entry point, starter*, or *launcher* class) is a class whose purpose is to drive the execution of another class, which often involves creating an instance of the class and calling one or more of its methods. The driver class typically requires only a single method to accomplish this task; this method is traditionally called main. Since it is the first method called by the program, the main method *must* be static, because when a program starts, there are no instances available to run instance-based methods. If the main method were not static, we would have a problem similar to the philosophical conundrum: Which came first: the chicken or the egg? Something has to be able to instantiate a class without itself being instantiated, and this is exactly what the static main method of a driver class does.

A standard "Hello, World!" program could be rewritten using a driver class as follows:

```java
public class Greeter
{
        public void sayHello()
        {
                System.out.print("Hello!");
        }
}

public class Launcher
{
        public static void main()
        {
                Greeter greta = new Greeter();
                greta.sayHello();
        }
}
```

Next, in the same project, create a class called HelloLauncher that contains the following code:

```java
import com.badlogic.gdx.backends.lwjgl.LwjglApplication;
public class HelloLauncher
{
    public static void main (String[] args)
    {
        HelloWorldImage myProgram = new HelloWorldImage();
        LwjglApplication launcher = new LwjglApplication( myProgram );
    }
}
```

As mentioned in the previous "Static Methods and Driver Classes" sidebar, this class first creates an instance of the HelloWorldImage class, called myProgram. Then, instead of running the methods of myProgram directly, the main method creates a LwjglApplication object, which takes myProgram as input; the constructor performs some initialization tasks, and then runs the create and render methods of myProgram as discussed previously.

The acronym *LWJGL* stands for the *Lightweight Java Game Library*, an open source Java library originally created by Caspian Rychlik-Prince to simplify game development in terms of accessing the desktop computer hardware resources. In LibGDX, LWJGL is used for the desktop back end to support all the major desktop operating systems, such as Windows, Linux, and Mac OS X.

Another benefit to having a driver class, separate from the classes that contain the game functionality, is the potential to create driver classes for other platforms, such as Android, which LibGDX also supports.

When you've entered all the code for both classes, return to the main window in BlueJ, and click the Compile button. Then right-click the orange rectangle for the HelloLauncher class, and in the list of methods that appears, select the method listed as void main(String[] args). A pop-up window appears, in which you could enter an array of strings as input if you needed to—but you don't. Click the OK button, and you should see a window as shown previously in Figure 1-5.

Congratulations on completing your first application using LibGDX!

Advantages to Using LibGDX

In addition to the ability to compile your game so that it can run on multiple platforms, there are many other advantages to using the LibGDX game development framework. LibGDX makes it easy to accomplish tasks such as these:

- Render 2D graphics, animations, bitmap-based fonts, and particle effects

- Stream music and play sound effects

- Process input from a keyboard, mouse, touch screens, accelerometer, or game pad

- Organize user interfaces using a scene graph and fully skinnable UI control library

- Integrate third-party plug-ins, such as the Box2D physics engine (box2d.org), the Tiled map editor file format (mapeditor.org), and the Spine 2D animation software (esotericsoftware.com)

- Render 3D graphics with materials and lighting effects, and load 3D models from common file formats such as OBJ and FBX

A complete list of LibGDX features can be found at the web site http://libgdx.badlogicgames.com/features.html.

Summary

In this chapter, you've set up BlueJ, an integrated development environment for Java programming, and configured BlueJ to use the LibGDX game development framework. Then you created your first application with LibGDX: a "Hello, World!" program that displays an image of the world in a window. This program involved extending LibGDX's Game class, and creating a driver class that runs the program on the desktop. Along the way, you learned about a few of the other classes involved in this program. Finally, you learned about some of the additional features of the LibGDX library, many of which are discussed in detail in future chapters.

CHAPTER 2

■ ■ ■

The LibGDX Framework

This chapter introduces many of the major features of the LibGDX library. It illustrates how to use them in the process of creating a game called *Cheese, Please!*, where you help the player's character, Mousey, scurry around the floor while looking for a tasty piece of cheese. A screenshot of this game in action appears in Figure 2-1. You'll see a few ways to accomplish standard game programming tasks, such as representing game entities. Then, you'll incrementally add a variety of features, such as animation, a user interface, and an introductory menu screen.

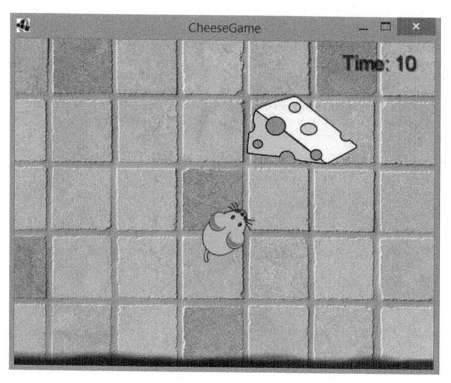

Figure 2-1. *The main screen for the game Cheese, Please!*

Understanding the Life Cycle of a Game

Before jumping into the programming aspect of game development, it is important to understand the overall structure of a game program: the major stages that a game program progresses through, and the tasks that a game program must perform in each stage. The stages are as follows:

- *Startup*: During this stage, any files needed (such as images or sounds) are loaded, game objects are created, and values are initialized.

- *The game loop*: A stage that repeats continuously while the game is running, and that consists of the following three substages:

    - *Process input*: The program checks to see if the user has performed any action that sends data to the computer: pressing keyboard keys, moving the mouse or clicking mouse buttons, touching or swiping on a touch screen, or pressing joysticks or buttons on a game pad.

    - *Update*: Performs tasks that involve the state of the game world and the entities within it. This could include changing positions of entities based on user input or physics simulations, performing collision detection to determine when two entities come in contact with each other and what action to perform in response, or selecting actions for nonplayer characters

    - *Render*: Draw all graphics on the screen, such as background images, game world entities, and the user interface (which typically overlays the game world).

- *Shutdown*: This stage begins when the player provides input to the computer indicating that he is finished using the software (for example, by clicking a Quit button), and may involve removing images or data from memory, saving player data or the game state, signaling the computer to stop monitoring hardware devices for user input, and closing any windows that were created by the game.

The flowchart in Figure 2-2 illustrates the order in which these stages occur.

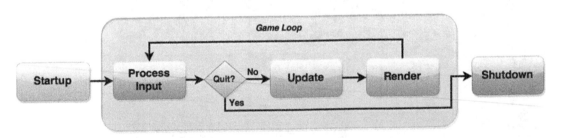

Figure 2-2. The stages of a game program

Some game developers may include additional stages in the game loop, such as these:

- A *sleep* stage that pauses the execution of the program for a given amount of time. Many game developers aim to write programs that can run at 60 frames per second (FPS), meaning that the game loop will run once every 16.67 milliseconds.[1] If the game loop can run faster than this, the program can be instructed to pause for whatever amount of time remains in the 16.67-millisecond interval, thus freeing up the CPU for any other applications that may be running in the background. LibGDX automatically handles this for us, so we won't worry about including it here.

- An *audio* stage, where any background music is streamed or sound effects are played. In this book, we will consider playing audio as part of the update stage, and we will discuss how to accomplish this in a later chapter.

Most of these stages are handled by a corresponding method in LibGDX. For example, the startup stage is carried out by the `create` method, the update and render stages are both handled by the `render` method,[2] and any shutdown actions are performed by a method named `dispose`.

In fact, when your driver class creates any kind of `Application` (such as a `LwjglApplication`), the application will work correctly only if given an object that contains a certain set of methods (including `create`, `render`, and `dispose`); this is a necessary convention so that the `Application` knows what to do during each stage of the game program's life cycle. The way you are able to enforce such requirements in Java programs is by using interfaces.

INTERFACES

Informally, you can think of an *interface* as a kind of contract that other classes can promise to fulfill. As a simple example, let's say that you write a `Player` class, which contains a method named `talkTo` that is used to interact with objects in your environment. The `talkTo` method takes a single input, called `creature`, and in the code that follows, you have

```
creature.speak();
```

For the `talkTo` method to work correctly, whatever type of object that `creature` is an instance of, it *must* have a method named `speak`. Maybe sometimes `creature` is an instance of a `Person` class, while at other times `creature` is an instance of a `Monster` class. In general, you would like the `talkTo` method to be as inclusive as possible—any object with a `speak` method should be permitted as input. You can accomplish this behavior by using interfaces.

First, you create an interface as follows:

```
public interface Speaker
{
    public void speak();
}
```

---

[1]Running faster than this is usually unnecessary, because most computer display hardware is incapable of displaying images at a greater rate than this.
[2]The next chapter covers how to organize code more intuitively, so that the update and render stages are handled by separate methods.

At first glance, an interface appears similar to a class, except that the methods are only declared; they do not contain any actual code. All that is required is the *signature* of the method: the name, the output type, the input types (if any), and any modifiers such as public. This information is followed by a semicolon instead of the familiar set of braces that encompass code. The classes that implement this interface will provide the code for their version of the speak function. I emphasize that since Speaker is not a class, you *cannot* create an instance of a Speaker object; instead, you write other classes that include the methods as specified in the Speaker interface.

A class indicates that it meets the requirements of an interface (that it contains all the indicated fields and methods) by including the keyword implements, followed by the name of interface, after the name of the class. Any class that implements the Speaker interface must provide the code for its version of the speak function. The following demonstrates with a class called Person and a class called Monster:

```
public class Person implements Speaker
{
    // additional code above
    public void speak()
    {   System.out.println( "Hello." );  }
    // additional code below
}

public class Monster implements Speaker
{
    // additional code above
    public void speak()
    { System.out.println("Grrr!");  }
    // additional code below
}
```

Always remember, when implementing an interface, you *must* write methods for everything declared in the interface; otherwise, there will be a compile-time error. You could even write a method that contains no code between the braces, as shown next (for a class that represents a particularly untalkative piece of furniture). This can be convenient when you need to use only part of the functionality of the interface.

```
public class Chair implements Speaker
{
    // additional code above
    public void speak() { }
    // additional code below
}
```

Finally, you write the method talkTo so that it takes a Speaker as input:

```
public class Player
{
        // additional code above

        public void talkTo(Speaker creature)
        {
                creature.speak();
        }

        // additional code below
}
```

Any class that implements the Speaker interface may be used as input for a Player object's talkTo method. For example, we present some code that creates instances of each of these classes, and describe the results in the accompanying comments:

```
Player dan = new Player();
Person chris = new Person();
Monster grez = new Monster();
Chair footstool = new Chair();
dan.talkTo(chris); // prints "Hello."
dan.talkTo(grez); // prints "Grrr!"
dan.talkTo(footstool); // does not print anything
```

An Application in LibGDX requires user-created classes to implement the ApplicationListener interface so that it can handle all stages of a game program's life cycle. You may recall, however, that in our example from Chapter 1, the HelloWorldImage class did not implement the ApplicationListener class; it only extended the Game class. Why didn't this result in an error when the class was compiled? If you take a look "under the hood" (which, in the context of computer programming, typically means to inspect the source code), you'll notice that the Game class itself implements the ApplicationListener class, and includes "empty" versions of the functions; there is no code between the braces that define the body of each function. This enables you to write only variations of the interface methods that you need to use in the class that extends the Game class, which will then *override* the versions in the Game class; any interface method that you don't write will default to the empty version in the Game class. (In fact, the ApplicationListener interface requires a total of six methods: create, render, resize, pause, resume, and dispose; in our example, you wrote only two of these.)

Working with User Input

This section introduces the game Cheese, Please!, where we help guide the player's character, Mousey, to a piece of cheese. Some of the code will be familiar from the HelloWorldImage example, such as the Texture and SpriteBatch classes, the purpose of the create and render methods, and the role of the driver class. There are a few new additions as well. Since the coordinates of Mousey may change, you use variables to store these values. Most significantly, you introduce some code that makes our program interactive—you will process keyboard input from the user. Finally, you'll include a Boolean variable that keeps track of whether the player has won, which becomes true when Mousey reaches the cheese, and also results in a You Win message being displayed on the screen.

In this section, as well as the sections that follow, you are invited to create a new project in BlueJ and enter the code that is presented, or alternatively, to simply download the source code from the web site for this book, and run the code via the included BlueJ project files. The online source code also contains all the images that you will need, stored in the assets folder in each project, referenced in the following code.

The source code for this initial version of our game, called CheesePlease1, appears next. Note in particular that for organizational purposes, all the image files are stored in a folder called assets, contained within the main project directory. There are also new import statements, which enable you to create a variety of new objects, which are also explained here.

```
import com.badlogic.gdx.Gdx;
import com.badlogic.gdx.Input.Keys;
import com.badlogic.gdx.graphics.GL20;
import com.badlogic.gdx.graphics.Texture;
import com.badlogic.gdx.graphics.g2d.SpriteBatch;
import com.badlogic.gdx.Game;
```

```java
public class CheesePlease1 extends Game
{
    private SpriteBatch batch;

    private Texture mouseyTexture;
    private float mouseyX;
    private float mouseyY;

    private Texture cheeseTexture;
    private float cheeseX;
    private float cheeseY;

    private Texture floorTexture;
    private Texture winMessage;

    private boolean win;

    public void create()
    {
        batch = new SpriteBatch();

        mouseyTexture = new Texture( Gdx.files.internal("assets/mouse.png") );
        mouseyX = 20;
        mouseyY = 20;

        cheeseTexture = new Texture( Gdx.files.internal("assets/cheese.png") );
        cheeseX = 400;
        cheeseY = 300;

        floorTexture = new Texture( Gdx.files.internal("assets/tiles.jpg") );
        winMessage = new Texture( Gdx.files.internal("assets/you-win.png") );

        win = false;
    }

    public void render()
    {
        // check user input
        if (Gdx.input.isKeyPressed(Keys.LEFT))
            mouseyX--;
        if (Gdx.input.isKeyPressed(Keys.RIGHT))
            mouseyX++;
        if (Gdx.input.isKeyPressed(Keys.UP))
            mouseyY++;
        if (Gdx.input.isKeyPressed(Keys.DOWN))
            mouseyY--;
```

```
        // check win condition: mousey must be overlapping cheese
        if ( (mouseyX > cheeseX)
          && (mouseyX + mouseyTexture.getWidth() < cheeseX + cheeseTexture.getWidth())
          && (mouseyY > cheeseY)
          && (mouseyY + mouseyTexture.getHeight() < cheeseY + cheeseTexture.getHeight()) )
            win = true;

        // clear screen and draw graphics
        Gdx.gl.glClearColor(0.8f, 0.8f, 1, 1);
        Gdx.gl.glClear(GL20.GL_COLOR_BUFFER_BIT);

        batch.begin();
        batch.draw( floorTexture, 0, 0 );
        batch.draw( cheeseTexture, cheeseX, cheeseY );
        batch.draw( mouseyTexture, mouseyX, mouseyY );
        if (win)
            batch.draw( winMessage, 170, 60 );
        batch.end();
    }
}
```

You also need a launcher-style class to create an instance of this class and run it; this can be accomplished with the following short class:

```
import com.badlogic.gdx.backends.lwjgl.LwjglApplication;
public class Launcher1
{
    public static void main (String[] args)
    {
        CheesePlease1 myProgram = new CheesePlease1();
        LwjglApplication launcher = new LwjglApplication( myProgram );
    }
}
```

In the class CheesePlease1, the create method initializes variables and loads textures. This program contains four images, stored as Texture objects: Mousey, the cheese, floor tiles for the background, and an image containing the words *You Win*. For brevity, instead of creating a new variable to store each of the FileHandle objects created by the internal method, you initialize them in the same line where you construct each new Texture object. The coordinates of Mousey's position are stored by using floating-point numbers, since you need to store decimal values, and the LibGDX game development framework uses float rather than double variables in its classes for a slight increase in program efficiency. Even though the coordinates of the cheese texture will not be changing, you store them by using variables anyway so that future code involving these values is more readable. The floorTexture and winMessage objects do not require variables to store their coordinates, as their positions will not be changing, and their positions will be specified in the render method (discussed later in this section).

The render method contains three main blocks of code that roughly correspond to the game loop substages: process input, update, and render.

First, a sequence of commands use a method named isKeyPressed, belonging to (an object belonging to) the Gdx class, which determines whether a key on the keyboard is currently being pressed. The names of each key are represented using constant values from the Keys class. When one of the arrow keys is pressed, the corresponding x or y coordinate of Mousey is adjusted accordingly; x values increase toward the right side of the window, while y values increase toward the top of the window.[3] Note that if the user presses the left and right arrow keys at the same time, the effects of the addition and subtraction cancel each other out, and the position of Mousey will not change; a similar situation also applies when the user presses the up and down arrow keys at the same time.

The second set of commands perform collision detection: they determine whether the rectangular region containing mouseyTexture is completely contained within the rectangular region containing cheeseTexture. To determine this, you need to compare the left, right, top, and bottom boundaries of the rectangles as indicated in Figure 2-3. The position of the left and bottom sides are given by the values of the x and y coordinates of the texture, respectively; the position of the right and top sides can be calculated by adding the width and height of the texture (obtained by using the getWidth and getHeight methods) to the x and y coordinates, respectively. As illustrated in Figure 2-3, rectangle A contains rectangle B exactly when these four conditions are true:

- A.x < B.x
- (B.x + B.width) < (A.x + A.width)
- A.y < B.y
- (B.y + B.height) < (A.y + A.height)

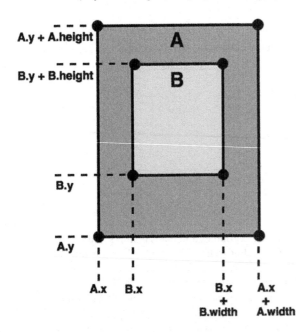

Figure 2-3. *Rectangle containment diagram*

This test is applied to mouseyTexture and cheeseTexture, and when true, the Boolean variable win is set to true, indicating that the player has won the game.

The third set of commands is where the actual rendering takes place. The glClear method draws a solid- colored rectangle on the screen, using the color specified in the glClearColor method (in terms of red/green/blue/alpha values). The screen must be cleared in this manner during every rendering pass,

---

[3]The design choice to have y increase toward the top, while consistent with mathematical conventions, is the opposite of most computer science coordinate system conventions, which place the origin point (0,0) at the top-left corner of a window, and the y value increases toward the bottom.

effectively "erasing" the screen, because the images from previous render calls might be visible otherwise. The order of the draw method calls is particularly important: textures that are rendered later appear on top of those rendered earlier. Thus, you typically want to draw the background elements first, followed by the main in-game entities, and the user interface elements are typically drawn last. The Batch class, used for drawing, optimizes graphics operations by sending multiple images at once to the computer's graphics processing unit (GPU).

Managing the Action

In the previous example—our first iteration of the game Cheese, Please!—you have seen that each game entity (such as Mousey and the cheese) has a lot of related information that you need to keep track of, such as textures and (x,y) coordinates. A central design principle in an object-oriented programming language like Java is to encapsulate related information in a single class. While you could create a Mousey class, a Cheese class, and so forth to manage this information, this approach would result in a lot of redundancy in your program, which is both inefficient and difficult to manage. Since another guiding principle in software engineering is to write reusable code, you want to implement a single class that contains the basic information common to all game entities, which you can then extend when necessary.

LibGDX demonstrates its flexibility in this regard by providing multiple ways to manage this information, two of which you'll explore in this section: the Sprite class and the Actor class.

The Sprite Class

The Sprite class contains everything you need to refactor the code from the class CheesePlease1. Sprites contain fields that store coordinates, a texture, and additional information such as angle of rotation and scaling factors. There is even an associated Rectangle object, which has built-in methods (such as contains and intersects) to perform collision detection, which will greatly simplify that part of our program. Each of these fields is accessed using standard get and set style functions. Some other available Sprite methods that will be useful include the methods translateX and translateY, which change the values of the x and y coordinates of the Sprite, and draw, which a Sprite can use to render itself (taking into account its position and rotation) using a given SpriteBatch. Following is the code for this new version of Cheese, Please!, the class CheesePlease2, using Sprite objects; in addition to importing the Sprite class, you also import the Rectangle class, which you will see simplifies collision detection.

```java
import com.badlogic.gdx.Game;
import com.badlogic.gdx.Gdx;
import com.badlogic.gdx.Input.Keys;
import com.badlogic.gdx.graphics.GL20;
import com.badlogic.gdx.graphics.Texture;
import com.badlogic.gdx.graphics.g2d.SpriteBatch;
import com.badlogic.gdx.graphics.g2d.Sprite;
import com.badlogic.gdx.math.Rectangle;

public class CheesePlease2 extends Game
{
    private SpriteBatch batch;
    private Sprite mouseySprite;
    private Sprite cheeseSprite;
    private Sprite floorSprite;
    private Sprite winTextSprite;
    private boolean win;
```

```
    public void create()
    {
        batch = new SpriteBatch();

        mouseySprite = new Sprite( new Texture(Gdx.files.internal("assets/mouse.png")) );
        mouseySprite.setPosition( 20, 20 );

        cheeseSprite = new Sprite( new Texture(Gdx.files.internal("assets/cheese.png")) );
        cheeseSprite.setPosition( 400, 300 );

        floorSprite = new Sprite( new Texture(Gdx.files.internal("assets/tiles.jpg")) );
        floorSprite.setPosition( 0, 0 );

        winTextSprite = new Sprite( new Texture(Gdx.files.internal("assets/you-win.png")) );
        winTextSprite.setPosition( 170, 60 );

        win = false;
    }

    public void render()
    {
        // process input
        if (Gdx.input.isKeyPressed(Keys.LEFT))
            mouseySprite.translateX( -1 );
        if (Gdx.input.isKeyPressed(Keys.RIGHT))
            mouseySprite.translateX( 1 );
        if (Gdx.input.isKeyPressed(Keys.UP))
            mouseySprite.translateY( 1 );
        if (Gdx.input.isKeyPressed(Keys.DOWN))
            mouseySprite.translateY( -1 );

        // check win condition
        Rectangle cheeseRectangle = cheeseSprite.getBoundingRectangle();
        Rectangle mouseyRectangle = mouseySprite.getBoundingRectangle();

        if ( cheeseRectangle.contains(mouseyRectangle) )
            win = true;

        // draw graphics
        Gdx.gl.glClearColor(0.8f, 0.8f, 1, 1);
        Gdx.gl.glClear(GL20.GL_COLOR_BUFFER_BIT);

        batch.begin();
        floorSprite.draw( batch );
        cheeseSprite.draw( batch );
        mouseySprite.draw( batch );
        if (win)
            winTextSprite.draw( batch );
        batch.end();
    }
}
```

For the most part, the lines of code for the CheesePlease2 class directly correspond to those in the CheesePlease1 class. You can observe a few minor differences: Sprites are initialized using a Texture object, and use of the Rectangle method greatly simplifies collision detection. The CheesePlease2 class will require its own launcher class, similar to the one for CheesePlease1 (but it should initialize a CheesePlease2 instance). Since the change is a minor one, I won't list the launcher code here, but as always, complete functioning source code for all examples can be downloaded from this book's web site.

For some games, the Sprite object may be sufficient for your needs; other times, you may need to write a customized class that extends the Sprite class in order to store additional data and provide extra functionality for your game entities. For example, the characters in your game might need to keep track of health points (HP); perhaps they can be damaged or healed, and you need to be able to check if they are "alive" (whether their HP is greater than zero). In this scenario, you could extend the Sprite class as follows:

```
public class SpriteWithHP extends Sprite
{
    private int HP;

    // constructor
    public SpriteWithHP(Texture t)
    {
        // activate constructor of the class being extended
        super(t);
        // set default amount of HP
        HP = 100;
    }
}

public int getHP()
{   return HP;   }

public void setHP(int amount)
{   HP = amount;   }

public void damage(int amount)
{   HP -= amount;   }

public void heal(int amount)
{   HP += amount;   }

public boolean isAlive()
{   return (HP > 0);   }

}
```

Since SpriteWithHP is an extension of the Sprite class, all the data and functions in the Sprite class can be used with one of these objects also!

The Actor Class

As mentioned previously, LibGDX provides multiple approaches to managing the information associated with game entities. With the core functionality provided by the Sprite class and the ability to extend this class as needed, at first thought it may be unclear how a second approach would be useful. Furthermore, checking the source code for the LibGDX Actor class, it may seem to be a poor substitute for the Sprite class, as it doesn't provide prebuilt functionality involving the Texture or Rectangle class. However, as you will come to see, this seeming "omission" ultimately turns out to be a strength of the Actor class. You are free to implement graphics, bounding shapes, a draw method, and any other features in any way that is convenient to you. For instance, you could emulate the single-texture approach of a Sprite object, presented in the following code:

```
public class SpritelikeActor extends Actor
{
    private Texture image;

    // constructor
    public SpritelikeActor()
    {  super();  }

    public void setTexture(Texture t)
    {  image = t;  }

    public Texture getTexture()
    {  return image;  }

    public void draw(Batch b)
    {
        b.draw( getTexture(), getX(), getY() );
    }
}
```

Alternatively, you could store multiple textures, and customize the draw method to select a texture to render based on the internal state of the object (for example, according to the number of health points the object has). This could be accomplished with the following code:

```
public class HealthyActor extends Actor
{
    public int HP;
    public Texture healthyImage;
    public Texture damagedImage;
    public Texture deceasedImage;

    // omitted: constructor
    // omitted: methods to get/set above fields

    public void draw(Batch b)
    {
        if (HP > 50)
            b.draw( healthyImage, getX(), getY() );
        else if (HP > 0 && HP <= 50)
            b.draw( damagedImage, getX(), getY() );
        else    // in this case, HP <= 0
            b.draw( deceasedImage, getX(), getY() );
    }
}
```

You could even store one or more animations in your actor; you'll see this variation later in this chapter.

A few other fundamental differences between the Sprite and Actor classes should be mentioned here. First, in addition to a draw method, the Actor class has an act method, which can serve as a form of an update method for the Actor. Second, the Actor class was designed to be used in concert with a class called Stage (that you will be using in the near future), which stores a list of Actor instances and contains methods (named act and draw) that call the act and draw methods of every actor that has been added to it.

Our next goal is to rewrite the Cheese, Please! game so that it uses the Actor class rather than the Sprite class to represent its game entities. Before proceeding, however, you first need to extend the Actor class so that it stores a Texture and a Rectangle. You will also include two float variables in our new class; they will represent the velocity (in pixels per second) in the x and y directions, and be used in the act method to automatically calculate the new position of the Actor. (For an Actor that does not move, you will leave the velocity variables set at their default value of 0.)

This new class, called BaseActor, is shown here:

```java
import com.badlogic.gdx.scenes.scene2d.Actor;
import com.badlogic.gdx.graphics.g2d.Batch;
import com.badlogic.gdx.graphics.Texture;
import com.badlogic.gdx.graphics.g2d.TextureRegion;
import com.badlogic.gdx.math.Rectangle;
import com.badlogic.gdx.graphics.Color;

public class BaseActor extends Actor
{
    public TextureRegion region;
    public Rectangle boundary;
    public float velocityX;
    public float velocityY;

    public BaseActor()
    {
        super();
        region = new TextureRegion();
        boundary = new Rectangle();
        velocityX = 0;
        velocityY = 0;
    }

    public void setTexture(Texture t)
    {
        int w = t.getWidth();
        int h = t.getHeight();
        setWidth( w );
        setHeight( h );
        region.setRegion( t );
    }

    public Rectangle getBoundingRectangle()
    {
        boundary.set( getX(), getY(), getWidth(), getHeight() );
        return boundary;
    }
```

```java
public void act(float dt)
{
    super.act( dt );
    moveBy( velocityX * dt, velocityY * dt );
}

public void draw(Batch batch, float parentAlpha)
{
    Color c = getColor();
    batch.setColor(c.r, c.g, c.b, c.a);
    if ( isVisible() )
        batch.draw( region, getX(), getY(), getOriginX(), getOriginY(),
            getWidth(), getHeight(), getScaleX(), getScaleY(), getRotation() );
}
}
```

The following are some observations about this code:

- Instead of using a Texture, you are using a TextureRegion to store your image, which will yield greater flexibility in future extensions of the BaseActor class. The main difference is that a TextureRegion can be used to store a Texture that contains multiple images or animation frames, and a TextureRegion also stores coordinates, called (u,v) coordinates, that determine which rectangular subarea of the Texture is to be used.

- First, in the act method, you include the method call super.act(dt). The causes the act method in the Actor class (the class being extended, sometimes called the *super class*) to be executed first.

- Next, in the act method, you calculate the distance the BaseActor has travelled (if any) since the last update. This amount is calculated using this physics formula:

  distance = rate × time

  The rate is the value of the velocity variable; the time elapsed since the last update is stored in the variable dt (which stands for *delta time*; in physics, delta often signifies the change in a value). The distance travelled along each axis is then added to the corresponding position variable.

- In the draw method, you set the Color values (red, green, blue, and alpha/transparency) of the Batch object to be equal to those of the Color stored in the Actor class. This is used for tinting the color of the BaseActor texture, which can vary the visual appearance of an image in many ways, without needing to load additional images. The default Color value of an Actor is white, which has no effect on the texture's appearance.

- Finally, in the draw method, after checking whether the Actor field visible is set to true (using the isVisible method), you draw the texture, taking into account its position, origin (center of rotation), width and height, scaling factors, and rotation angle.

Next, is the new version of our game's source code, which uses the new BaseActor class throughout. There are a few changes from the Sprite-based version of the code. In particular:

- Actor objects must be added to the Stage, and the act and draw methods of the Stage must be called (recall that calling the act and draw methods on a Stage results in the Stage object calling the act and draw methods of all the Actor objects that have been added to it).

- We set the initial visibility of winText to false, because the player should not be able to see that particular image until later, when she has won the game.

- Mousey's position is not changed directly; the change in position is calculated using velocity and elapsed time since the last update, the latter of which is given by the method getDeltaTime. A velocity of 100 (pixels per second) may seem large, but if the game is running at a rate of 60 frames per second, then getDeltaTime will return a value of approximately 0.016; this means Mousey will move about 1.6 pixels each time the update method is called. This is comparable to Mousey's speed in the version of the game from the class CheesePlease1.

```
import com.badlogic.gdx.Game;
import com.badlogic.gdx.Gdx;
import com.badlogic.gdx.Input.Keys;
import com.badlogic.gdx.graphics.GL20;
import com.badlogic.gdx.graphics.Texture;
import com.badlogic.gdx.graphics.g2d.SpriteBatch;
import com.badlogic.gdx.math.Rectangle;
import com.badlogic.gdx.scenes.scene2d.Stage;

public class CheesePlease3 extends Game
{
    public Stage mainStage;
    private BaseActor mousey;
    private BaseActor cheese;
    private BaseActor floor;
    private BaseActor winText;

    public void create()
    {
        mainStage = new Stage();

        floor = new BaseActor();
        floor.setTexture( new Texture(Gdx.files.internal("assets/tiles.jpg")) );
        floor.setPosition( 0, 0 );
        mainStage.addActor( floor );

        cheese = new BaseActor();
        cheese.setTexture( new Texture(Gdx.files.internal("assets/cheese.png")) );
        cheese.setPosition( 400, 300 );
        mainStage.addActor( cheese );
```

```java
        mousey = new BaseActor();
        mousey.setTexture( new Texture(Gdx.files.internal("assets/mouse.png")) );
        mousey.setPosition( 20, 20 );
        mainStage.addActor( mousey );

        winText = new BaseActor();
        winText.setTexture( new Texture(Gdx.files.internal("assets/you-win.png")) );
        winText.setPosition( 170, 60 );
        winText.setVisible( false );
        mainStage.addActor( winText );
    }

    public void render()
    {
        // process input
        mousey.velocityX = 0;
        mousey.velocityY = 0;

        if (Gdx.input.isKeyPressed(Keys.LEFT))
            mousey.velocityX -= 100;
        if (Gdx.input.isKeyPressed(Keys.RIGHT))
            mousey.velocityX += 100;
        if (Gdx.input.isKeyPressed(Keys.UP))
            mousey.velocityY += 100;
        if (Gdx.input.isKeyPressed(Keys.DOWN))
            mousey.velocityY -= 100;

        // update
        float dt = Gdx.graphics.getDeltaTime();
        mainStage.act(dt);

        // check win condition: mousey must be overlapping cheese
        Rectangle cheeseRectangle = cheese.getBoundingRectangle();
        Rectangle mouseyRectangle = mousey.getBoundingRectangle();

        if ( cheeseRectangle.contains(mouseyRectangle) )
            winText.setVisible( true );

        // draw graphics
        Gdx.gl.glClearColor(0.8f, 0.8f, 1, 1);
        Gdx.gl.glClear(GL20.GL_COLOR_BUFFER_BIT);

        mainStage.draw();
    }
}
```

In the next section, you'll see how using the Actor class enables you to implement various types of animations for your game entities.

Implementing Visual Effects

This section shows how to implement two types of animation: value-based animation and image-based animation.

Value-Based Animations

Many visual effects can be achieved by continuously changing values associated with a game entity, such as the following:

- A movement effect can be created by changing the position coordinate values.

- A spinning effect can be created by changing the rotation value.

- A growing or shrinking effect can be created by changing the scale factors.

- A color-cycling effect can be created by changing the color red/green/blue component values.

- A fading in/out effect can be created by changing the alpha (transparency) value.

These effects can easily be added to your game by using LibGDX's Action class. An Action is an object that can be added to an Actor, which automatically changes the values of various fields (position, rotation, scale, color) over time. The code that accomplishes this is contained within the act method of the Actor class (and this is why you needed to call super.act(dt) when writing the act method of the BaseActor class—to make sure that this code was executed). To create an Action, it is recommended to use the static methods available in the Actions class. We'll see many examples of these methods in what follows; for a complete listing, see the documentation for the LibGDX Actions class.

You can also create complex, compound visual effects by combining Action objects. These effects can be configured to run one after the other (*in sequence*) or all at the same time (*in parallel*). Additionally, actions can be set to repeat a finite or infinite number of times. Once again, the methods of the Actions class greatly simplify this process.

You will add two value-based animation effects to the program, both of which will occur (that is, they will be created and added to the corresponding actors) when the player wins the game.

You start by creating a new class, called CheesePlease4, that contains all of the code from the class CheesePlease3. To this new class, you begin by declaring a Boolean variable called win, and in the create method, initialize it to false. To check whether the player has won the game, you use the following code, which is structured so that win is set to true only once:

```
Rectangle cheeseRectangle = cheese.getBoundingRectangle();
Rectangle mouseyRectangle = mousey.getBoundingRectangle();
if ( !win && cheeseRectangle.contains( mouseyRectangle ) )
{
    win = true;
}
```

The following code listings should be added into the preceding block of code, where win is set to true.

Next, you will create an effect that will cause the cheese image to rotate (360 degrees per 1 second), shrink (change both scaling factors to 0 over the course of 1 second), and fade out (over the course of 1 second); furthermore, these actions will all occur in parallel. This also requires you to import the Action and Actions classes; the full import paths can be found in the LibGDX documentation, or seen in the source code accompanying this chapter.

```
Action spinShrinkFadeOut = Actions.parallel(
    Actions.alpha(1),            // set transparency value
    Actions.rotateBy(360, 1),    // rotation amount, duration
    Actions.scaleTo(0, 0, 1),    // x amount, y amount, duration
    Actions.fadeOut(1)           // duration of fade out
);
cheese.addAction( spinShrinkFadeOut );
```

In order for the cheese image to rotate around its center (rather than a corner), you need to set the origin point of the Actor, which serves as the center of rotation. This can be accomplished by adding the following line of code to the create method, after setting the Texture of the cheese object:

```
mousey.setOrigin( mousey.getWidth()/2, mousey.getHeight()/2 );
```

You now create a sequence of effects that causes the You Win graphic to become visible, and then fade in (over the course of 2 seconds). The last step will be an infinite loop containing a two-step sequence: shift the color tint to red, and then shift the color tint to blue, each of these steps occurring over the course of 1 second. (This will also require you to import the Color class.) Since the nesting of these method calls can be complicated, I've used indentation to make the code more readable:

```
Action fadeInColorCycleForever = Actions.sequence(
    Actions.alpha(0),    // set transparency value
    Actions.show(),      // set visible to true
    Actions.fadeIn(2),   // duration of fade in
    Actions.forever(
        Actions.sequence(
            // color shade to approach, duration
            Actions.color( new Color(1,0,0,1), 1 ),
            Actions.color( new Color(0,0,1,1), 1 )
        )
    )
);
winText.addAction( fadeInColorCycleForever );
```

Image-Based Animations

An *image-based animation* is created from images that are rapidly displayed in sequence to create the illusion of movement. In LibGDX, this can be accomplished using the Animation class. Creating an animation requires three pieces of information:

- An Array of TextureRegion objects (the images to be used in the animation)

- The amount of time that each image should be displayed

- A value that indicates how the frames should be played—in the order given, in reverse order, from first to last to first again (*ping-pong order*), and whether to repeat (loop) the animation

The following code presents an example of creating an animation that will be used for the Mousey character later. You initialize a standard array to store textures. Next, you use a for loop to load textures from image files (the images displayed in Figure 2-4), set the filter type (which controls how pixel colors are interpolated when the image is rotated or stretched), and store the textures in an array. For the images to load, you must make sure that they have been copied into the project's assets folder (the images are included with the source code for this chapter). Then you convert the standard Java array into a LibGDX Array instance. Finally, you initialize an Animation. This requires four additional import statements to be added, for the TextureRegion, TextureFilter, Array, and Animation classes.

```java
TextureRegion[] frames = new TextureRegion[4];
for (int n = 0; n < 4; n++)
{
    String fileName = "assets/mouse" + n + ".png";
    Texture tex = new Texture(Gdx.files.internal(fileName));
    tex.setFilter(TextureFilter.Linear, TextureFilter.Linear);
    frames[n] = new TextureRegion( tex );
}
Array<TextureRegion> framesArray = new Array<TextureRegion>(frames);
Animation anim = new Animation(0.1f, framesArray, Animation.PlayMode.LOOP_PINGPONG);
```

Figure 2-4. *Images used to animate Mousey: mouse0.png through mouse3.png*

Next, you will create a new class, AnimatedActor, which extends the BaseActor class and uses this newly created Animation data in its draw method. The additional information this class needs to store includes the total elapsed time the animation has been playing (to determine the correct image to use at each point in time), and of course the Animation itself. In the act method, you will increment elapsedTime. For an extra bit of polish, here you'll set the rotation of the Actor texture to match the direction of movement. (This value is calculated using the velocity, an arctangent function, and a conversion factor from radians to degrees; we'll discuss the derivation of this formula at a later time.) Finally, in the draw method, *before* you call the draw method of the BaseActor class, you use the getKeyFrame method of the Animation class to retrieve the correct image based on the current value of elapsedTime. The complete source code for this method appears here:

```java
import com.badlogic.gdx.graphics.g2d.Batch;
import com.badlogic.gdx.graphics.Texture;
import com.badlogic.gdx.graphics.g2d.Animation;
import com.badlogic.gdx.math.MathUtils;

public class AnimatedActor extends BaseActor
{
    public float elapsedTime;
    public Animation anim;

    public AnimatedActor()
    {
        super();
        elapsedTime = 0;
    }
```

```
    public void setAnimation(Animation a)
    {
        Texture t = a.getKeyFrame(0).getTexture();
        setTexture( t );
        anim = a;
    }

    public void act(float dt)
    {
        super.act( dt );
        elapsedTime += dt;
        if (velocityX != 0 || velocityY != 0)
            setRotation( MathUtils.atan2( velocityY, velocityX ) * MathUtils.
radiansToDegrees );
    }

    public void draw(Batch batch, float parentAlpha)
    {
        region.setRegion( anim.getKeyFrame(elapsedTime) );
        super.draw(batch, parentAlpha);
    }
}
```

Now that you have created a class that handles animations, you can rewrite the initialization code for Mousey to use the AnimatedActor class. You declare the mousey instance as follows:

```
private AnimatedActor mousey;
```

And finally, *after* anim (Mousey's Animation) is initialized in the create method, you replace Mousey's initialization code with the following code. (Note that you need to set Mousey's origin coordinates to be the center of the image, so that rotations appear as expected.)

```
mousey = new AnimatedActor();
mousey.setAnimation( anim );
mousey.setOrigin( mousey.getWidth()/2, mousey.getHeight()/2 );
mousey.setPosition( 20, 20 );
mainStage.addActor(mousey);
```

The complete source code for this example, which incorporates all of these changes to introduce both types of animations, can be found in the file CheesePlease4.java. When you run this version, you should see that Mousey's whiskers twitch, her tail swings back and forth, and she faces the direction that she is moving in.

Introducing User Interfaces

The *user interface* of a game typically displays information about the game world or the player's status, using a combination of graphics and text. We've previously discussed how to display graphics in great detail, and so in this section we discuss a simple method for displaying image-based text. You'll also add a second Stage to contain user-interface elements: both the You Win texture, as well as a text-based object that displays how long the game has been running. Finally, you'll enlarge the size of your game world so that it is larger than the program window, and then see how to adjust the area of the Stage that is being drawn to the window. You'll create a new class, called CheesePlease5, that contains all the code from CheesePlease4 as a starting point.

Along the way, you'll learn about some new LibGDX classes, so you need to add the following import statements to the code:

```
import com.badlogic.gdx.scenes.scene2d.ui.Label;
import com.badlogic.gdx.scenes.scene2d.ui.Label.LabelStyle;
import com.badlogic.gdx.graphics.g2d.BitmapFont;
import com.badlogic.gdx.graphics.Camera;
import com.badlogic.gdx.math.MathUtils;
```

Labels and Bitmap Fonts

To display text in LibGDX, the most straightforward approach is to use the Label class, which also happens to be an extension of the Actor class (and thus gets added to a Stage in the same way). A Label is initialized with (at least) two pieces of information: some text to display (normally in String format), and a LabelStyle. A LabelStyle itself requires two pieces of information when being initialized: a BitmapFont, and a Color used to tint the font graphics.

The data for a computer-generated font is typically stored in one of two ways: either as a set of mathematical curves and formulas (these are called *outline fonts* or *vector fonts*, and include standards such as TrueType font), or as a set of images. The latter is referred to as a *bitmap font*, and is the format used by the LabelStyle class.

There are many ways to initialize a BitmapFont object, which are discussed at length in a future chapter. For now, you use the constructor with no arguments, which defaults to the size 15 Arial font file included in the LibGDX libraries.

The additions to the CheesePlease5 class are as follows:

First, initialize a float variable to keep track of the total elapsed time, and a Label variable that will display this information:

```
private float timeElapsed;
private Label timeLabel;
```

Next, in the create method, you initialize both of these variables. At the start of the program, the timeElapsed should be set to 0. Before you initialize the Label, you first initialize the default BitmapFont, and then create a label containing the text Time: 0 and use a LabelStyle with your font, tinted with a navy blue color. You can make the font appear larger by using the method setFontScale,[4] and the coordinates of the text can be set by using the setPosition method, just as with any Actor object.

```
timeElapsed = 0;
BitmapFont font = new BitmapFont();
String text = "Time: 0";
LabelStyle style = new LabelStyle( font, Color.NAVY );
timeLabel = new Label( text, style );
timeLabel.setFontScale(2);
timeLabel.setPosition(500, 440);
```

---

[4]For enlarging font, this method should be used sparingly, as it may cause images to look pixelated. This effect can be lessened by using a linear texture filter on the bitmap font image, but the best practice would be to simply use a high-resolution image for the font whenever possible.

Updating these variables (timeElapsed and timeLabel) is fairly straightforward. There are two additional tasks to perform in the update section: increment the time elapsed, and change the text of the label (using the Label class setText method, and rounding timeElapsed to a whole number by casting it to the int type). The following code demonstrates these additions. Since these changes should take place only while the game is still ongoing (meaning, the player did *not* yet win the game), the code is placed within a conditional block:

```
if (!win)
{
    timeElapsed += dt;
    timeLabel.setText( "Time: " + (int)timeElapsed );
}
```

Layering with Stage Objects

Generally, user interface elements are drawn on top of game world entities. In previous examples, I have been careful in choosing the order in which the Actors are added to the Stage,[5] so that background images are rendered first, followed by the main game entities, followed by the user interface elements. An easier method is to create multiple Stage objects that represent these groups, and then render the Stage objects in the correct order.

Adding a second Stage is a straightforward process: most of the code mirrors that of the already existing Stage object called mainStage. Right after mainStage is declared, you'll declare a new Stage called uiStage:

```
private Stage uiStage;
```

You need to initialize uiStage in the create method (in the line after mainStage is initialized):

```
uiStage = new Stage();
```

Also during the create method, you'll add the timeLabel object to uiStage, and also change a line of code so that winText is added to uiStage instead of mainStage:

```
uiStage.addActor( winText );
uiStage.addActor( timeLabel );
```

In the update section of the game loop, right after the call to the act method of mainStage, you do the same for uiStage:

```
uiStage.act(dt);
```

Similarly, after drawing the mainStage elements, you need to draw the uiStage elements:

```
uiStage.draw();
```

At this point, you can try compiling and running the code to see how the text appears onscreen.

---

[5]However, it is possible to rearrange the rendering order of an Actor after it has been added to a Stage by using the setZIndex method of the Actor class.

Cameras and Scrolling

Up to this point, we've implicitly assumed that the dimensions (length and width) of the game world are exactly the same as the dimensions of the program window, which are 640 by 480 pixels by default. In this section, you'll begin by increasing the size of the game world to 800 by 800 pixels, which will later lead us to a discussion of scrolling and cameras. To this end, your first modification to the code will be to declare some constants to store these values, using the final keyword to guarantee that their values cannot accidentally be changed later. This will also make the code that follows more readable.

```
// game world dimensions
final int mapWidth = 800;
final int mapHeight = 800;

// window dimensions
final int viewWidth = 640;
final int viewHeight = 480;
```

You'll also change the background texture (the floor tiles) to a new image file that is 800 by 800 pixels, which will fit the game world exactly. You've made the edges of this image a bit darker as well so that it is clear to the player where the boundaries of the game world are.

```
floor.setTexture( new Texture(Gdx.files.internal("assets/tiles-800-800.jpg")) );
```

Next, you'll address and fix a small game-play detail: as it stands, Mousey can move beyond the dimensions of the game world. You could stop Mousey from wandering past the left boundary of the game world with this code:

```
if ( mousey.getX() < 0 )
    mousey.setX(0);
```

You also want the right edge of Mousey's texture to be bounded by the right edge of the screen; this can be expressed with the inequality mousey.getX() + mousey.getWidth() < mapWidth, or equivalently, Mousey's x coordinate should always be less than mapWidth - mousey.getWidth(). This restriction can be accomplished with this line of code:

```
if ( mousey.getX() > mapWidth - mousey.getWidth() )
    mousey.setX( mapWidth - mousey.getWidth();
```

Effectively, what you're doing is restricting the value of mousey.x to the interval [0, mapWidth - mousey.width]. This mathematical function is called *clamping*, and is one of the functions provided by the MathUtils class in LibGDX. The method call clamp(x,a,b) will return

- a, when x < a

- x, when a <= x and x <= b

- b, when x > b

Using this method, you can condense the previous two lines of code into the following:

```
mousey.setX( MathUtils.clamp( mousey.getX(), 0, mapWidth - mousey.getWidth() ));
```

Similarly, to keep Mousey within the game world in the vertical direction, you need to restrict Mousey's y coordinate to the interval [0, mapHeight - mousey.height]. This can be accomplished with this code:

```
mousey.setY( MathUtils.clamp( mousey.getY(), 0,  mapHeight - mousey.getHeight() ));
```

The previous two lines of code can be inserted right after the line containing mainStage.act(dt).

This point is another good time to compile and test the code, and verify that Mousey can no longer pass completely beyond the boundaries of the screen.

Next, you need to use the Camera class, for it determines which part of a Stage is rendered; this is now important, since only a portion of the game world can be displayed in the program window at a time. In the render part of the game loop, before you draw mainStage, you'll get the Camera object associated with mainStage and center it on (by setting its position to) the player's (Mousey's) position.

However, when Mousey approaches the edge of the game world, if the camera remains centered on Mousey, then the region the camera is displaying might include areas outside the boundary of the game world, which would be unacceptable. Therefore, you need to make a second adjustment to the camera's position: you need to bound the camera position so that it stays in the central area of the game world. More precisely, as illustrated in Figure 2-5, the x coordinate of the camera must always be at least viewWidth/2 pixels away from the left and right boundaries of the game world. The division by 2 occurs because the camera is in the center of the screen, and therefore needs a buffer of only half the width on each side. Similarly, the y coordinate must be at least viewHeight/2 pixels away from the top and bottom boundaries of the game world.

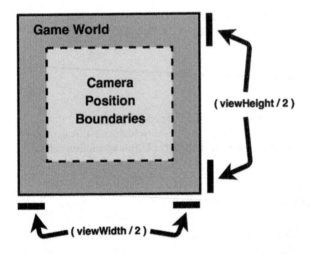

Figure 2-5. *Boundaries for the camera position*

This can be efficiently accomplished using the clamp method, similarly to when you bounded the position of Mousey to the game world. The code to accomplish this is listed next, and should appear right before the call to mainStage.draw():

```
Camera cam = mainStage.getCamera();

// center camera on player
cam.position.set( mousey.getX() + mousey.getOriginX(),
    mousey.getY() + mousey.getOriginY(), 0 );
```

```
// bound camera to layout
cam.position.x = MathUtils.clamp(cam.position.x, viewWidth/2,  mapWidth - viewWidth/2);
cam.position.y = MathUtils.clamp(cam.position.y, viewHeight/2, mapHeight - viewHeight/2);
cam.update();
```

Note that you don't need to perform any similar adjustments to the stage that contains the user interface, as the contents of the UI do not scroll as the game world does.

The complete source code for this example is not listed here; it can be viewed from the book web site, in the file CheesePlease5.java. Try running the code now, and observe how the camera always centers on Mousey whenever possible.

Handling Multiple Screens

One major component of video game software that you have not yet implemented is the ability to handle multiple screens. Almost every game has a *title screen* displaying the name of the game, perhaps with menu items or buttons that bring the player to a help screen with instructions or load a new screen where the game play begins. The Game class of the LibGDX library enables you to accomplish these goals.

Recall that the Game class implements the ApplicationListener interface, so that it can handle all the tasks of the game life cycle. The Game class also has the ability to delegate these functions to another object, but this object must contain a particular set of methods for this approach to work correctly. As you've seen previously, this kind of convention is enforced by using interfaces; the particular interface provided by LibGDX for this task is called Screen. It is quite similar to the ApplicationListener interface, except for the following differences:

- The create method is not required. Instead, you could call a create-style method from the constructor of the class implementing the interface.

- Two new methods, called show and hide, are required. These methods are called when the implementing class gains or loses focus, respectively.

To adapt the current version of your game to this new framework, the basic steps are as follows:

You create a new class, called CheeseLevel, which contains all the code from the previous iteration of our main example (CheesePlease5), and all the changes discussed next should be applied to this new class. CheeseLevel should also import the class com.badlogic.gdx.Screen.

The class declaration should no longer extend the Game class; rather, it implements the Screen interface, so it should read as follows: public class CheeseLevel implements Screen. Also, you will need to include code for each of the methods required by the interface; for now, you'll leave each method body empty, as follows:

```
public void resize(int width, int height) {   }
public void pause()    {   }
public void resume()   {   }
public void dispose() {   }
public void show()     {   }
public void hide()     {   }
```

The interface also assumes that the render method is passed a float method that represents the time elapsed since the last frame (which means you no longer need to calculate it). You rewrite the method declaration for render as public void render(float dt), and you can delete the following (now redundant) line of code from the render method:

```
float dt = Gdx.graphics.getDeltaTime();
```

You also want to store a reference to the Game that created this screen, which will enable you to switch screens later. After the existing variable declarations, you add this:

```
public Game game;
```

You write a constructor method for this class; it will take a Game object as a parameter, to store for later access as mentioned previously, and it will also call the create method, as follows:

```
public CheeseLevel(Game g)
{
    game = g;
    create();
}
```

The complete code for this new, final version of your game, containing all of the additions listed previously, is given here:

```
import com.badlogic.gdx.Game;
import com.badlogic.gdx.Gdx;
import com.badlogic.gdx.Input.Keys;
import com.badlogic.gdx.graphics.Color;
import com.badlogic.gdx.graphics.GL20;
import com.badlogic.gdx.graphics.Texture;
import com.badlogic.gdx.math.Rectangle;
import com.badlogic.gdx.scenes.scene2d.Stage;
import com.badlogic.gdx.scenes.scene2d.actions.Actions;
import com.badlogic.gdx.graphics.Texture.TextureFilter;
import com.badlogic.gdx.graphics.g2d.TextureRegion;
import com.badlogic.gdx.graphics.g2d.Animation;
import com.badlogic.gdx.graphics.g2d.Animation.PlayMode;
import com.badlogic.gdx.utils.Array;

import com.badlogic.gdx.scenes.scene2d.ui.Label;
import com.badlogic.gdx.scenes.scene2d.ui.Label.LabelStyle;
import com.badlogic.gdx.graphics.g2d.BitmapFont;
import com.badlogic.gdx.graphics.Camera;
import com.badlogic.gdx.math.MathUtils;

import com.badlogic.gdx.Screen;

public class CheeseLevel implements Screen
{
    private Stage mainStage;
    private Stage uiStage;

    private AnimatedActor mousey;
    private BaseActor cheese;
    private BaseActor floor;
    private BaseActor winText;
    private boolean win;
```

```java
private float timeElapsed;
private Label timeLabel;

// game world dimensions
final int mapWidth = 800;
final int mapHeight = 800;
// window dimensions
final int viewWidth = 640;
final int viewHeight = 480;

public Game game;
public CheeseLevel(Game g)
{
    game = g;
    create();
}

public void create()
{
    mainStage = new Stage();
    uiStage = new Stage();
    timeElapsed = 0;

    floor = new BaseActor();
    floor.setTexture( new Texture(Gdx.files.internal("assets/tiles-800-800.jpg")) );
    floor.setPosition( 0, 0 );
    mainStage.addActor( floor );

    cheese = new BaseActor();
    cheese.setTexture( new Texture(Gdx.files.internal("assets/cheese.png")) );
    cheese.setPosition( 400, 300 );
    cheese.setOrigin( cheese.getWidth()/2, cheese.getHeight()/2 );
    mainStage.addActor( cheese );

    mousey = new AnimatedActor();

    TextureRegion[] frames = new TextureRegion[4];
    for (int n = 0; n < 4; n++)
    {
        String fileName = "assets/mouse" + n + ".png";
        Texture tex = new Texture(Gdx.files.internal(fileName));
        tex.setFilter(TextureFilter.Linear, TextureFilter.Linear);
        frames[n] = new TextureRegion( tex );
    }
    Array<TextureRegion> framesArray = new Array<TextureRegion>(frames);

    Animation anim = new Animation(0.1f, framesArray, Animation.PlayMode.LOOP_PINGPONG);

    mousey.setAnimation( anim );
    mousey.setOrigin( mousey.getWidth()/2, mousey.getHeight()/2 );
    mousey.setPosition( 20, 20 );
    mainStage.addActor(mousey);
```

```
    winText = new BaseActor();
    winText.setTexture( new Texture(Gdx.files.internal("assets/you-win.png")) );
    winText.setPosition( 170, 60 );
    winText.setVisible( false );
    uiStage.addActor( winText );

    BitmapFont font = new BitmapFont();
    String text = "Time: 0";
    LabelStyle style = new LabelStyle( font, Color.NAVY );
    timeLabel = new Label( text, style );
    timeLabel.setFontScale(2);
    timeLabel.setPosition(500,440); // sets bottom left (baseline) corner?
    uiStage.addActor( timeLabel );

    win = false;
}

public void render(float dt)
{
    // process input
    mousey.velocityX = 0;
    mousey.velocityY = 0;

    if (Gdx.input.isKeyPressed(Keys.LEFT))
        mousey.velocityX -= 100;
    if (Gdx.input.isKeyPressed(Keys.RIGHT))
        mousey.velocityX += 100;;
    if (Gdx.input.isKeyPressed(Keys.UP))
        mousey.velocityY += 100;
    if (Gdx.input.isKeyPressed(Keys.DOWN))
        mousey.velocityY -= 100;
    if (Gdx.input.isKeyPressed(Keys.M))
        game.setScreen( new CheeseMenu(game) );

    // update
    mainStage.act(dt);
    uiStage.act(dt);

    // bound mousey to the rectangle defined by mapWidth, mapHeight
    mousey.setX( MathUtils.clamp( mousey.getX(), 0,  mapWidth - mousey.getWidth() ));
    mousey.setY( MathUtils.clamp( mousey.getY(), 0,  mapHeight - mousey.getHeight() ));

    // check win condition: mousey must be overlapping cheese
    Rectangle cheeseRectangle = cheese.getBoundingRectangle();
    Rectangle mouseyRectangle = mousey.getBoundingRectangle();
```

```java
if ( !win && cheeseRectangle.contains( mouseyRectangle ) )
{
    win = true;
    winText.addAction( Actions.sequence(
            Actions.alpha(0),
            Actions.show(),
            Actions.fadeIn(2),
            Actions.forever( Actions.sequence(
                    Actions.color( new Color(1,0,0,1), 1 ),
                    Actions.color( new Color(0,0,1,1), 1 )
                ))
        ));

    cheese.addAction( Actions.parallel(
            Actions.alpha(1),
            Actions.rotateBy(360f, 1),
            Actions.scaleTo(0,0, 2), // xAmt, yAmt, duration
            Actions.fadeOut(1)
        ));
}

if (!win)
{
    timeElapsed += dt;
    timeLabel.setText( "Time: " + (int)timeElapsed );
}

// draw graphics
Gdx.gl.glClearColor(0.8f, 0.8f, 1, 1);
Gdx.gl.glClear(GL20.GL_COLOR_BUFFER_BIT);

// camera adjustment
Camera cam = mainStage.getCamera();

// center camera on player
cam.position.set( mousey.getX() + mousey.getOriginX(),
    mousey.getY() + mousey.getOriginY(), 0 );

// bound camera to layout
cam.position.x = MathUtils.clamp(cam.position.x, viewWidth/2,  mapWidth - viewWidth/2);
cam.position.y = MathUtils.clamp(cam.position.y, viewHeight/2, mapHeight - viewHeight/2);
cam.update();

mainStage.draw();
uiStage.draw();
}
```

```
    public void resize(int width, int height) {  }
    public void pause()    {  }
    public void resume()   {  }
    public void dispose()  {  }
    public void show()     {  }
    public void hide()     {  }
}
```

With this groundwork laid, you will now create an extension of the Game class that creates an instance of the CheeseLevel class (passing itself as an argument in the process), and sets it to be the active Screen:

```
import com.badlogic.gdx.Game;
public class CheeseGame extends Game
{
    public void create()
    {
        CheeseLevel cl = new CheeseLevel(this);
        setScreen( cl );
    }
}
```

And, as usual, you need to write a new driver class:

```
import com.badlogic.gdx.backends.lwjgl.LwjglApplication;
public class CheeseLauncher
{
    public static void main (String[] args)
    {
        CheeseGame myProgram = new CheeseGame();
        LwjglApplication launcher = new LwjglApplication( myProgram );
    }
}
```

Now is a good time to test the new version of the code, to verify that all the changes have been implemented correctly.

Next, you'll create another class that also implements the Screen interface; this class will serve as your start menu, and is illustrated in Figure 2-6.

Figure 2-6. *The start menu screen for the game Cheese, Please!*

In this class, you need only one Stage to contain all the elements of the user interface. You will use a BaseActor for the background floor tile image, and another for the title graphic, both of which need to be copied to the assets folder. You'll use a Label to create the instruction text, and since it is an extension of the Actor class, you can and will add a repeating sequence of actions to give the text a pulsing effect. The source code for this class is listed here; you start by listing the import statements, variable declarations, and method names:

```
import com.badlogic.gdx.Game;
import com.badlogic.gdx.Gdx;
import com.badlogic.gdx.Input.Keys;
import com.badlogic.gdx.graphics.Color;
import com.badlogic.gdx.graphics.GL20;
import com.badlogic.gdx.graphics.Texture;
import com.badlogic.gdx.scenes.scene2d.Stage;
import com.badlogic.gdx.scenes.scene2d.ui.Label;
import com.badlogic.gdx.scenes.scene2d.ui.Label.LabelStyle;
import com.badlogic.gdx.scenes.scene2d.actions.Actions;
import com.badlogic.gdx.graphics.g2d.BitmapFont;
import com.badlogic.gdx.Screen;
```

```
public class CheeseMenu implements Screen
{
    private Stage uiStage;
    private Game game;

    public CheeseMenu(Game g)
    {
        game = g;
        create();
    }

    public void create()
    {   }

    public void render(float dt)
    {   }

    public void resize(int width, int height) {  }
    public void pause()   {  }
    public void resume()  {  }
    public void dispose() {  }
    public void show()    {  }
    public void hide()    {  }
}
```

In the create method, you initialize the Stage and the BaseActor objects that will contain the title screen images, as well as the BitmapFont and Label that display the instructions and the associated effect, with the following code:

```
uiStage  = new Stage();

BaseActor background = new BaseActor();
background.setTexture( new Texture(Gdx.files.internal("assets/tiles-menu.jpg")) );
uiStage.addActor( background );

BaseActor titleText = new BaseActor();
titleText.setTexture( new Texture(Gdx.files.internal("assets/cheese-please.png")) );
titleText.setPosition( 20, 100 );
uiStage.addActor( titleText );

BitmapFont font = new BitmapFont();
String text = " Press S to start, M for main menu ";
LabelStyle style = new LatbelStyle( font, Color.YELLOW );
Label instructions = new Label( text, style );
instructions.setFontScale(2);
instructions.setPosition(100, 50);
// repeating color pulse effect
```

```
instructions.addAction(
    Actions.forever(
        Actions.sequence(
            Actions.color( new Color(1, 1, 0, 1), 0.5f ),
            Actions.delay( 0.5f ),
            Actions.color( new Color(0.5f, 0.5f, 0, 1), 0.5f )
        )
    )
);
uiStage.addActor( instructions );
```

In the render method, you'll check to see whether the user is pressing the S key, in which case you'll use the setScreen method of the Game class to switch the Screen to a CheeseLevel instance, which is where the game is played. In addition, you perform the standard tasks of calling the act method of any Stage objects being used, and drawing the graphics to the screen, as follows:

```
// process input
if (Gdx.input.isKeyPressed(Keys.S))
    game.setScreen( new CheeseLevel(game) );

// update
uiStage.act(dt);

// draw graphics
Gdx.gl.glClearColor(0.8f, 0.8f, 1, 1);
Gdx.gl.glClear(GL20.GL_COLOR_BUFFER_BIT);
uiStage.draw();
```

Now that the CheeseMenu class has been configured, you can return to the previously created CheeseLevel class. You'd like to give the user the ability to return to the main menu by pressing the M key, and so you add the following code to the update section of the render method in the CheeseLevel class:

```
if (Gdx.input.isKeyPressed(Keys.M))
    game.setScreen( new CheeseMenu(game) );
```

Finally, you need to rewrite the CheeseGame class to use an instance of CheeseMenu (rather than CheeseLevel) as the first screen that will be loaded, as follows:

```
import com.badlogic.gdx.Game;
public class CheeseGame extends Game
{
    public void create()
    {
        CheeseMenu cm = new CheeseMenu(this);
        setScreen( cm );
    }
}
```

This completes the "Cheese, Please!" game!

Summary

This chapter introduced many features of the LibGDX library. You began with an overview of the life cycle of a game program, and learned how the stages are performed by methods with a particular naming convention, enforced by an interface. You learned how to process keyboard input by using the Gdx class, and how to encapsulate game entity data by using either the Sprite class or the Actor class. You learned how the Stage class can be used to manage Actor instances, and how to extend the Actor class for greater functionality. Next, you saw how to make actors more visually interesting by using value-based animations provided by the Actions class, and image-based animations via the Animation class. Then, I introduced the Label, LabelStyle, and BitmapFont classes to help you create a user interface on a second Stage. You also increased the size of the game world and learned how to use the Camera associated with a Stage to display the correct part of the game world. Finally, the chapter introduced the Screen interface that enabled you to create a start menu in a class separate from the class containing the game-play code; and you saw how the Game class manages multiple screens.

In the next chapter, you'll create your own extensions of these classes that capture the common features in many games, and see how to use these as the basis of a completely new game.

CHAPTER 3

■ ■ ■

Extending the Framework

This chapter begins by reviewing the code for the *Cheese, Please!* game from the previous chapter. Your main focus will be streamlining your code from the previous chapter by refactoring common elements into new classes that can be reused as needed. This will also make it easier to introduce more-advanced features, such as new methods for processing user input. Then you will see how your new classes can be used as a basis for additional game projects. Finally, you will improve your custom extensions of the Actor class by adding improved collision detection and response, managing multiple animations, and implementing physics-based movement.

Cheese, Please! Revisited

Looking at the final version of the code from the previous chapter's game (Cheese, Please!), you can observe that the Screen-implementing classes contain similar data (such as Stage objects) and perform similar tasks (such as calling the act and draw methods of the stages). In computer programming, you'd like to remove repetition and create reusable code whenever possible, so that your code is easier to understand and maintain. You'll address this issue in this section. In addition, you'll introduce some new functionality to each of these classes:

- The ability to handle discrete input events—actions that occur only once when a key is pressed or a mouse button is clicked

- The ability to pause the game, which requires the Boolean variable paused to determine whether the game is currently paused, and some associated helper methods: isPaused, setPaused, and togglePaused

- The ability to resize the window and have the game world entities scale appropriately in response

To this end, you'll create a new class, called BaseScreen, which manages the data and handles the new and old tasks that your classes have in common. Then, your other game-play-centric classes will extend the BaseScreen class, which will simplify your code greatly. Before you start writing this class, however, you need to learn about two implementation-related issues in detail: discrete input and abstract class design.

Discrete Input

Previously, the method you used to process input is called *polling*: checking the state of the input hardware devices (such as the keyboard) during *every* iteration of the game loop. This approach is particularly well-suited for *continuous actions*—those that continue to happen during an interval of time, as long as the corresponding trigger is active. For instance, the player's character should continue to move (barring the presence of solid obstacles such as walls) for as long as the player is pressing an arrow key.

In contrast, an action such as jumping is called a *discrete action*, since it happens only once per key press. Even if the player continues to hold down the jump key, the player's character will *not* jump again until the jump key is released and pressed a second time (provided that the character is on the ground again!).

Discrete actions are tricky to handle using the polling approach, and so the LibGDX library provides an event-driven approach. This involves writing functions that are automatically called when certain events occur (such as the initial press or release of a key, or click of a mouse button).

Any object can be assigned the responsibility of responding to input events, but in order to do so correctly, it must contain a particular set of methods: those specified by the InputProcessor interface. There are eight of these methods altogether: keyDown, keyUp, and keyTyped to handle keyboard events; touchDown, touchUp, and touchDragged to handle both mouse and touch-screen events; mouseMoved and scrolled to handle mouse events. We'll discuss these methods further during the source code listing for the BaseScreen class.

The final question we need to address in this section is this: which component of your program should bear the responsibility of responding to input events? For example, the Stage class implements the InputProcessor interface; this is particularly helpful for a Stage that contains user interface elements, because it enables button-like objects to activate methods when they are clicked. At the same time, you are planning for the BaseScreen class to also implement the InputProcessor interface so that it can handle discrete input as described earlier. Should the Stage class or the BaseScreen class be in charge of responding to input events? In practice, you want both objects to have the opportunity to do so. The way this arrangement will be implemented in your code is via the InputMultiplexer class. An InputMultiplexer object is itself an InputProcessor that contains a list of other InputProcessors. You can add the Stage and BaseScreen objects to an InputMultiplexer, and when input events occur, the InputMultiplexer will forward along the information to each of these objects and give them the opportunity to respond accordingly.

Abstract Class Design

Another design consideration you have to address is which classes should implement which methods. In the BaseScreen class you will be writing, you will be providing the code for some methods, such as the constructor and render methods. For other methods, such as create, the classes extending BaseScreen should be required to provide the code. Conceptually, the role of BaseScreen lies somewhere between a standard class, where all of the methods are fully implemented, and an interface, where the methods are only declared. In Java, this functionality can be achieved by an *abstract class*.

ABSTRACT CLASSES

Often in programming, we'll try to reduce redundant code by refactoring repeated features in a base class, and then extending that class with specialized subclasses. Sometimes, we'll know that all of the extending classes will need to implement a particular method—but they will all do it in a different way, so we can't write the code ahead of time in the base class, but we do need to declare the method in the base class.

For example, we might create a fantasy-style role-playing game. Our base class, Person, will contain some standard fields and methods that all Person objects should have, like a String called name that stores the name of the person, and get and set methods to access this information. There may be two classes, Wizard and Warrior, that extend the Person class. The user interface of this game contains a Sword button that activates the useSword method of the Person class, while a Spell button activates a useSpell method.

Although the `Person` class will declare these methods, their implementation will differ greatly in the `Wizard` and `Warrior` classes. Traditionally, warriors wield swords, and wizards do not; wizards cast magic spells, and warriors do not. If the player clicks a button corresponding to an action that a character is unable to perform, we may want a message to display onscreen explaining this.

The programming difficulty is that we want to require extensions of the `Person` class to be required to provide code for the methods `useSword` and `useSpell`, as an interface does; however, `Person` *cannot* be an interface because it provides code for some of its methods, such as getting and setting the `name` field. In an interface, methods are only declared, not written.

The solution to this scenario is to declare the method, as we would in an interface, with the additional modifier that the method is `abstract`, which is written as follows:

```
public abstract void useSword();
public abstract void useSpell();
```

When one or more methods are declared in this way, this has an effect on the class as well. Since not all of the code is provided, we cannot create an instance of this class (again, similar to an interface). We must indicate this by declaring the class to abstract as well:

```
public abstract class Person
{
    private String name;
    public void setName(String n)  { name = n; }
    public String getName()  { return name; }
    public abstract void useSword();
    public abstract void useSpell();
}
```

Now, the classes that extend `Person` must provide an implementation of each abstract method. For example:

```
public class Wizard extends Person
{
    public void useSword()
    {
        System.out.print("You are unable to wield a sword...");
    }

    public void useSpell()
    {
        // insert code here that damages enemies
    }
}

public class Warrior extends Person
{
    public void useSword()
    {
        // insert code here that damages enemies
    }
```

```
    public void useSpell()
    {
        System.out.print("You are unable to use magic…");
    }
}
```

In this way, an abstract class combines the advantages of a standard class and an interface.

You want every class that extends the BaseScreen class to be required to implement its own create method, since create will be called by the constructor method of the BaseScreen class. Therefore, you will write the method signature and declare it to be abstract:

```
public abstract void create();
```

Additionally, the use of abstract methods enables you to address a design concern from the previous chapter. When we discussed the stages of the life cycle of a game program, you observed that LibGDX uses the render method to perform the game-loop tasks. However, rendering graphics is really only one of three tasks performed in the game loop, the others being processing input and updating the state of the game world. You can use abstract classes to help separate out the update and render functionality. Within the render method of the BaseScreen class, you'll start by calling an abstract method named update, and then the BaseScreen class will proceed to perform all the rendering code. Overall, this greatly reduces the complexity for the developers who write the classes that extend BaseScreen; their primary focus is to write the methods create and update.

Refactoring the Project

This section introduces the BaseScreen class. In particular, the code you write will handle the following tasks, in common to all your Screen–extending classes:

- Provide a reference to the Game object that instantiated the current class

- Initialize the mainStage and uiStage objects

- In the render method, call the act method of the stages, clear the screen, and then call the draw method of the stages

- Provide empty methods for all the Screen interface methods and InputProcessor interface methods not needed by your program

- Provide methods for pausing the game and resizing the window

At this point, create a new project in BlueJ, and copy all of the classes from the previous version of the Cheese, Please! game project. Then create a new class called BaseScreen, as described next.

First, you present the core of the BaseScreen class, which contains the import statements and variable declarations needed. The various methods of this class will be explained in the subsequent code listings.

```
import com.badlogic.gdx.Screen;
import com.badlogic.gdx.InputProcessor;
import com.badlogic.gdx.Game;
import com.badlogic.gdx.Gdx;
import com.badlogic.gdx.graphics.GL20;
```

```
import com.badlogic.gdx.scenes.scene2d.Stage;
import com.badlogic.gdx.utils.viewport.FitViewport;
import com.badlogic.gdx.InputMultiplexer;

public abstract class BaseScreen implements Screen, InputProcessor
{
    protected Game game;

    protected Stage mainStage;
    protected Stage uiStage;

    public final int viewWidth  = 640;
    public final int viewHeight = 480;

    private boolean paused;
}
```

Next, you have the constructor, which stores a reference to the Game object, initializes the Stage objects, sets pause to false, sets up the InputMultiplexer to receive all input data and pass it along to this class and the stages, and calls the create method. Note that each Stage is initialized with a FitViewport object; this object scales each Stage and its contents to fit the current window size, and if the aspect ratio of the window does not match that of the Stage, then the extra region is filled in with solid black.

```
public BaseScreen(Game g)
{
    game = g;

    mainStage = new Stage( new FitViewport(viewWidth, viewHeight) );
    uiStage   = new Stage( new FitViewport(viewWidth, viewHeight) );

    paused = false;

    InputMultiplexer im = new InputMultiplexer(this, uiStage, mainStage);
    Gdx.input.setInputProcessor( im );

    create();
}
```

After this, you include the abstract methods create and update, which must be implemented by any classes that extend BaseScreen:

```
public abstract void create();
```

```
public abstract void update(float dt);
```

Following this is the render method, which runs the game loop. You include the code that updates the stages, calls the update method, and draws the graphics:

```
// gameloop code; update, then render.
public void render(float dt)
{
    uiStage.act(dt);

    // only pause gameplay events, not UI events
    if ( !isPaused() )
    {
        mainStage.act(dt);
        update(dt);
    }

    // render
    Gdx.gl.glClearColor(0,0,0,1);
    Gdx.gl.glClear(GL20.GL_COLOR_BUFFER_BIT);
    mainStage.draw();
    uiStage.draw();
}
```

Then you have the methods that provide pausing functionality for your games:

```
// pause methods
public boolean isPaused()
{   return paused;   }

public void setPaused(boolean b)
{   paused = b;   }

public void togglePaused()
{   paused = !paused;   }
```

Also, you enter code in the resize method of the Screen interface to adjust the size of the stages' Viewport objects whenever the window size is changed:

```
public void resize(int width, int height)
    {
        mainStage.getViewport().update(width, height, true);
        uiStage.getViewport().update(width, height, true);
    }
```

Finally, you write empty versions of the remaining methods required by the Screen and InputProcessor interfaces, so that the classes extending BaseScreen don't have to do so:

```
// methods required by Screen interface
public void pause()   {  }
public void resume()  {  }
public void dispose() {  }
public void show()    {  }
public void hide()    {  }
```

```
// methods required by InputProcessor interface
public boolean keyDown(int keycode)
{   return false;   }
public boolean keyUp(int keycode)
{   return false;   }
public boolean keyTyped(char c)
{   return false;   }
public boolean mouseMoved(int screenX, int screenY)
{   return false;   }
public boolean scrolled(int amount)
{   return false;   }

public boolean touchDown(int screenX, int screenY, int pointer, int button)
{   return false;   }
public boolean touchDragged(int screenX, int screenY, int pointer)
{   return false;   }
public boolean touchUp(int screenX, int screenY, int pointer, int button)
{   return false;   }
```

Now, you will see how the BaseScreen class can be used to simplify the classes CheeseMenu and CheeseLevel from the previous version of the Cheese, Please! game. The game-specific classes no longer need to deal with much of the infrastructure, such as declaring and initializing Game and Stage variables. Each is required to contain only two methods: create and update. The update method contains much of the code originally present in the render method, notable exceptions being the absence of the calls to the each stage's act methods, and all the code that actually performed rendering operations. For demonstration purposes, you will also overwrite the keyDown method; it is particularly well suited for the discrete event of switching screens, and using the new pause functionality (which is triggered in the game by pressing the P key). To implement this code, it may be easiest to start with the code from the previous version of the class and make modifications and deletions where necessary.

The following is the rewritten code for the CheeseMenu class, starting with the core code: the import statements and constructor. Note in particular that there are fewer import statements; you are now extending the BaseScreen class rather than the Screen class, and you don't need to declare a Game or Stage variable (as the BaseScreen class handles this for you):

```
import com.badlogic.gdx.Game;
import com.badlogic.gdx.Gdx;
import com.badlogic.gdx.Input.Keys;
import com.badlogic.gdx.graphics.Color;
import com.badlogic.gdx.graphics.Texture;
import com.badlogic.gdx.scenes.scene2d.ui.Label;
import com.badlogic.gdx.scenes.scene2d.ui.Label.LabelStyle;
import com.badlogic.gdx.scenes.scene2d.actions.Actions;
import com.badlogic.gdx.graphics.g2d.BitmapFont;

public class CheeseMenu extends BaseScreen
{
    public CheeseMenu(Game g)
    {   super(g);   }

}
```

The create method of the BaseScreen class follows; here, note that you don't need to initialize the Stage object:

```
public void create()
{
    BaseActor background = new BaseActor();
    background.setTexture( new Texture(Gdx.files.internal("assets/tiles-menu.jpg")) );
    uiStage.addActor( background );

    BaseActor titleText = new BaseActor();
    titleText.setTexture( new Texture(Gdx.files.internal("assets/cheese-please.png")) );
    titleText.setPosition( 20, 100 );
    uiStage.addActor( titleText );

    BitmapFont font = new BitmapFont();
    String text = " Press S to start, M for main menu ";
    LabelStyle style = new LabelStyle( font, Color.YELLOW );
    Label instructions = new Label( text, style );
    instructions.setFontScale(2);
    instructions.setPosition(100, 50);
    // repeating color pulse effect
    instructions.addAction(
        Actions.forever(
            Actions.sequence(
                Actions.color( new Color(1, 1, 0, 1), 0.5f ),
                Actions.delay( 0.5f ),
                Actions.color( new Color(0.5f, 0.5f, 0, 1), 0.5f )
            )
        )
    );
    uiStage.addActor( instructions );
}
```

Finally, the following is the code for the remaining two methods. First you have the update method, which replaces the render method from the previous version of this class and contains only the code pertaining to the game logic; note the absence of the drawing code. The only input you processed in the previous version was checking to see whether the S key was being held down. Since this is more accurately represented as a discrete event, you'll move this code into the keyDown method of the InputProcessor interface, overriding the empty version from the BaseScreen class. As it turns out, this means that no code is left within the update method, but you must include the method even though the body is empty, because it was declared abstract in the BaseScreen class.

```
public void update(float dt)
{

}

// InputProcessor methods for handling discrete input
public boolean keyDown(int keycode)
{
```

```
    if (keycode == Keys.S)
        game.setScreen( new CheeseLevel(game) );

    return false;
}
```

This completes the code for the CheeseMenu class. Next is the code for the rewritten CheeseLevel class. As before, you start with the core of the class: import statements, variable declarations, and the constructor:

```
import com.badlogic.gdx.Game;
import com.badlogic.gdx.Gdx;
import com.badlogic.gdx.Input.Keys;
import com.badlogic.gdx.graphics.Color;
import com.badlogic.gdx.graphics.Texture;
import com.badlogic.gdx.math.Rectangle;;
import com.badlogic.gdx.scenes.scene2d.Action;
import com.badlogic.gdx.scenes.scene2d.actions.Actions;
import com.badlogic.gdx.graphics.Texture.TextureFilter;
import com.badlogic.gdx.graphics.g2d.TextureRegion;
import com.badlogic.gdx.graphics.g2d.Animation;
import com.badlogic.gdx.graphics.g2d.Animation.PlayMode;
import com.badlogic.gdx.utils.Array;
import com.badlogic.gdx.scenes.scene2d.ui.Label;
import com.badlogic.gdx.scenes.scene2d.ui.Label.LabelStyle;
import com.badlogic.gdx.graphics.g2d.BitmapFont;
import com.badlogic.gdx.graphics.Camera;
import com.badlogic.gdx.math.MathUtils;

public class CheeseLevel extends BaseScreen
{
    private AnimatedActor mousey;
    private BaseActor cheese;
    private BaseActor floor;
    private BaseActor winText;
    private boolean win;
    private float timeElapsed;
    private Label timeLabel;

    // game world dimensions
    final int mapWidth = 800;
    final int mapHeight = 800;

    public CheeseLevel(Game g)
    {  super(g);   }
```

```
}
```

Next, is the code for the create method, once again devoid of initializing the Stage objects:

```
public void create()
{
    timeElapsed = 0;

    floor = new BaseActor();
    floor.setTexture( new Texture(Gdx.files.internal("assets/tiles-800-800.jpg")) );
    floor.setPosition( 0, 0 );
    mainStage.addActor( floor );

    cheese = new BaseActor();
    cheese.setTexture( new Texture(Gdx.files.internal("assets/cheese.png")) );
    cheese.setPosition( 400, 300 );
    cheese.setOrigin( cheese.getWidth()/2, cheese.getHeight()/2 );
    mainStage.addActor( cheese );

    mousey = new AnimatedActor();

    TextureRegion[] frames = new TextureRegion[4];
    for (int n = 0; n < 4; n++)
    {
        String fileName = "assets/mouse" + n + ".png";
        Texture tex = new Texture(Gdx.files.internal(fileName));
        tex.setFilter(TextureFilter.Linear, TextureFilter.Linear);
        frames[n] = new TextureRegion( tex );
    }
    Array<TextureRegion> framesArray = new Array<TextureRegion>(frames);

    Animation anim = new Animation(0.1f, framesArray, Animation.PlayMode.LOOP_PINGPONG);

    mousey.setAnimation( anim );
    mousey.setOrigin( mousey.getWidth()/2, mousey.getHeight()/2 );
    mousey.setPosition( 20, 20 );
    mainStage.addActor(mousey);

    winText = new BaseActor();
    winText.setTexture( new Texture(Gdx.files.internal("assets/you-win.png")) );
    winText.setPosition( 170, 60 );
    winText.setVisible( false );
    uiStage.addActor( winText );

    BitmapFont font = new BitmapFont();
    String text = "Time: 0";
    LabelStyle style = new LabelStyle( font, Color.NAVY );
    timeLabel = new Label( text, style );
    timeLabel.setFontScale(2);
    timeLabel.setPosition(500,440); // sets bottom left (baseline) corner?
    uiStage.addActor( timeLabel );

    win = false;
```

```
}
```

Finally, you have the code for the update method, which is a subset of the code of the render method of the previous version. As was the case with the previous update method, you no longer need to call the act or draw methods of the stages. The code that processes input pertaining to movement of the player, a continuous action, remains in the update method; the code for discrete actions (switching screens and pausing the game) is moved to a keyDown method, also presented here:

```
public void update(float dt)
{
    // process input
    mousey.velocityX = 0;
    mousey.velocityY = 0;

    if (Gdx.input.isKeyPressed(Keys.LEFT))
        mousey.velocityX -= 100;
    if (Gdx.input.isKeyPressed(Keys.RIGHT))
        mousey.velocityX += 100;;
    if (Gdx.input.isKeyPressed(Keys.UP))
        mousey.velocityY += 100;
    if (Gdx.input.isKeyPressed(Keys.DOWN))
        mousey.velocityY -= 100;

    // bound mousey to the rectangle defined by mapWidth, mapHeight
    mousey.setX( MathUtils.clamp( mousey.getX(), 0,  mapWidth - mousey.getWidth() ));
    mousey.setY( MathUtils.clamp( mousey.getY(), 0,  mapHeight - mousey.getHeight() ));

    // check win condition: mousey must be overlapping cheese
    Rectangle cheeseRectangle = cheese.getBoundingRectangle();
    Rectangle mouseyRectangle = mousey.getBoundingRectangle();

    if ( !win && cheeseRectangle.contains( mouseyRectangle ) )
    {
        win = true;

        Action spinShrinkFadeOut = Actions.parallel(
            Actions.alpha(1),          // set transparency value
            Actions.rotateBy(360, 1), // rotation amount, duration
            Actions.scaleTo(0,0, 2),  // x amount, y amount, duration
            Actions.fadeOut(1)         // duration of fade in
        );
        cheese.addAction( spinShrinkFadeOut );

        Action fadeInColorCycleForever = Actions.sequence(
            Actions.alpha(0),    // set transparency value
            Actions.show(),      // set visible to true
            Actions.fadeIn(2),   // duration of fade out
```

```
            Actions.forever(
                Actions.sequence(
                    // color shade to approach, duration
                    Actions.color( new Color(1,0,0,1), 1 ),
                    Actions.color( new Color(0,0,1,1), 1 )
                )
            )
        );
        winText.addAction( fadeInColorCycleForever );
    }

    if (!win)
    {
        timeElapsed += dt;
        timeLabel.setText( "Time: " + (int)timeElapsed );
    }

    // camera adjustment
    Camera cam = mainStage.getCamera();

    // center camera on player
    cam.position.set( mousey.getX() + mousey.getOriginX(),
        mousey.getY() + mousey.getOriginY(), 0 );

    // bound camera to layout
    cam.position.x = MathUtils.clamp(cam.position.x, viewWidth/2,  mapWidth-viewWidth/2);
    cam.position.y = MathUtils.clamp(cam.position.y, viewHeight/2, mapHeight-viewHeight/2);
    cam.update();
}

// InputProcessor methods for handling discrete input
public boolean keyDown(int keycode)
{
    if (keycode == Keys.M)
        game.setScreen( new CheeseMenu(game) );

    if (keycode == Keys.P)
        togglePaused();

    return false;
}
```

This completes the refactoring of the code for the Cheese, Please! game.

At this point, your project contains many classes that depend on each other in various ways. The BlueJ window represents each class with an orange rectangle, and the relationships between the classes are indicated by arrows. Dashed arrows indicate that one class creates an instance of another, while solid arrows indicate that one class extends another. You can drag and drop the orange rectangles to rearrange them so

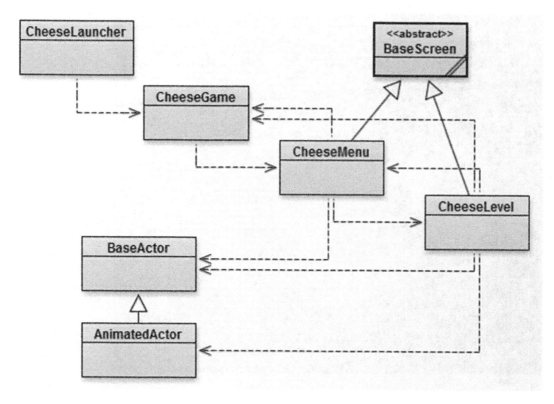

Figure 3-1. *Relationships between classes in the refactored Cheese, Please! game project*

that the interrelationships are more clear; one possible such arrangement appears in Figure 3-1. Note in particular that you can visually deduce that CheeseLevel and CheeseMenu extend the BaseScreen class.

Now that you see how the BaseScreen class enables you to streamline your previous code, in the next section you'll see how it simplifies the creation of a completely new game, with an entirely different (mouse-driven) control scheme.

Balloon Buster: A Mouse-Driven Game

This section presents a game called *Balloon Buster*, which serves two purposes: first, to illustrate the general applicability of the BaseScreen class from the previous section, and second, to present a game that is played using only the mouse (in contrast to Cheese, Please!, which was played using only the keyboard).

In Balloon Buster, illustrated in Figure 3-2, the player's goal is to pop as many balloons as possible. Balloons spawn to the left of the screen at regular intervals, and then drift across the screen to the right, following various randomized patterns. Game play continues until the player decides to quit. The program keeps track of and displays various statistics: the total number of balloons that have been popped, the

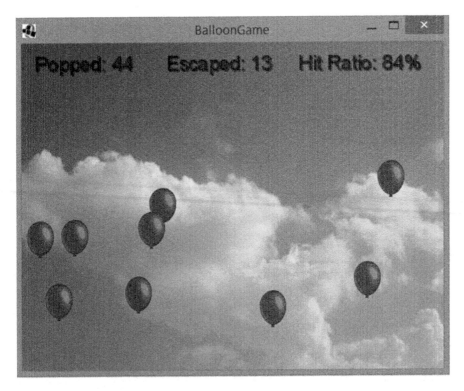

Figure 3-2. *A screenshot of the game Balloon Buster*

number that have escaped off-screen, and the *hit ratio* (the ratio of popped balloons to mouse clicks). The closer the hit ratio value is to 100%, the more accurate the player is.

At this point, you create a new project in BlueJ. Into this project, you need to copy the code for the BaseScreen and BaseActor classes. In addition, you need a launcher class, as well as a class that extends Game and initializes and sets the first (and in this game, only) screen to be displayed, BalloonLevel (described next). The corresponding classes can also be copied over from the previous project and changed as needed.

You will write a class called BalloonLevel that extends the BaseScreen class, and you will also reuse the BaseActor class from the previous game. This allows you to focus on determining the fields required by the BalloonLevel class, and the contents of the create and update methods.

In Balloon Buster, the only game entities that appear on the main stage are a background image (of the sky) and the balloons that the player will be popping. You'll need a variable to keep track of how much time has passed since the previous balloon was spawned, to know when it is time to spawn another. You'll also need to keep track of the number of popped balloons, escaped balloons, and mouse clicks; Label objects will be used to display each of these values on the user interface stage. Finally, you'll store the width and height of the game world, as they will be needed to determine when a balloon has flown off-screen. The following is the code for the BalloonLevel class that includes these variables, as well as all the import statements you will eventually need. The create and update methods are blank for now; you will fill them in later in this section.

```
import com.badlogic.gdx.Game;
import com.badlogic.gdx.Gdx;
import com.badlogic.gdx.graphics.Color;
```

```
import com.badlogic.gdx.graphics.Texture;
import com.badlogic.gdx.scenes.scene2d.Actor;
import com.badlogic.gdx.scenes.scene2d.ui.Label;
import com.badlogic.gdx.scenes.scene2d.ui.Label.LabelStyle;
import com.badlogic.gdx.graphics.g2d.BitmapFont;
import com.badlogic.gdx.scenes.scene2d.InputListener;
import com.badlogic.gdx.scenes.scene2d.InputEvent;

public class BalloonLevel extends BaseScreen
{
    private BaseActor background;

    private float spawnTimer;
    private float spawnInterval;

    private int popped;
    private int escaped;
    private int clickCount;

    private Label poppedLabel;
    private Label escapedLabel;
    private Label hitRatioLabel;

    // game world dimensions
    final int mapWidth = 640;
    final int mapHeight = 480;

    public BalloonLevel(Game g)
    {  super(g);  }

    public void create()
    {       }

    public void update(float dt)
    {       }
}
```

Balloons

The balloon entities are particularly interesting, from a coding standpoint. You'd like each balloon to move a little differently, according to a set of parameters that are randomly generated at the time the balloon is created. Because you need each balloon to store this information, and the information is unique to each instance, you need to write a class (named Balloon) that extends the BaseActor class. This class will also have its own act method that sets the position of the actor to follow a sine wave–based path across the screen. You calculate the position of each balloon *parametrically*: the x and the y coordinates are each a function of another variable, time, which represents the amount of time that has passed since the Balloon object was created. As time passes, the x coordinate of the balloon steadily increases, while the y coordinate is calculated according to this formula:

$$y = A \times \sin(B \times x) + C$$

where A controls the amplitude (or height) of the sine wave (illustrated in Figure 3-3), B affects the rate of oscillation (illustrated in Figure 3-4), and C controls the initial height.

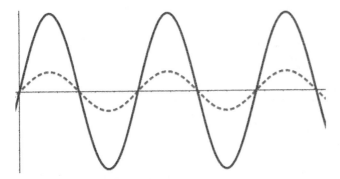

Figure 3-3. *Sine waves with different amplitudes: small (dashed line) and large (solid line)*

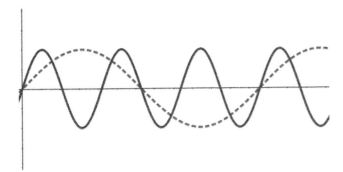

Figure 3-4. *Sine waves with different rates of oscillation: small (dashed line) and large (solid line)*

The constructor of the Balloon object initializes and randomizes the values used in this formula (and also loads a texture). You use some functions from the MathUtils class. The random method produces a randomly generated float value between the two given inputs, which you use to introduce some variation in the parameters that control the path of the balloon. The sin method calculates the values of a sine wave function. You also initially offset the x position to beyond the left edge of the screen so that the balloon objects don't suddenly appear in the middle of the sky. The source code for this class is given here:

```
import com.badlogic.gdx.Gdx;
import com.badlogic.gdx.math.MathUtils;
import com.badlogic.gdx.graphics.Texture;

public class Balloon extends BaseActor
{
    public float speed;
    public float amplitude;
    public float oscillation;
    public float initialY;
    public float time;
    public int offset;
```

```
public Balloon()
{
    speed       = 80    * MathUtils.random(0.5f, 2.0f);
    amplitude   = 50    * MathUtils.random(0.5f, 2.0f);
    oscillation = 0.01f * MathUtils.random(0.5f, 2.0f);
    initialY    = 120   * MathUtils.random(0.5f, 2.0f);
    time = 0;
    offsetX = -100;
    setTexture( new Texture( Gdx.files.internal("assets/red-balloon.png")) );

    // initial spawn location off-screen
    setX(offsetX);
}

public void act(float dt)
{
    super.act(dt);
    time += dt;
    // set starting location to left of window
    float xPos = speed * time + offsetX;
    float yPos = amplitude * MathUtils.sin(oscillation * xPos) + initialY;
    setPosition( xPos, yPos );
}
}
```

Next, you'll learn about the create method of the BalloonLevel class. This initializes most of the variables discussed previously, adding a background image to the main stage, creating a BitmapFont and LabelStyle for the Label objects to use, and then adding each Label object to the stage containing the user interface elements. The one object that is not initialized here is the Balloon object; these are handled by the update method, which is discussed later.

```
public void create()
{
    background = new BaseActor();
    background.setTexture( new Texture(Gdx.files.internal("assets/sky.jpg")) );
    background.setPosition( 0, 0 );
    mainStage.addActor( background );

    spawnTimer = 0;
    spawnInterval = 0.5f;

    // set up user interface
    BitmapFont font = new BitmapFont();
    LabelStyle style = new LabelStyle( font, Color.NAVY );

    popped = 0;
    poppedLabel = new Label( "Popped: 0", style );
    poppedLabel.setFontScale(2);
    poppedLabel.setPosition(20, 440);
    uiStage.addActor( poppedLabel );
```

```
    escaped = 0;
    escapedLabel = new Label( "Escaped: 0", style );
    escapedLabel.setFontScale(2);
    escapedLabel.setPosition(220, 440);
    uiStage.addActor( escapedLabel );

    clickCount = 0;
    hitRatioLabel = new Label( "Hit Ratio: ---", style );
    hitRatioLabel.setFontScale(2);
    hitRatioLabel.setPosition(420, 440);
    uiStage.addActor( hitRatioLabel );
}
```

Adding Interactivity

This section covers the contents of the update method. You update the spawnTimer, and once it exceeds a predefined period (stored in spawnInterval), you create a new Balloon instance. Most significantly in this portion of the code, you add an object to the Balloon that allows it to process input. You may recall from our discussion of the InputMultiplexer object earlier in this chapter that discrete input events can be processed by classes implementing the InputProcessor interface, as well as Actor objects (and for this reason, you included the Stage objects when creating the InputMultiplexer). You specify how an Actor should respond to an input event via an InputListener object, which contains methods corresponding to the different types of input that can be handled. Since each custom InputListener object is used within only a single line of code in our program, you can simplify your code by creating anonymous inner classes.

ANONYMOUS INNER CLASSES

One of the reasons we create variables when writing a program is so that we can refer to them again at a later point in the code. Sometimes, however, we need to use an instance only once in a program, and there is no need to refer to it later. For example, we might want to use a Scanner object to process the contents of a text file. To this end, we can create a File object that provides access to the text file, and pass this to the Scanner object, as follows:

```
File f = new File( "data.txt" );
Scanner s = new Scanner( f );
```

However, since we never need to access the File object later in this program, we could alternatively create an *anonymous*[1] File instance at the single point in the code where it is needed: during the initialization of the Scanner object.

```
Scanner s = new Scanner( new File("data.txt") );
```

---

[1]It is called anonymous because it is not assigned a name, and thus can't be accessed again for later use.

In Java, not only can preexisting classes be initialized in this way, but also new classes can be created as well. For example, perhaps you are creating a game in which a character collects Scroll objects, via a method called addScroll; each Scroll can display a different message. The Scroll class is given as follows:

```java
public class Scroll
{
    public void displayMessage() {  }
}
```

This class is meant to be extended so that the displayMessage method can be overwritten. However, if every Scroll-derived object is instantiated at only a single point in the program, creating files for all these classes results in a lot of unnecessary extra code. For example, we could create a class called TreasureScroll as follows:

```java
public class TreasureScroll extends Scroll
{
    public void displayMessage()
    {  System.out.print("The treasure is buried in the castle garden.");  }
}
```

Then we could create an anonymous instance of this object when the player adds it to their Scroll collection:

```java
player.addScroll( new TreasureScroll() );
```

We can create an *anonymous inner class* to accomplish the same goal with the following code:

```java
player.addScroll(
    new Scroll()
    {
        public void displayMessage()
        {  System.out.print("The treasure is buried in the castle garden.");  }
    }
);
```

Within the call to addScroll, we've created an instance of a new object, which extends the Scroll class, and includes a set of braces where fields and method declarations can be placed, just as with a regular class. This new object is *anonymous*, since neither the instance nor the class are named, and is an *inner class* because it is a class defined within another class.

The same approach is also valid when working with interfaces. For example, assume that Scroll had been defined as an interface instead of a class, as follows:

```java
public interface Scroll
{
    public void displayMessage();
}
```

In this situation, when an anonymous inner class is created and passed as a parameter to the addScroll method, the parameter will be interpreted as a class that implements the Scroll interface.

This programming pattern is particularly useful when creating objects that contain code detailing how to respond to user input, since such objects are typically needed only once, as an argument to an input-processing method.

You will create an anonymous inner class that extends the InputListener class and contains a single method, named touchDown, that is called when the user touches or clicks within the rectangular region defined by the actor. Within this method, you make the actor remove itself from the stage that contains it. You also increment the number of popped balloons; this latter instruction is why the InputListener is added within the BalloonLevel class rather than the Balloon class: it needs to access the popped variable in the BalloonLevel class.

Next, in the update method, you use a for-each loop that iterates through the set of all actors stored in the mainStage object, checks whether they have passed beyond the boundaries of the screen, and if so, removes them from the stage and increments escaped, the number of escaped balloons.[2]

Finally, in the update method, you update the text of the Label objects in the user interface. You are particularly careful to update only the Label displaying the hit ratio information after clickCount is greater than 0, to avoid a division-by-zero runtime error.

You're now ready for the complete source code of the update method:

```java
public void update(float dt)
{
    spawnTimer += dt;
    // check time for next balloon spawn
    if (spawnTimer > spawnInterval)
    {
        spawnTimer -= spawnInterval;
        Balloon b = new Balloon();
        b.addListener(
          new InputListener()
          {
              public boolean touchDown (InputEvent ev, float x, float y, int pointer, int button)
              {
                  popped++;
                  b.remove();
                  return true;
              }
          });
        mainStage.addActor(b);
    }

    // remove balloons that are off-screen
    for ( Actor a : mainStage.getActors() )
    {
        if (a.getX() > mapWidth || a.getY() > mapHeight)
        {
            escaped++;
            a.remove();
        }
    }
}
```

---

[2]Technically, you're really interested in only whether Balloon objects pass beyond the boundary of the screen, and mainStage also stores the BaseActor that stores the background image. Fortunately, the background can't move off-screen and so you can use the Stage's internal list for your purposes. In future programs, you'll be forced to be more precise, and keep track of and process different types of game entities using different lists.

```
    // update user interface
    poppedLabel.setText( "Popped: " + popped );
    escapedLabel.setText( "Escaped: " + escaped );
    if ( clickCount > 0 )
    {
        int percent = (int)(100.0 * popped / clickCount);
        hitRatioLabel.setText( "Hit Ratio: " + percent + "%" );
    }
}
```

You may have noticed that you didn't change the value of clickCount, the number of mouse clicks, anywhere within the update method. This is because clicking a mouse button is a discrete action, and is best handled by the touchDown method in the BalloonLevel class. (Recall that all classes that implement the InputProcessor interface have a touchDown method, and because of our use of the InputMultiplexer class, each one of these classes will have a chance to process user input.) To accomplish this, you add the following code immediately following the update method:

```
public boolean touchDown(int screenX, int screenY, int pointer, int button)
{
    clickCount++;
    return false;
}
```

In addition, as usual, you need to create a new class that extends the Game class:

```
import com.badlogic.gdx.Game;
public class BalloonGame extends Game
{
    public void create()
    {
        BalloonLevel z = new BalloonLevel(this);
        setScreen( z );
    }
}
```

And also as usual, you need to create a new driver class:

```
import com.badlogic.gdx.backends.lwjgl.LwjglApplication;
public class BalloonLauncher
{
    public static void main ()
    {
        BalloonGame myProgram = new BalloonGame();
        LwjglApplication launcher = new LwjglApplication( myProgram );
    }
}
```

This completes the core mechanics of the Balloon Buster game. Now is a good time to test out the game, and see how many balloons you can pop!

Next Steps

Although this game is fully functional, many features still could be changed or added to the game to make it more interesting or visually appealing. The following are some ideas and suggestions that you could implement, or that may inspire you to create other modifications:

- Add a start screen containing a button image to click that starts the game.

- Use the gray-balloon.png image instead, and select a random Color to tint the balloon image when it is spawned.

- When a balloon is popped, add an Action that makes the balloon fade out slowly instead of just disappearing.

- Add an ending condition—perhaps the game ends after a fixed amount of time, or after a fixed number of balloons have escaped, or after 100 total balloons have been spawned.

- Change the game-play mechanic entirely: randomly spawn red and green balloons; popping green balloons adds to your score, while popping red balloons subtracts from your score or ends the game.

- Anything else you can think of—the sky's the limit!

Starfish Collector: A Game with Improved Actor Classes

This section introduces another new game, and the final game of this chapter: Starfish Collector. Developing this game will involve rearranging and adding some features to the BaseActor and AnimatedActor classes, as well as creating a new class, PhysicsActor, for improved realistic motion. In these classes and in our new game program, you will also use some of Java's built-in data structure classes.

DATA STRUCTURES

Data structures are specialized formats for storing, organizing, and accessing data.

The first data structure typically encountered in Java programming is the *array*, which can store a fixed number of objects of a single type; the values stored in the array can be later accessed by an integer that refers to the position index within the array. While simple to understand, arrays have a few drawbacks, such as having a fixed size when they are created, and the possibly unintuitive association of a number to each array element.

Java provides a variety of data structures that address these problems, two of which are introduced here (and both of which you will use in this chapter and beyond).

One of these data structures is the ArrayList class. It can be used to store any number of objects of a single type; its size is not fixed and does not need to be specified when it is created. Objects can be added to a particular position, similar to arrays, but objects can also be added to the end of an ArrayList by using the method add (which also increases the size of the ArrayList by 1).

Another convenience to using an ArrayList is that if you want to use a loop to perform some action with each of the elements, you can use a for-each loop (illustrated in the following code), which allows you to create an index variable that iterates through the *objects* stored in the ArrayList; this is in

---

contrast to looping through a standard array, where your index variable must be an int that iterates over the *positions* of the objects stored in the array, and retrieving the objects themselves requires an extra line of code.

Finally, objects can be removed from an ArrayList by using the method remove and the object itself (which will also decrease the size of the ArrayList by 1). To accomplish the same task with an array is much more difficult: first, we have to somehow determine the index of the object that is to be removed; second, the object can't really even be removed—it is typically replaced with a null object, and the size of the array isn't changed.

For comparison, the following are two variations of the same code. First, we use an array:

```
// initialize array
String[] names = new String[3];

// add data to array
names[0] = "Lee";
names[1] = "Dan";
names[2] = "Chris";

// print the names
for (int i = 0; i < names.length; i++)
{
    String n = names[i];
    System.out.println( n );
}

// delete "Lee" from array
names[0] = null;

// names.length still equals 3
```

Next, we write some equivalent code that instead uses the ArrayList class:

```
// initialize ArrayList
ArrayList<String> names = new ArrayList<String>();

// add data to ArrayList
names.add("Lee");
names.add("Dan");
names.add("Chris");

// print the names
for (String n : names)
{
    System.out.println( n );
}

// delete "Lee" from ArrayList
names.delete("Lee");

// now, names.size() equals 2
```

In many cases, the ArrayList version of the preceding code is more intuitive and easier to maintain.

Another useful data structure is called an *associative array*, which stores pairs of objects. The first object in the pair is called the *key*; the second object is called the *value*. All the keys are the same type of object, as are all the values (but the key type may be different from the value type). A standard Java array is a special case of an associative array, where the keys are consecutive integers, ranging from 0 to some number *n*.

The HashMap class in Java provides all the functionality of an associative array. For example, perhaps we would like to store a list of names (each a String) and their associated high scores (each an Integer) in a game. We initialize a HashMap object similarly to the way we initialize an ArrayList object, except that the angle brackets contain the names of both the key type and the value type. Key-value pairs can be stored using the put method, values can be retrieved using the get method, and the name of the associated key, and key-value pairs can be deleted by using the remove method and the name of the key. You can also check whether a given key or value exists in the HashMap by using the containsKey and containsValue methods. The following example demonstrates some of these methods:

```
// initialize HashMap
HashMap<String,Integer> highScores = new HashMap<String,Integer>();

// add data to HashMap
highScores.put( "Lee", 337 );
highScores.put( "Dan", 9001 );
highScores.put( "Chris", 3333361 );

// retrieve a value
int danScore = highScores.get( "Dan" );

// delete an entry
highScores.remove( "Chris" );

// now, highScores.size() equals 2

//   and highScores.containsKey( "Chris" ) returns false
```

At this point, you will start a new project in BlueJ for the Starfish Collector game. To begin, copy the code from the previous project for the BaseActor and AnimatedActor classes, which you will modify over the course of the following sections.

The BaseActor Class

First, you will work on the BaseActor class. The purpose of this class is to manage a single texture and a collision polygon; you remove the velocity-related code (which will become part of the PhysicsActor class instead). You also replace the Rectangle object with a Polygon object. A Polygon is a data structure that defines a shape in terms of the coordinates of its vertices (corners); it is initialized with an array of float values that define the coordinates of the vertices, one after the other. For example, if the vertices of a polygon are (x0,y0), (x1,y1), ... , (xN,yN), then the corresponding Polygon object would be initialized with the array {x0, y0, x1, y1, ... , xN, yN}. Also, unlike a Rectangle object, a Polygon can be translated and rotated, which will come in useful later. You begin our presentation of the BaseActor class by listing the code for the import statements, declaring the variables you need, writing the constructor to initialize these variables, and you also repeat the methods that haven't changed since the previous version: setTexture, act, and draw.

```java
import com.badlogic.gdx.scenes.scene2d.Actor;
import com.badlogic.gdx.graphics.g2d.Batch;
import com.badlogic.gdx.graphics.Texture;
import com.badlogic.gdx.graphics.g2d.TextureRegion;
import com.badlogic.gdx.graphics.Color;
import com.badlogic.gdx.math.Rectangle;
import com.badlogic.gdx.math.Polygon;
import com.badlogic.gdx.math.MathUtils;
import com.badlogic.gdx.math.Intersector;
import com.badlogic.gdx.math.Intersector.MinimumTranslationVector;

public class BaseActor extends Actor
{
    public TextureRegion region;
    public Polygon boundingPolygon;

    public BaseActor()
    {
        super();
        region = new TextureRegion();
        boundingPolygon = null;
    }

    public void setTexture(Texture t)
    {
        int w = t.getWidth();
        int h = t.getHeight();
        setWidth( w );
        setHeight( h );
        region.setRegion( t );
    }
    public void act(float dt)
    {
        super.act( dt );
    }

    public void draw(Batch batch, float parentAlpha)
    {
        Color c = getColor();
        batch.setColor(c.r, c.g, c.b, c.a);
        if ( isVisible() )
            batch.draw( region, getX(), getY(), getOriginX(), getOriginY(),
                getWidth(), getHeight(), getScaleX(), getScaleY(), getRotation() );
    }

}
```

Specifying the coordinates of a polygon can be a laborious task, so in the BaseActor class you will include a pair of methods that can be used to initialize a Polygon object, either with a rectangular shape, or with a shape approximating a circle or an ellipse.

The coordinates of a rectangle are easy to calculate. If the rectangle has width w and height h, then (as illustrated in Figure 3-5), the coordinates of the vertices, in counterclockwise order, are (0,0), (w,0), (w,h), and (0,h). You initialize this polygon with the float array {0,0, w,0, w,h, h,0}. The method setRectangleBoundary will set this up for you.

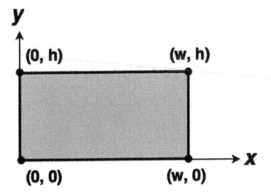

Figure 3-5. *Vertices of a rectangle*

Your other method, setEllipseBoundary, will be used to initialize a polygon that approximates the shape of an ellipse[3] contained within the rectangular region pictured in Figure 3-5. This method involves some mathematical equations to calculate the coordinates of the vertices. The trigonometric functions, sine and cosine, can be used to *parameterize* a circle or an ellipse, which means you can write functions for the x and y coordinates in terms of another variable, t. For example, if we let x = cos(t) and y = sin(t), then as the variable t takes on values ranging from 0 to 2 × pi (approximately 6.28),[4] the corresponding (x,y) points will trace out the shape of a circle with radius 1. You can adapt these equations to generate an ellipse that fits snugly within the given rectangular region, as illustrated in Figure 3-6. First, you must scale (multiply) x by w/2, and y by h/2, so the ellipse has the correct size. However, the resulting ellipse is centered at the origin, and you want the ellipse to be centered at (w/2, h/2); therefore, you add these values to the x and y equations, respectively. The final form of the equations are as follows:

```
x = w/2 * cos(t) + w/2
y = h/2 * sin(t) + h/2
```

The setEllipseBoundary method contains a loop to generate a set of n equally spaced values for t in the interval [0, 6.28], then calculates the corresponding x and y coordinates, and stores them in an array that will be used to initialize the polygon. If n = 4, the polygon will be a diamond shape; if n = 8, the polygon will be an octagon shape, and so forth. The larger the value of n, the smoother the shape will be. However, there is a trade-off: collision detection for general polygons is computationally intensive; large values of n can drastically slow down your program. For the game you're going to create, you'll be content with n = 8; an ellipse alongside a polygon approximation is illustrated in Figure 3-7.

---

[3]Although LibGDX contains an Ellipse class, there are no classes or methods in LibGDX that perform collision detection with ellipse shapes; however, Polygon objects do have such functionality available.
[4]The interval extends from 0 to 6.28 because mathematical functions typically use radian measure for angles rather than degree measure. 6.28 radians roughly corresponds to 360 degrees, which represents a full rotation around the origin, which we need when calculating the values of points all the way around the ellipse.

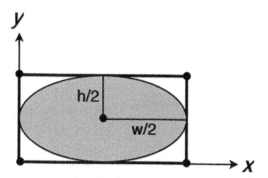

Figure 3-6. *Ellipse contained within a rectangle*

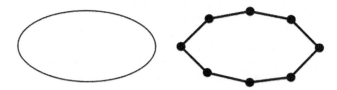

Figure 3-7. *An ellipse and a polygon approximation of the ellipse*

The code for setRectangleBoundary and setEllipseBoundary are given next, along with a method getBoundingPolygon that returns the collision polygon for this actor, adjusting it according to the actor's current position and rotation.

```
public void setRectangleBoundary()
{
    float w = getWidth();
    float h = getHeight();
    float[] vertices = {0,0, w,0, w,h, 0,h};
    boundingPolygon = new Polygon(vertices);
    boundingPolygon.setOrigin( getOriginX(), getOriginY() );
}

public void setEllipseBoundary()
{
    int n = 8; // number of vertices
    float w = getWidth();
    float h = getHeight();
    float[] vertices = new float[2*n];
    for (int i = 0; i < n; i++)
    {
        float t = i * 6.28f / n;
        // x-coordinate
        vertices[2*i] = w/2 * MathUtils.cos(t) + w/2;
        // y-coordinate
        vertices[2*i+1] = h/2 * MathUtils.sin(t) + h/2;
    }
```

```
    boundingPolygon = new Polygon(vertices);
    boundingPolygon.setOrigin( getOriginX(), getOriginY() );
}

public Polygon getBoundingPolygon()
{
    boundingPolygon.setPosition( getX(), getY() );
    boundingPolygon.setRotation( getRotation() );
    return boundingPolygon;
}
```

Now that you've defined the collision polygons for the BaseActor class, there is still the matter of detecting when two polygons overlap. Unlike the Rectangle class, which has its own overlaps method, the Polygon class does not. Fortunately, another utility class provided by LibGDX, called Intersector, does have such a method. Even more significantly, the Intersector class also has the functionality to deal with collision *response*. If a character overlaps with an item or power-up, the typical response is to add an item to an inventory or increase character stats, respectively. If a character overlaps with a solid object such as a wall, then instead you need to calculate how to adjust that character's position. There are many ways to adjust the position, many of which are mathematically complex, and so we'll relegate a more comprehensive discussion to future chapters. For now, you'll just provide the code for a function named overlaps, which determines whether this BaseActor overlaps with another. The overlaps method also takes a second input, a Boolean variable that indicates whether the collision should be treated as solid; if set to true, the position of this BaseActor will be adjusted so that it no longer overlaps the other BaseActor. The code for this method is as follows:

```
/**
 *  Determine if the collision polygons of two BaseActor objects overlap.
 *  If (resolve == true), then when there is overlap, move this BaseActor
 *    along minimum translation vector until there is no overlap.
 */
public boolean overlaps(BaseActor other, boolean resolve)
{
    Polygon poly1 = this.getBoundingPolygon();
    Polygon poly2 = other.getBoundingPolygon();

    if ( !poly1.getBoundingRectangle().overlaps(poly2.getBoundingRectangle()) )
        return false;

    MinimumTranslationVector mtv = new MinimumTranslationVector();
    boolean polyOverlap = Intersector.overlapConvexPolygons(poly1, poly2, mtv);
    if (polyOverlap && resolve)
    {
        this.moveBy( mtv.normal.x * mtv.depth, mtv.normal.y * mtv.depth );
    }
    float significant = 0.5f;
    return (polyOverlap && (mtv.depth > significant));
}
```

Finally, you introduce a pair of general-purpose methods, called copy and clone. The clone method will create and return a new BaseActor, and make this new object an exact duplicate of the BaseActor calling the method. This process is carried out via the copy method, which copies the data from one

BaseActor into another (and in fact, this is really the only situation in which copy will need to be called). These methods will be helpful when you want to create multiple instances of an object that have only slight variations; you can create a base version of an object, clone it, and then change whatever properties need to be changed. The code for these two methods is as follows:

```
public void copy(BaseActor original)
{
    this.region = new TextureRegion( original.region );
    if (original.boundingPolygon != null)
    {
        this.boundingPolygon = new Polygon( original.boundingPolygon.getVertices() );
        this.boundingPolygon.setOrigin( original.getOriginX(), original.getOriginY() );
    }
    this.setPosition( original.getX(), original.getY() );
    this.setOriginX( original.getOriginX() );
    this.setOriginY( original.getOriginY() );
    this.setWidth( original.getWidth() );
    this.setHeight( original.getHeight() );
    this.setColor( original.getColor() );
    this.setVisible( original.isVisible() );
}

public BaseActor clone()
{
    BaseActor newbie = new BaseActor();
    newbie.copy( this );
    return newbie;
}
```

This completes the methods for the BaseActor class.

The AnimatedActor Class

Next, you'll modify the AnimatedActor class. The main purpose of this class is to manage a set of animations, and select the correct image from the active animation (by *active*, I mean the animation that is currently being rendered). For simplicity, to each Animation you'd like to associate a String that represents its name. For example, in a top-view adventure game, the main character might have four animations named north, south, east, and west, one for each direction she might be walking in. In a platformer action game, the main character might have animations named stand, walk, and jump that correspond to each of these actions in the game.

To store this information, you'll use the HashMap data structure, as discussed previously. String objects will be used as keys, and Animation objects will be the associated values; therefore, the full data type is HashMap<String,Animation>. You'll include a method named storeAnimation that puts this data into the HashMap, and a method named setActiveAnimation that gets an animation from the HashMap and sets it to be the currently active animation. You'll also have a field named activeName that stores the name of the currently active animation, to make it easier to check what's currently playing. You'll also add a few nice touches for convenience: the first animation loaded will be set as the default, and there will be a version of the storeAnimation method that takes a Texture as input and will automatically convert it to a one-frame, or *still*, animation.

75

Here is the code for the AnimatedActor class:

```
import com.badlogic.gdx.graphics.g2d.Batch;
import com.badlogic.gdx.graphics.Texture;
import com.badlogic.gdx.graphics.g2d.TextureRegion;
import com.badlogic.gdx.graphics.g2d.Animation;
import java.util.HashMap;

public class AnimatedActor extends BaseActor
{
    private float elapsedTime;
    private Animation activeAnim;
    private String activeName;
    private HashMap<String,Animation> animationStorage;

    public AnimatedActor()
    {
        super();
        elapsedTime = 0;
        activeAnim = null;
        activeName = null;
        animationStorage = new HashMap<String,Animation>();
    }

    public void storeAnimation(String name, Animation anim)
    {
        animationStorage.put(name, anim);
        if (activeName == null)
            setActiveAnimation(name);
    }

    public void storeAnimation(String name, Texture tex)
    {
        TextureRegion reg = new TextureRegion(tex);
        TextureRegion[] frames = { reg };
        Animation anim = new Animation(1.0f, frames);
        storeAnimation(name, anim);
    }

    public void setActiveAnimation(String name)
    {
        if ( !animationStorage.containsKey(name) )
        {
            System.out.println("No animation: " + name);
            return;
        }

        // no need to set animation if already running
        if ( activeName.equals(name) )
            return;
```

```
        activeName = name;
        activeAnim = animationStorage.get(name);
        elapsedTime = 0;

        Texture tex = activeAnim.getKeyFrame(0).getTexture();
        setWidth( tex.getWidth() );
        setHeight( tex.getHeight() );
    }

    public String getAnimationName()
    {
        return activeName;
    }

    public void act(float dt)
    {
        super.act( dt );
        elapsedTime += dt;
    }

    public void draw(Batch batch, float parentAlpha)
    {
        region.setRegion( activeAnim.getKeyFrame(elapsedTime) );
        super.draw(batch, parentAlpha);
    }
}
```

The PhysicsActor Class

Finally, we come to the topic of the brand new PhysicsActor class, which extends the AnimatedActor class. This class will store velocity as well as acceleration data, which will make movement appear much smoother. Instead of setting velocity when a movement key is pressed, you can choose to set acceleration, which causes the actor to slowly gain speed (much like a car does when the gas pedal, also known as the accelerator, is pressed). This data will be stored using the Vector2 class, which stores two-dimensional vector data, both an x and a y component; there are also convenience methods for operations such as adding two vectors together, or calculating the length of a vector. In the PhysicsActor class, you'll store a maxSpeed value, which will be used to stop the actor from gaining speed indefinitely, and also a deceleration value, which will control how quickly the character slows down (its speed decreases) when not accelerating. Finally, a Boolean variable autoAngle will determine whether an actor's image should be rotated to match the direction of motion. The following are the import statements, variable declarations, and constructor method for this class:

```
import com.badlogic.gdx.math.Vector2;
import com.badlogic.gdx.math.MathUtils;

public class PhysicsActor extends AnimatedActor
{
    private Vector2 velocity;
    private Vector2 acceleration;
```

```
// maximum speed
private float maxSpeed;

// speed reduction, in pixels/second, when not accelerating
private float deceleration;

// should image rotate to match velocity?
private boolean autoAngle;

public PhysicsActor()
{
    velocity = new Vector2();
    acceleration = new Vector2();
    maxSpeed = 9999;
    deceleration = 0;
    autoAngle = false;
}
}
```

This PhysicsActor class contains many methods for getting and setting this information. For the Vector2 variables, velocity and acceleration, we provide two ways to set their data: either in terms of the x and y components, or in terms of the angle and magnitude (or size), which the methods then convert to x and y components by using trigonometry, as illustrated in Figure 3-8. If the vector's direction angle is given by A, and the magnitude is given by M, then the x component of the vector is calculated by the formula $x = M \times \cos(A)$, and similarly, the y component is given by $y = M \times \sin(A)$.

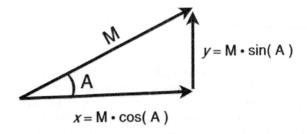

Figure 3-8. *Converting a vector's angle and magnitude to x and y components*

The methods involving velocity and acceleration are as follows:

```
// velocity methods

public void setVelocityXY(float vx, float vy)
{ velocity.set(vx,vy); }

public void addVelocityXY(float vx, float vy)
{ velocity.add(vx,vy); }
```

```java
    // set velocity from angle and speed
    public void setVelocityAS(float angleDeg, float speed)
    {
        velocity.x = speed * MathUtils.cosDeg(angleDeg);
        velocity.y = speed * MathUtils.sinDeg(angleDeg);
    }
```

```java
// acceleration/deceleration methods

    public void setAccelerationXY(float ax, float ay)
    {  acceleration.set(ax,ay);  }

    public void addAccelerationXY(float ax, float ay)
    {  acceleration.add(ax,ay);  }

    // set acceleration from angle and speed
    public void setAccelerationAS(float angleDeg, float speed)
    {
        acceleration.x = speed * MathUtils.cosDeg(angleDeg);
        acceleration.y = speed * MathUtils.sinDeg(angleDeg);
    }
    public void setDeceleration(float d)
    {  deceleration = d;  }
```

In addition, related utility methods determine the speed and angle of motion of the actor, change the current speed, and accelerate in the direction the actor is currently facing:

```java
    public float getSpeed()
    {  return velocity.len();  }

    public void setSpeed(float s)
    {  velocity.setLength(s);  }

    public void setMaxSpeed(float ms)
    {  maxSpeed = ms;  }

    public float getMotionAngle()
    {  return MathUtils.atan2(velocity.y, velocity.x) * MathUtils.radiansToDegrees;  }

    public void setAutoAngle(boolean b)
    {  autoAngle = b;  }

    public void accelerateForward(float speed)
    {  setAccelerationAS( getRotation(), speed );  }
```

Most fundamental to the PhysicsActor class is the act method, which processes and updates the actor's position and velocity data. The five steps of the act method are as follows:

- Change velocity according to acceleration and the time passed (dt)

- Decrease the speed (decelerate) when not accelerating

- If the current speed is greater than maxSpeed, reduce it to this amount

- Change the position according to velocity and the time passed (dt)

- When autoAngle is true, set the actor rotation equal to the direction of motion

Finally, here is the code for the act method:

```java
public void act(float dt)
{
    super.act(dt);

    // apply acceleration
    velocity.add( acceleration.x * dt, acceleration.y * dt );

    // decrease velocity when not accelerating
    if (acceleration.len() < 0.01)
    {
        float decelerateAmount = deceleration * dt;
        if ( getSpeed() < decelerateAmount )
            setSpeed(0);
        else
            setSpeed( getSpeed() - decelerateAmount );
    }

    // cap at max speed
    if ( getSpeed() > maxSpeed )
        setSpeed(maxSpeed);

    // apply velocity
    moveBy( velocity.x * dt, velocity.y * dt );

    // rotate image when moving
    if (autoAngle && getSpeed() > 0.1 )
        setRotation( getMotionAngle() );
}
```

Creating the Game

Now, with these new general-purpose Actor-based classes at your disposal, you will put them through their paces with a new game called Starfish Collector. In this game, the player guides a turtle around a set of rocks to aid her in her quest of collecting all the starfish she can see. Figure 3-9 features a screenshot of this game in action.

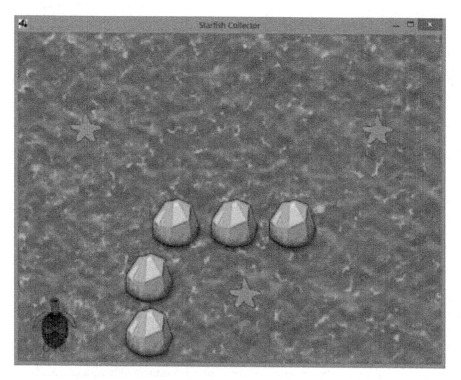

Figure 3-9. *The Starfish Collector game*

As usual, you'll need a driver class and a class extending Game; these can be copied from the previous project and modified as necessary. In this project, you also need to include a copy of the BaseScreen class created earlier in this chapter. The main game play will be handled by a class named TurtleLevel that will extend the BaseScreen class. The three main parts of the TurtleLevel class you must develop are the list of fields you need to declare, the contents of the create method, and the contents of the update method.

First, in this game, you'll use a BaseActor for the ocean background, and a PhysicsActor for the turtle character controlled by the player. The rock and starfish objects do not move and are not animated, so these will both be BaseActor objects; since you need many copies of each, you'll create two ArrayList objects. One will store the rock entities to process for collision detection, and the other will store the starfish entities that the turtle can collect. Variables will store the dimensions of the game world. At this point, the code for the TurtleLevel class (including all the import statements you will require in the future) is as follows:

```
import com.badlogic.gdx.Game;
import com.badlogic.gdx.Gdx;
import com.badlogic.gdx.Input.Keys;
import com.badlogic.gdx.graphics.Texture;
import com.badlogic.gdx.graphics.Texture.TextureFilter;
import com.badlogic.gdx.graphics.g2d.TextureRegion;
import com.badlogic.gdx.graphics.g2d.Animation;
import com.badlogic.gdx.graphics.g2d.Animation.PlayMode;
import com.badlogic.gdx.utils.Array;
import com.badlogic.gdx.math.MathUtils;
import java.util.ArrayList;
```

```java
public class TurtleLevel extends BaseScreen
{
    private BaseActor ocean;
    private ArrayList<BaseActor> rockList;
    private ArrayList<BaseActor> starfishList;
    private PhysicsActor turtle;
    private int mapWidth = 800;
    private int mapHeight = 600;

    public TurtleLevel(Game g)
    {  super(g);  }

    public void create()
    {    }

    public void update(float dt)
    {    }
}
```

Next, you will develop the create method. The images referred to in this section can be obtained from the StarfishCollector/assets folder containing the source code for this chapter, and should be copied into your project's assets folder. You start by creating the BaseActor that contains the background image of water. You also clone this BaseActor, offset the position, set its Color so that it will appear translucent, and add it to the uiStage so all the objects on the mainStage will appear to be underwater. Next, you create the BaseActor representing a rock, and set its collision polygon to be elliptical. You then initialize an ArrayList and use it to store cloned versions of the rock entity, each with slightly different positions, which were stored in the rockCoords array. This is followed by completely analogous code for creating a set of starfish objects. Finally in the create method, you set up turtle, which is a PhysicsActor object. You create and store a multiframe animation (similar to how you created Mousey's animation in Cheese, Please!), and you also store a texture, which is converted to a single-frame animation by the AnimatedActor class. You set the initial position and rotation of the turtle, and you set the origin so that the turtle will rotate around its center. You also initialize the collision boundary to be an ellipse, set the maximum speed to be 100 (pixels/second), and set deceleration to be 200 (pixels/second), so that once the player releases the arrow keys, the turtle will glide to a stop in about half a second. The code for the create method is given here:

```java
public void create()
{
    ocean = new BaseActor();
    ocean.setTexture( new Texture(Gdx.files.internal("assets/water.jpg")) );
    ocean.setPosition( 0, 0 );
    mainStage.addActor( ocean );

    BaseActor overlay = ocean.clone();
    overlay.setPosition(-50,-50);
    overlay.setColor(1,1,1, 0.25f);
    uiStage.addActor(overlay);

    BaseActor rock = new BaseActor();
    rock.setTexture( new Texture(Gdx.files.internal("assets/rock.png")) );
    rock.setEllipseBoundary();
```

```
rockList = new ArrayList<BaseActor>();
int[] rockCoords = {200,0, 200,100, 250,200, 360,200, 470,200};
for (int i = 0; i < 5; i++)
{
    BaseActor r = rock.clone();
    // obtain coordinates from the array, both x and y, at the same time
    r.setPosition( rockCoords[2*i], rockCoords[2*i+1] );
    mainStage.addActor( r );
    rockList.add( r );
}

BaseActor starfish = new BaseActor();
starfish.setTexture( new Texture(Gdx.files.internal("assets/starfish.png")) );
starfish.setEllipseBoundary();

starfishList = new ArrayList<BaseActor>();
int[] starfishCoords = {400,100, 100,400, 650,400};
for (int i = 0; i < 3; i++)
{
    BaseActor s = starfish.clone();
    s.setPosition( starfishCoords[2*i], starfishCoords[2*i+1] );
    mainStage.addActor( s );
    starfishList.add( s );
}

turtle = new PhysicsActor();
TextureRegion[] frames = new TextureRegion[6];
for (int n = 1; n <= 6; n++)
{
    String fileName = "assets/turtle-" + n + ".png";
    Texture tex = new Texture(Gdx.files.internal(fileName));
    tex.setFilter(TextureFilter.Linear, TextureFilter.Linear);
    frames[n-1] = new TextureRegion( tex );
}
Array<TextureRegion> framesArray = new Array<TextureRegion>(frames);

Animation anim = new Animation(0.1f, framesArray, Animation.PlayMode.LOOP);
turtle.storeAnimation( "swim", anim );

Texture frame1 = new Texture(Gdx.files.internal("assets/turtle-1.png"));
turtle.storeAnimation( "rest", frame1 );

turtle.setOrigin( turtle.getWidth()/2, turtle.getHeight()/2 );
turtle.setPosition( 20, 20 );
turtle.setRotation( 90 );
turtle.setEllipseBoundary();
turtle.setMaxSpeed(100);
turtle.setDeceleration(200);
mainStage.addActor(turtle);
}
```

Finally, you design and create the update method. The turtle is controlled by the arrow keys, but the movement is from the perspective of the turtle. The left and right arrow keys rotate the turtle to the left and right, and the up arrow key accelerates the turtle forward, in whatever direction the turtle is currently facing. The next lines of code switch the turtle's animation to rest or swim, if necessary, based on the turtle's current speed. After that, the turtle object is bound to the game-world area, so that it can't move off-screen. Then you check to see whether the turtle is overlapping any of the rock objects, and resolve the position of the turtle if so. Finally, you check to see whether the turtle is overlapping any of the starfish objects (the starfish are not solid, so you don't need to resolve the turtle's position in this case). When there is an overlap, you want to remove the starfish from the game: both from the Stage that is rendering it, and from the ArrayList that is used for collision detection. This last step is tricky, because you can't remove an object from a list at the same time that you are iterating through the list; this would be like someone tearing the pages out of a book while you're trying to read it (in Java, this is called a ConcurrentModificationException error). Therefore, when you identify a starfish that you want to remove from the game, you add it to a list of objects to delete later, and then afterward you iterate through this second list, at which time you can safely remove the starfish from the Stage and the original ArrayList. The code for the update method is shown here:

```java
public void update(float dt)
{
    // process input
    turtle.setAccelerationXY(0,0);

    if (Gdx.input.isKeyPressed(Keys.LEFT))
        turtle.rotateBy(90 * dt);
    if (Gdx.input.isKeyPressed(Keys.RIGHT))
        turtle.rotateBy(-90 * dt);
    if (Gdx.input.isKeyPressed(Keys.UP))
        turtle.accelerateForward(100);

    // set correct animation
    if ( turtle.getSpeed() > 1 && turtle.getAnimationName().equals("rest") )
        turtle.setActiveAnimation("swim");
    if ( turtle.getSpeed() < 1 && turtle.getAnimationName().equals("swim") )
        turtle.setActiveAnimation("rest");

    // bound turtle to the screen
    turtle.setX( MathUtils.clamp( turtle.getX(), 0,  mapWidth - turtle.getWidth() ));
    turtle.setY( MathUtils.clamp( turtle.getY(), 0,  mapHeight - turtle.getHeight() ));

    for (BaseActor r : rockList)
    {
        turtle.overlaps(r, true);
    }

    ArrayList<BaseActor> removeList = new ArrayList<BaseActor>();
    for (BaseActor s : starfishList)
    {
        if ( turtle.overlaps(s, false) )
            removeList.add(s);
    }
```

```
    for (BaseActor b : removeList)
    {
        b.remove();                // remove from stage
        starfishList.remove(b); // remove from list used by update
    }
}
```

As usual, you need a class that extends Game, as follows:

```
import com.badlogic.gdx.Game;
public class TurtleGame extends Game
{
    public void create()
    {
        TurtleLevel tl = new TurtleLevel(this);
        setScreen( tl );
    }
}
```

Also as usual, each project requires a driver class. This time, you create a driver class that contains an additional feature: a LwjglApplicationConfiguration object. This class contains fields that can be set, which allow you to change the window-specific settings such as the width and height of the game window, and the text displayed in the title bar. This object can be passed in as a second parameter to the LwjglApplication constructor.

```
import com.badlogic.gdx.backends.lwjgl.LwjglApplication;
import com.badlogic.gdx.backends.lwjgl.LwjglApplicationConfiguration;
public class TurtleLauncher
{
    public static void main (String[] args)
    {
        LwjglApplicationConfiguration config = new LwjglApplicationConfiguration();
        // change configuration settings
        config.width = 1000;
        config.height = 800;
        config.title = "Starfish Collector";

        TurtleGame myProgram = new TurtleGame();
        LwjglApplication launcher = new LwjglApplication( myProgram, config );
    }
}
```

This covers the core mechanics of the Starfish Collector game.

Next Steps

Despite the advanced mechanics, by no means is this a finished product, similar to the situation at the end of the Balloon Buster game section. However, with what you've covered in the previous examples, you're ready to add more features yourself, such as these:

- A start screen, which contains directions and a lists of keys to press, or has a button image to click in order to load the TurtleLevel screen and start the game.

- A Label in the user interface that states how many starfish remain to be collected.

- For added challenge, make the game world larger than the window, so that not all the starfish are visible at the same time, and add extra rocks to make the game world more maze-like and extra starfish that are located in regions of the game world not immediately visible at the start of the game.

- Add some special effects using the Actions class, such as making that starfish slowly rotate, and once a starfish is collected, have it fade out before it is removed from the stage.

- Add a You Win message to the game that fades in after all the starfish have been collected.

Summary

In this chapter, you created a set of reusable classes that can greatly streamline the code development process for future projects. You refactored the code from the previous chapter and created the BaseScreen class, which contains standard data and startup tasks common to many games, such as storing and initializing Stage objects. You saw how to handle discrete input, such as the initial press of a key or the click of a mouse, and created the Balloon Buster game. Finally, you created a trio of extensions of the Actor class: BaseActor, which performs collision detection and resolution with a generalized polygon shape; AnimatedActor, which manages a collection of animations; and PhysicsActor, which stores and processes motion-related data such as velocity and acceleration. The use of these classes was illustrated with the game Starfish Collector. You've come a long way already, and in the next chapter you'll take another leap forward by learning how to incorporate sounds and music into your games.

CHAPTER 4

■ ■ ■

Adding Polish to Your Game

This chapter builds on the Starfish Collector game introduced in the previous chapter. The core game play remains the same; the additions include background music and sound effects, as well as a user interface with customized bitmap fonts, image-based buttons, and other UI controls.

Audio

Incorporating audio into your game is a straightforward process, thanks to the built-in functionality of the LibGDX libraries. Supported file types include MP3, OGG, and WAV. LibGDX provides two interfaces for this purpose, Sound and Music, each of which can be created from the audio object of the Gdx class. (The classes that implement the interfaces depend on the platform being used; happily, these details are handled for you by LibGDX.)

The Sound interface is provided for sound effects: small audio files that are played when discrete game events occur, such as when an item is collected, a character jumps, or two objects collide. Sound effects are typically short (a few seconds or less), and the corresponding files should not be larger than 1MB. (For larger audio clips, you should consider using the Music interface, given next.) To load a sound effect into memory, for example, you use this code:

```
Sound beep = Gdx.audio.newSound( Gdx.files.internal("beep.wav") );
```

After the sound has been loaded into memory, it can be played with the following:

```
beep.play(volume);
```

The variable volume is a float between 0 and 1, which determines how loudly the sound will be played (0 is silent, and 1 is full volume). A single sound effect can be played multiple times in rapid succession; the sounds will simply overlap each other in this case.

The Music interface is provided for longer audio sequences, such as background music or ambient sounds. To prepare music for streaming, you use this code:

```
Music song = Gdx.audio.newSound( Gdx.files.internal("song.ogg") );
```

The volume can be set using the setVolume method, which takes a float value just as a Sound objects do. If you would like the audio to loop, use setLooping(true). To control playback, there are play, pause, and stop methods. To retrieve information about the current state of playback, you use the methods isPlaying, isLooping, and getPosition, the latter of which returns the current position in seconds.

Sound and Music instances should be *disposed*—removed from memory—when the game is finished, which can be accomplished using their provided dispose methods.

Next, you'll see how to add music and sound effects to the Starfish Collector game created in the previous chapter. All the code that follows should be added to the TurtleLevel class. You begin by adding the following import statements:

```
import com.badlogic.gdx.audio.Sound;
import com.badlogic.gdx.audio.Music;
```

Then you declare the following variables:

```
private float audioVolume;
private Sound waterDrop;
private Music instrumental;
private Music oceanSurf;
```

At the end of the create method, you initialize these variables and start playing the music with the following code. The sound files referenced in the code can be downloaded from the assets directory containing the source code from this chapter, and should be added to your local project's assets folder:

```
waterDrop    = Gdx.audio.newSound(Gdx.files.internal("assets/Water_Drop.ogg"));
instrumental = Gdx.audio.newMusic(Gdx.files.internal("assets/Master_of_the_Feast.ogg"));
oceanSurf    = Gdx.audio.newMusic(Gdx.files.internal("assets/Ocean_Waves.ogg"));

audioVolume = 0.80f;
instrumental.setLooping(true);
instrumental.setVolume(audioVolume);
instrumental.play();
oceanSurf.setLooping(true);
oceanSurf.setVolume(audioVolume);
oceanSurf.play();
```

In the update method, during the collision detection, you play the water-drop sound effect whenever a starfish disappears. This section of code is given next; only the line that appears in bold font needs to be added:

```
for (BaseActor b : removeList)
{
    b.remove();
    starfishList.remove(b);
    waterDrop.play(audioVolume);
}
```

Finally, you add a dispose method, which in turn calls the dispose method of each audio object, so as to free up memory when the screen is closed:

```
public void dispose()
{
    waterDrop.dispose();
    instrumental.dispose();
    oceanSurf.dispose();
}
```

This method should be activated when the user exits the program; later in this chapter, you'll see where this takes place.

You may have noticed that you're using the variable audioVolume to store the volume for playing sounds and music, but nowhere in the provided code is there a mechanism for changing this value. You will implement volume control in the next section, which covers advanced user-interface controls.

Advanced User-Interface Design

Our next goal is to create a polished user interface.

First, you'll create a title screen that includes the name of your game, buttons to start or quit the game, and a graphic that credits the LibGDX library. This is illustrated in Figure 4-1.

Figure 4-1. *Title screen layout*

Next, in the main game screen (where the game is played), you want to add some text that states how many starfish remain to be collected, and a Pause button. These elements should appear in the upper corners of the window so that they do not block the player's view of the game world, which could interfere with the game play, resulting in a diminished player experience. This is illustrated in Figure 4-2.

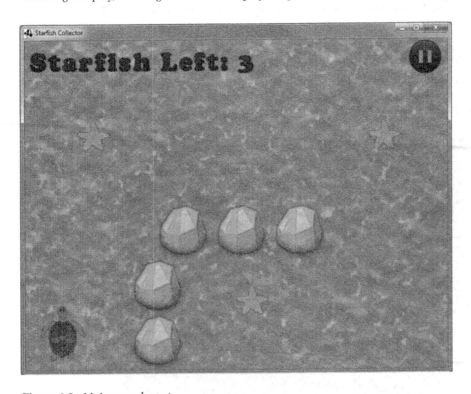

Figure 4-2. Main game layout

Finally, when the user clicks the Pause button, in addition to pausing the game play, a pause menu should appear. This menu dims the view of the game world by overlaying a translucent black rectangle on top of it; on top of this is text indicating the game is paused, buttons to resume or quit the game, and a slider to control the audio volume, as shown in Figure 4-3.

Figure 4-3. *Pause game layout*

In the subsections that follow, you'll design and implement layouts with the Table class, manage image and style resources with the Skin class, and learn about classes that provide commonly needed user-interface elements, such as Label, Image, Button (and its subclass TextButton), and Slider.

Arranging UI Elements

In Chapter 2, you created a game called Cheese, Please! that had a simple user interface: the menu screen contained a title image and some text instructions, and the main game screen contained text that displayed the time elapsed. Determining the exact screen coordinates where those items should be displayed, taking into account the size of the items being placed, can be tedious to calculate. Fortunately, the LibGDX libraries provide a class named Table that greatly simplifies this process by automatically placing these elements for you.

Table is a subclass of Actor, so it can be added to Stage objects; furthermore, Table is also a subclass of Group, so objects can be added to a Table as well. In particular, a Table consists of Cell objects, laid out in rows and columns, each Cell containing an Actor. The add method creates a new Cell (containing an Actor, if one is specified), and adds it to the end of the current row. The add method returns the Cell object that is created, and thus can be immediately formatted by calling any combination of the following methods on the result:

- left, center, and right to set the horizontal alignment of the Cell contents

- bottom and top to set the vertical alignment

- padLeft, padRight, padBottom, padTop to add an amount of padding (in pixels) to the contents of the current Cell, or the pad method to apply padding in all directions

- width and height to set the size of the Cell (the size of the Cell affects the size of its contents)

- expandX and expandY to force a Cell to increase its size to fill the remaining table size in that direction

- colspan to declare that a given Cell will span multiple columns

All tables contain a single row by default. To create a new row in the Table, positioned beneath the current row, you call the row method.

For example, let's create a Table named t with contents laid out in the style of the title screen shown previously in Figure 4-1. For simplicity in this section and in the accompanying diagram, we will name the Actor objects a, b, c, and d; a represents the title image, b and c represent the Start and Quit buttons, and d represents the LibGDX image. Figure 4-4 illustrates the layout.

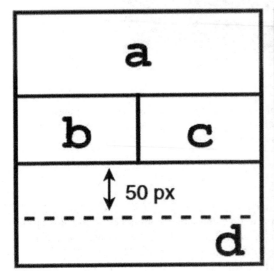

Figure 4-4. *Abstract table layout for the Start screen*

The diagram indicates that you will need a Table with three rows and two columns. Every row that doesn't require two separate cells should have its single cell set to span two columns. The final cell is the trickiest to configure: not only does it span two columns, but its contents are aligned to the right, and there should be 50 pixels of padding between itself and the row above. The following code illustrates how this layout can be achieved; however, you won't add any code to the project at this time. Later, you will add code based on this template (with a, b, c, and d replaced by the variables corresponding to these objects).

```
Table t = new Table();
t.add(a).colspan(2);
t.row();
t.add(b);
t.add(c);
t.row();
t.add(d).colspan(2).right().padTop(50);
```

As another example of the Table class, you'll learn how to create the layout for the main game screen (shown previously in Figure 4-2). The abstract version of this layout appears in Figure 4-5.

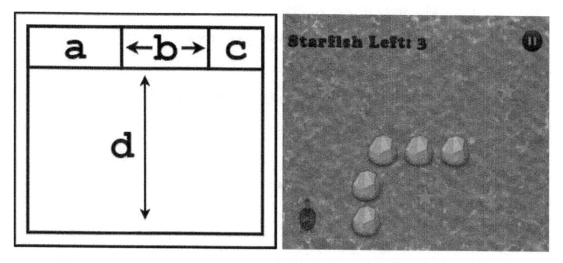

Figure 4-5. *Abstract table layout for the main game screen*

In Figure 4-5, the entire table has 10 pixels of padding on all sides (represented by the empty border area). Cell a contains the Starfish Left label, and cell c contains the Pause button. Cell b does not contain an actor; it will be extended in the horizontal (x) direction to fill all remaining space in the first row, so that cells a and c will be positioned on the left and right sides of the screen, respectively. Similarly, cell d is also used for positioning purposes and does not contain an actor; it spans all three columns in the second row, and is extended to fill all the remaining space in the vertical (y) direction, so that the first row will appear at the top of the screen. The code that yields the layout from Figure 4-5 is presented here (and as before, it will serve as a template to be added to the project later):

```
Table t = new Table();
t.pad(10);
t.add(a);
t.add().expandX();
t.add(c);
t.row();
t.add().colspan(3).expandY();
```

Creating the content that will be added to these Table objects—instances of the Label, Image, and Button classes—is discussed later in this chapter. Even before we discuss this topic, note that because multiple screens will use a Table object, you will write and add the corresponding code to the BaseScreen class.

First you need the corresponding import statement:

```
import com.badlogic.gdx.scenes.scene2d.ui.Table;
```

Next, you declare a Table object, named uiTable, following the declaration of the Stage objects:

```
protected Table uiTable;
```

Finally, you initialize this object in the constructor of the BaseScreen class, and attach it to the uiStage:

```
uiTable = new Table();
uiTable.setFillParent(true);
uiStage.addActor(uiTable);
```

Next, you will lay additional groundwork before creating the user interface objects. You'll see how to efficiently store and reuse UI components.

Managing Resources

When designing a user interface, you typically want to have a consistent theme. You want to use the same set of fonts, styles, and so forth in the many screens the game will have. In the interests of efficiency, you do not want to re-create these game objects repeatedly. What you will do instead is to create the common UI elements when the Game class is initialized, and store them in a data structure that can be accessed by the Screen objects at a later time. Conveniently, the LibGDX libraries provide a class for precisely this purpose: the Skin class.

A Skin object stores objects in a way similar to a HashMap (discussed in Chapter 3), using String objects as keys and any object type as values. Objects can be stored using the add method and retrieved using the get method. For example, the following code creates a new Skin, and then creates a new Color and stores it using the name LightGreen, and finally retrieves it and assigns it to a new Color variable.

```
Skin uiSkin = new Skin();
Color greenish = new Color(0.5f, 1.0f, 0.5f, 1.0f);
uiSkin.add( "LightGreen", greenish );
Color textColor = uiSkin.get( "LightGreen", Color.class );
```

Note that the second parameter passed in the get method is the class field, which is used to determine the type of object being retrieved. If this parameter is not included, the return type is Object, and the returned value would need to be manually cast to the appropriate class type, as follows:

```
Color textColor = (Color)( uiSkin.get("LightGreen") );
```

Frequently stored object types have their own get-style methods. For instance, you could also retrieve the color stored previously by using the code getColor("LightGreen"). Using these methods can make the code slightly easier to read, because the value returned would not need to be cast into the required type. For a complete list of the provided get-related methods of the Skin class, please consult the LibGDX documentation.

Because you may use a Skin object in most games that you will create in the future, you will add a new class to your framework code that extends the core classes provided by LibGDX. Just as your BaseScreen class extended the Screen class, you will create a BaseGame class that extends the Game class. BaseGame will contain a Skin object that is initialized by the constructor. You will override the empty dispose method provided by the Game class and write a method that calls the dispose method of the skin, so memory is freed up when the BaseGame object is no longer needed (similar to the disposal of audio objects, discussed earlier in this chapter). In addition, extensions of the Game class must include a create method, but as BaseGame is never meant to be instantiated directly (similar to BaseScreen), you will declare the create method to be abstract, which in turn requires the BaseGame class itself to be abstract. The code for the BaseGame class is as follows:

```
import com.badlogic.gdx.Game;
import com.badlogic.gdx.scenes.scene2d.ui.Skin;

public abstract class BaseGame extends Game
{
    // used to store resources common to multiple screens
    Skin skin;

    public BaseGame()
    {
        skin = new Skin();
    }

    public abstract void create();

    public void dispose()
    {
        skin.dispose();
    }
}
```

Following this addition, you must change the BaseScreen class so that every occurrence of the Game type is replaced by the BaseGame type: the game variable and constructor parameter should both be of type BaseGame. Similarly, in the TurtleLevel class, the constructor parameter should be a BaseGame object. In addition, your TurtleGame class should now extend BaseGame, rather than Game. In the create method of TurtleGame, eventually you will include code to initialize the resources common to multiple screens, store these resources using the Skin object, and only after these tasks are complete should you initialize and set the first screen to appear in the game.

Using Customized Bitmap Fonts

Bitmap-based fonts were briefly mentioned in Chapter 2; this section discusses them in much greater detail.

To create a `BitmapFont`, you need two things: an image that contains all the characters you may want to represent in your application (Figure 4-6 contains an example), and an associated data file that lists the region (position and size) corresponding to each character. For example, the region in Figure 4-6 corresponding to A is located at x=319, y=134, and has width 45 and height 41. When a bitmap font is used to display text, the image region corresponding to each character of the text is extracted, and these image regions are aligned side by side to produce the result seen onscreen.

Figure 4-6. *An image file (512 by 256 pixels) used to create a bitmap font*

LibGDX uses the BMFont format for storing this data, developed by Andreas Jönsson.[1] An application named Hiero is provided by LibGDX that can be used to generate bitmap font data using fonts installed on your computer. The first version of Hiero was created by Kevin Glass for use with his Java game development library, Slick2D. Since then, Hiero has been ported to LibGDX by Nathan Sweet, one of the major contributors to the LibGDX libraries. Hiero is packaged as an executable JAR file; the current link to download it is posted on the LibGDX wiki page.[2]

For this project, I've created a custom font data file and bitmap file (`cooper.fnt` and `cooper.png`, respectively) that you can download from the `assets` folder in the source code directory for the chapter and copy to your own project. If you would prefer to create your own font using Hiero, I briefly discuss the operation of this program in the next paragraph; otherwise, you can skip to the paragraph afterward.

When you start Hiero, a variety of options are presented. Figure 4-7 contains a screenshot of the program in action. In the upper-left area, you may select a locally installed font; in the center region, you can enter the characters whose images you wish to generate; in the upper-right area, you can select various effects to apply to the image, including solid coloring, gradient coloring, outline, and drop shadow. Parameters for effects can be altered by clicking their values and entering or selecting a new value. When finished, select Save BMFont files from the File menu, and you'll have a PNG and FNT file ready to be used by the LibGDX `BitmapFont` class.

---

[1]See `www.angelcode.com/products/bmfont/` for additional details.
[2]Available at `https://github.com/libgdx/libgdx/wiki/Hiero` .

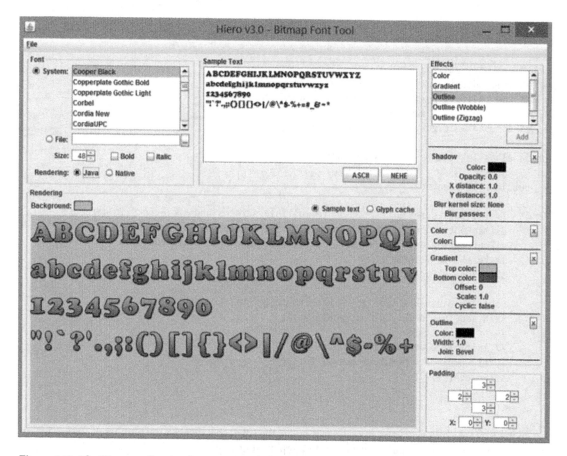

Figure 4-7. *The Hiero application for generating bitmap font data*

To use a custom-generated bitmap font in LibGDX, you initialize the BitmapFont object with a FileHandle to the FNT file generated. (The name of the associated PNG file is stored within the FNT file and thus does not need to be stated directly in the code.) For example:

```
BitmapFont myFont = new BitmapFont( Gdx.files.internal("myCustomFont.fnt") );
```

If desired, it is possible to access the Texture data contained within the BitmapFont object. You may want to do this, for example, in order to set the filter to obtain a smoother appearance when images are scaled. To accomplish this, you can include the following code after myFont is created:

```
myFont.getRegion().getTexture().setFilter(TextureFilter.Linear, TextureFilter.Linear);
```

After creating a BitmapFont, you can then use it as part of a LabelStyle, to be applied to Label objects in your game. With the new structure provided by the BaseGame class, you'll create the style objects in your BaseGame extension, and use these objects in your BaseScreen extensions.

First, here is the code for the completely overhauled TurtleGame class, which now extends BaseGame and creates and stores the shared resources:

```
import com.badlogic.gdx.Gdx;
import com.badlogic.gdx.graphics.Texture.TextureFilter;
import com.badlogic.gdx.scenes.scene2d.ui.Label.LabelStyle;
import com.badlogic.gdx.graphics.Color;
import com.badlogic.gdx.graphics.g2d.BitmapFont;

public class TurtleGame extends BaseGame
{
    public void create()
    {
        // initialize resources common to multiple screens and store to skin database
        BitmapFont uiFont = new BitmapFont(Gdx.files.internal("assets/cooper.fnt"));
        uiFont.getRegion().getTexture().setFilter(TextureFilter.Linear,
        TextureFilter.Linear);
        skin.add("uiFont", uiFont);

        LabelStyle uiLabelStyle = new LabelStyle(uiFont, Color.BLUE);
        skin.add("uiLabelStyle", uiLabelStyle);

        // initialize and start main game
        TurtleLevel tl = new TurtleLevel(this);
        setScreen( tl );
    }
}
```

In the TurtleLevel class, you can now easily create the Label that displays the number of starfish left to collect. First you need to include the corresponding import statement:

```
import com.badlogic.gdx.scenes.scene2d.ui.Label;
```

Next, you declare the Label, named starfishLeftLabel. Since this will be used in both the create and update methods, you declare it globally in the class:

```
Label starfishLeftLabel;
```

You then initialize this Label in the create method. At first glance, it may be surprising that the Skin class does not contain any get methods to retrieve style-related objects. However, this wasn't a development oversight; instead, the Label constructor method has an overloaded variation that allows you to pass in the Skin object itself, as well as the name of the style object to be used. The constructor itself will automatically retrieve and convert the corresponding data as necessary. Thus, the following code can be placed in the create method to initialize the Label with the LabelStyle you created in the TurtleGame class:

```
starfishLeftLabel = new Label("Starfish Left: --", game.skin, "uiLabelStyle");
```

Finally, at the end of the update method, you can update the text displayed by this Label so that it displays the correct number of starfish left to collect, using the following line of code:

```
starfishLeftLabel.setText( "Starfish Left: " + starfishList.size() );
```

At this point, the TurtleLevel class compiles, but no change is visible on the screen, as the label has not been added to a stage yet; you will do so in a later section, after exploring the remaining components for the user interface. The next user-interface control you need for the TurtleLevel class is provided by the Button class.

Creating Buttons

A button is one of the most basic user-interface controls that gets input from a user. There are multiple ways to customize the appearance and behavior of a button, as well as extensions of the Button class (such as TextButton and CheckBox), some of which you will explore in this chapter.

First, you will initialize a basic Button object together with a ButtonStyle. A ButtonStyle object can store one or more images, one of which will be displayed, depending on the current state of the button. An image stored in the up field serves as the default image. Image data for UI elements must be stored using a class that implements the Drawable interface, which has methods that resize and draw an image to fit in a given rectangular region. (TextureRegionDrawable is an example of one of many such classes.) The easiest way to initialize such an object is using the Skin class, which in addition to being an excellent way to manage resources, contains many methods for converting image data. For example, it is possible to store a Texture under a given name, and then retrieving that data using the same name and the getDrawable method will automatically create a Drawable object.

Adding interactivity to a Button object is a process you have seen before, in the Balloon Buster game from Chapter 3. In that game, the balloon objects were derived from the Actor class, and thus had the ability to listen for input events (such as being clicked/touched). The code that was executed in this event was contained in a method called touchDown, part of an anonymous inner class derived from the InputListener class. Since the Button class is also an extension of the Actor class, you can (and will) use the same approach here.

First, you require the following import statements to be added to the class:

```
import com.badlogic.gdx.scenes.scene2d.ui.Button;
import com.badlogic.gdx.scenes.scene2d.ui.Button.ButtonStyle;
import com.badlogic.gdx.scenes.scene2d.InputEvent;
import com.badlogic.gdx.scenes.scene2d.InputListener;
```

The following code creates a Button that will be used to pause and unpause the Starfish Collector game play (but not the music). Since you don't need to reference this object later in the update method, you can declare and initialize it within the create method of the TurtleLevel class. First, you load a Texture into the skin stored by game, and convert it to a Drawable for use in a ButtonStyle object. (As usual, the image you use can be downloaded from the source code assets folder.) Then you initialize the Button and add an InputListener which will activate the togglePause method, which was defined by the BaseScreen class.

```
Texture pauseTexture = new Texture(Gdx.files.internal("assets/pause.png"));
game.skin.add("pauseImage", pauseTexture );

ButtonStyle pauseStyle = new ButtonStyle();
pauseStyle.up = game.skin.getDrawable("pauseImage");

Button pauseButton = new Button( pauseStyle );
```

```
pauseButton.addListener(
    new InputListener()
    {
        public boolean touchDown (InputEvent event, float x, float y, int pointer, int button)
        {
            togglePaused();
            return true;
        }
    });
```

Now that you have created the objects starfishLeftLabel and pauseButton, and uiTable is provided by the BaseScreen class, you are now ready and able to implement the user-interface layout for the TurtleLevel class described earlier in this chapter. At the end of the create method in the TurtleLevel class, you simply add this code:

```
uiTable.pad(10);
uiTable.add(starfishLeftLabel);
uiTable.add().expandX();
uiTable.add(pauseButton);
uiTable.row();
uiTable.add().colspan(3).expandY();
```

Finally, there is one subtle but vital detail to address. In the create method, you previously added an object called overlay to the uiStage. This object contains a semitransparent image of water for the purpose of making all the game entities rendered underneath it appear underwater. Since this object was added to uiStage *after* uiTable was added, it is currently covering the button object, and thus preventing the button from registering user input (such as the touchDown event). To remedy this situation, you must rearrange the elements on the uiStage so that overlay appears underneath the button; visually speaking, you need to send it to the back of the layer. This is accomplished by adding the following line of code to the create method, *after* overlay has been added to uiStage:

```
overlay.toBack();
```

Setting Up the Start Screen

Next, you will set up the start screen, which appears when the user first starts the program (as depicted previously in Figure 4-1). You will create a new class for this purpose, called TurtleMenu. This class does not require you to use the mainStage object at all—just the uiTable is used to arrange objects. In this class, you use two new classes: Image and TextButton. Even before you introduce these classes, you can write skeleton code for the TurtleMenu class, as presented here:

```
import com.badlogic.gdx.Gdx;
import com.badlogic.gdx.graphics.Texture;
import com.badlogic.gdx.graphics.Texture.TextureFilter;
import com.badlogic.gdx.scenes.scene2d.ui.Image;
import com.badlogic.gdx.scenes.scene2d.ui.TextButton;
import com.badlogic.gdx.scenes.scene2d.InputEvent;
import com.badlogic.gdx.scenes.scene2d.InputListener;
```

```
public class TurtleMenu extends BaseScreen
{
    public TurtleMenu(BaseGame g)
    {  super(g);  }

    public void create()
    {    }

    public void update(float dt)
    {    }
}
```

Each picture that you want to display on this screen will be loaded initially as a Texture. To ensure that each image scales smoothly, you will consistently specify that linear filtering should be used each time. You can use a repeated image for the table background, provided you convert it to a Drawable first (which you do using the skin object). All other Texture objects that you would like to include in the uiTable will be displayed using Image objects, which exist for exactly this purpose. Recall that all user-interface objects store images using the Drawable interface so that they can be resized as needed. The Texture class does *not* implement the Drawable interface, but conveniently, the Image constructor accepts a Texture as input and can convert it to a Drawable object automatically. As usual, the image files referenced here can be download from the source code assets folder:

```
Texture waterTex = new Texture(Gdx.files.internal("assets/water.jpg"));
waterTex.setFilter(TextureFilter.Linear, TextureFilter.Linear);
game.skin.add( "waterTex", waterTex );
uiTable.background( game.skin.getDrawable("waterTex") );

Texture titleTex = new Texture(Gdx.files.internal("assets/starfish-collector.png"));
titleTex.setFilter(TextureFilter.Linear, TextureFilter.Linear);
Image titleImage = new Image( titleTex );

Texture libgdxTex = new Texture(Gdx.files.internal("assets/created-libgdx.png"));
libgdxTex.setFilter(TextureFilter.Linear, TextureFilter.Linear);
Image libgdxImage = new Image( libgdxTex );
```

Next, you introduce an extension of the Button class, called TextButton, which is a Button that has a Label on top to display the associated text. The associated style object, TextButtonStyle, requires both a Drawable for the button graphic, and a BitmapFont and Color to draw the label.

One potential complication with creating a TextButton arises when the button's text is larger than the provided image, in which case the text will overflow past the borders of the button. To alleviate this problem, you can use the NinePatch class, which allows you to scale an image in a particular way. A NinePatch object can be initialized using a Texture followed by four integers, as follows:

```
NinePatch np = new NinePatch( texture, left, right, top, bottom );
```

The integers represent distances, measured in pixels, from the correspondingly named edge of the image. They are used to divide the texture into nine regions, as illustrated in Figure 4-8.

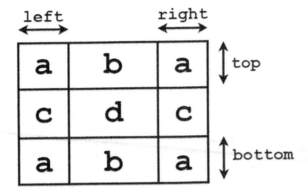

Figure 4-8. *Dividing a texture into nine regions*

When converted to a Drawable, the corners of the image (the regions labeled with a in Figure 4-8) will never be scaled; the b regions can scale horizontally, the c regions can scale vertically, and the central region d can scale in both directions. This is particularly useful for button-like images, so that the edges of the image do not appear distorted. Figure 4-9 illustrates a small image that is scaled using standard methods, and also scaled using nine-patch methods. Notice in particular that using standard scaling, the border of the enlarged image appears thicker, while nine-patch scaling more closely preserves the appearance of the original border, as it only scales each edge in the direction along which it is oriented.

Figure 4-9. *A button-like image, scaled using standard methods and using nine-patch methods*

At this point, you can turn your attention to the TurtleGame class. You will write the code that initializes the TextButtonStyle object, and store it using the skin object, so that it can be used by all the screens in your program. First, you need to add the following import statements:

```
import com.badlogic.gdx.graphics.Texture;
import com.badlogic.gdx.scenes.scene2d.ui.TextButton.TextButtonStyle;
import com.badlogic.gdx.graphics.g2d.NinePatch;
```

After downloading the nine patch–related images into the assets folder, the code you need to add to the create method is as follows:

```
TextButtonStyle uiTextButtonStyle = new TextButtonStyle();

uiTextButtonStyle.font      = uiFont;
uiTextButtonStyle.fontColor = Color.NAVY;

Texture upTex = new Texture(Gdx.files.internal("assets/ninepatch-1.png"));
skin.add("buttonUp", new NinePatch(upTex, 26,26,16,20));
uiTextButtonStyle.up = skin.getDrawable("buttonUp");
```

To add a bit more polish to the TextButton objects, you'll also add some information to the TextButtonStyle objects. Often the appearance of a button may change depending on how the user is interacting with it. For instance, when the mouse pointer is hovering over a button, it may become lighter in appearance, and while the button is being pressed, the background image may be changed to make the button look more "flat." These variations in appearance are illustrated in Figure 4-10.

Figure 4-10. *Different button appearances, based on state: default/up, hover/over, and pressed/down*

To provide a TextButton with the same style, you simply store additional image data to the over and down fields of the TextButtonStyle object, and you may change the font colors as well, if desired. These additions are accomplished, and the style object is added to the skin object, with the code presented here:

```
Texture overTex = new Texture(Gdx.files.internal("assets/ninepatch-2.png"));
skin.add("buttonOver", new NinePatch(overTex, 26,26,16,20) );
uiTextButtonStyle.over = skin.getDrawable("buttonOver");
uiTextButtonStyle.overFontColor = Color.BLUE;

Texture downTex = new Texture(Gdx.files.internal("assets/ninepatch-3.png"));
skin.add("buttonDown", new NinePatch(downTex, 26,26,16,20) );
uiTextButtonStyle.down = skin.getDrawable("buttonDown");
uiTextButtonStyle.downFontColor = Color.BLUE;

skin.add("uiTextButtonStyle", uiTextButtonStyle);
```

With this style data stored, you are now ready to create the TextButton objects in the TurtleMenu class. The Start button will initialize the TurtleLevel class and set it to be the active screen, while the Quit button will exit the application. This listener contains two methods, each of which is activated for different events: touchDown is called when the object is initially touched or when the mouse button is pressed down while over this object; touchUp is called immediately after the touching action stops or when the mouse button is released. The touchUp methods are used to execute these actions, so that they occur when the buttons are released.

```
TextButton startButton = new TextButton("Start", game.skin, "uiTextButtonStyle");
startButton.addListener(
    new InputListener()
    {
        public boolean touchDown (InputEvent event, float x, float y, int pointer,
        int button)
        {  return true;  }

        public void touchUp (InputEvent event, float x, float y, int pointer, int button)
        {
            game.setScreen( new TurtleLevel(game) );
        }
    });

TextButton quitButton = new TextButton("Quit", game.skin, "uiTextButtonStyle");
quitButton.addListener(
    new InputListener()
    {
        public boolean touchDown (InputEvent event, float x, float y, int pointer,
        int button)
        {  return true;  }

        public void touchUp (InputEvent event, float x, float y, int pointer, int button)
        {
            Gdx.app.exit();
        }
    });
```

Finally, with all the user-interface objects created, you are now ready to place them on the screen by adding them to the uiTable object. You use the same code from our earlier discussion of laying out the Start menu, with one addition: in the interests of symmetry, you'd like the two buttons to have the same width, but because of the text being displayed, the Start button will be wider by default. You can change the width of the Quit button to match the width of the Start button, by setting the width of the cell that contains it:

```
float w = startButton.getWidth();
uiTable.add(titleImage).colspan(2);
uiTable.row();
uiTable.add(startButton);
uiTable.add(quitButton).width(w);
uiTable.row();
uiTable.add(libgdxImage).colspan(2).right().padTop(50);
```

Finally, to load the menu screen (rather than the game-play screen) when the program starts, you need to make a change to the TurtleGame class. At the end of the create method, instead of creating an instance of the TurtleLevel class (and setting this to be the active screen), you'd like to use the TurtleMenu class. To this end, change the last two lines of the create method to the following:

```
TurtleMenu tm = new TurtleMenu(this);
setScreen(tm);
```

Creating an Overlay Menu

Now that you've finished setting up your two main user interfaces, you have one final addition to the Starfish Collector game. You'd like to create an overlay-style menu that appears on top of the main UI on the TurtleLevel screen when the game is paused, as illustrated in Figure 4-11. As with the previous user-interface discussion, you show the desired result side by side with an abstract layout diagram indicating the placement of the UI elements. In Figure 4-11, cells a and d contain labels, cells b and c contain buttons, and cell e contains a slider. There will also be a translucent black background that dims the user's view of the game, which also makes the Pause menu contents more easily identifiable. You are already familiar with two of the classes you need: Label and TextButton. The new control element you need is a Slider, which will be used to change the audioVolume variable that sets the volume of sound effects and background music, introduced in the beginning of this chapter.

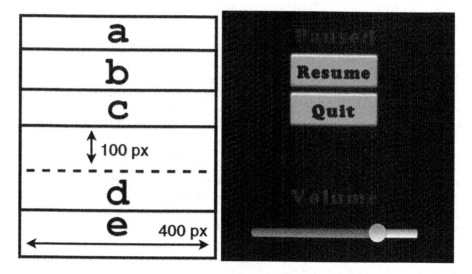

Figure 4-11. *Abstract table layout for the pause overlay*

For consistency, you'll initialize and store the associated SliderStyle object in the TurtleGame class, alongside the other style objects. As usual, you'll also use the methods of the Skin class to convert the needed Texture objects into Drawable objects. The two fields of the SliderStyle object you must include are images for the background and the knob that is dragged back and forth along the slider itself. You may also include two additional images that are set to appear on top of the background, before and after the knob image, which can be seen in Figure 4-11. The knob is the circular image; the "before" and "after" images are the colored horizontal images that appear to the left and right of the knob, respectively. All the necessary images can be downloaded from the source code assets folder. You need to add the following import to the TurtleGame class:

```
import com.badlogic.gdx.scenes.scene2d.ui.Slider.SliderStyle;
```

Then, in the create method, the code you will include to initialize your SliderStyle object appears here:

```
SliderStyle uiSliderStyle = new SliderStyle();

skin.add("sliderBack",   new Texture(Gdx.files.internal("assets/slider-after.png")) );
skin.add("sliderKnob",   new Texture(Gdx.files.internal("assets/slider-knob.png")) );
skin.add("sliderAfter",  new Texture(Gdx.files.internal("assets/slider-after.png")) );
skin.add("sliderBefore", new Texture(Gdx.files.internal("assets/slider-before.png")) );

uiSliderStyle.background = skin.getDrawable("sliderBack");
uiSliderStyle.knob       = skin.getDrawable("sliderKnob");
uiSliderStyle.knobAfter  = skin.getDrawable("sliderAfter");
uiSliderStyle.knobBefore = skin.getDrawable("sliderBefore");

skin.add("uiSliderStyle", uiSliderStyle);
```

Since each point along a slider corresponds to a numerical value, to initialize the Slider object in the TurtleLevel class, you must provide the minimum and maximum values that your Slider will represent (in our case, 0 and 1), as well as the smallest possible increment between values. You also must include a Boolean variable that determines whether the Slider should be displayed vertically (you leave this set to false to obtain a horizontal slider). The final arguments involve style data; in our case, since you stored the data using a Skin, you provide a reference to the Skin object and the corresponding name that was used to store the SliderStyle object.

Next, you add the code that will be executed when the user interacts with the Slider. In this case, you diverge from your previous approach of using an EventListener, because of the different way in which the user interacts with this particular user-interface element. Multiple changes may occur between the touchDown and touchUp events registered by an Actor; these intermediate changes are observed by the ChangeListener class, which then calls its changed method.

At this point, you return to the TurtleLevel class to make your final changes. First, you have the remaining import statements to add:

```
import com.badlogic.gdx.scenes.scene2d.ui.Slider;
import com.badlogic.gdx.scenes.scene2d.utils.ChangeListener;
import com.badlogic.gdx.scenes.scene2d.Actor;
import com.badlogic.gdx.scenes.scene2d.ui.Table;
import com.badlogic.gdx.scenes.scene2d.ui.Stack;
import com.badlogic.gdx.scenes.scene2d.utils.Drawable;
import com.badlogic.gdx.graphics.Color;
import com.badlogic.gdx.scenes.scene2d.ui.TextButton;
```

The following code creates a Slider using your previously created SliderStyle object, sets the coordinates of the slider's knob to the position corresponding to the initial value of audioVolume, and adds a ChangeListener object that adjusts the volume of the audio objects whenever the user interacts with the Slider. This code should be added after the audioVolume variable has been initialized:

```
Slider audioSlider = new Slider(0, 1, 0.005f, false, game.skin, "uiSliderStyle" );
audioSlider.setValue( audioVolume );
audioSlider.addListener(
    new ChangeListener()
    {
        public void changed(ChangeEvent event, Actor actor)
        {
            audioVolume = audioSlidergetValue();
            instrumental.setVolume(audioVolume);
            oceanSurf.setVolume(audioVolume);
        }
    });
```

Next, you want to create the pause overlay menu itself. Note that you can't just add these new elements into the preexisting uiTable. What you need is a second Table object, whose visibility depends on whether the game is paused, and when visible, renders on top of uiTable. The former goal can be accomplished using the setVisible method of the table; the latter can be arranged with a Stack object that, as the name suggests, places (stacks) one object above another.

You create a new Table in the TurtleLevel class:

```
private Table pauseOverlay;
```

And then in the create method, you initialize it:

```
pauseOverlay = new Table();
pauseOverlay.setFillParent(true);
```

Then you create a Stack object and add it to the uiStage. After this, you add the uiTable and the pauseOverlay table to it, which will cause them to render in that order:

```
Stack stacker = new Stack();
stacker.setFillParent(true);
uiStage.addActor(stacker);
stacker.add(uiTable);
stacker.add(pauseOverlay);
```

Next, you'll add a white texture to the skin, and use the newDrawable method to create a tinted version of this texture using a translucent black color, based on a simple image (which can be downloaded from the source code assets folder):

```
game.skin.add("white", new Texture( Gdx.files.internal("assets/white4px.png")) );
Drawable pauseBackground = game.skin.newDrawable("white", new Color(0,0,0,0.8f) );
```

Next, you create the remaining Label and TextButton objects for the pause overlay menu, and remember to call the previously written dispose method to free up memory when quitting the game:

```
Label pauseLabel = new Label("Paused", game.skin, "uiLabelStyle");

TextButton resumeButton = new TextButton("Resume", game.skin, "uiTextButtonStyle");
resumeButton.addListener(
    new InputListener()
    {
        public boolean touchDown (InputEvent event, float x, float y, int pointer,
        int button)
        {  return true;  }

        public void touchUp (InputEvent event, float x, float y, int pointer, int button)
        {
            togglePaused();
            pauseOverlay.setVisible( isPaused() );
        }
});

TextButton quitButton = new TextButton("Quit", game.skin, "uiTextButtonStyle");
quitButton.addListener(
    new InputListener()
    {
        public boolean touchDown (InputEvent event, float x, float y, int pointer,
        int button)
        {  return true;  }

        public void touchUp (InputEvent event, float x, float y, int pointer, int button)
        {
            dispose();
            Gdx.app.exit();
        }
});

Label volumeLabel = new Label("Volume", game.skin, "uiLabelStyle");
```

With all the user-interface objects created, you will add them to the pauseOverlay table, one object per row for simplicity. You also force the buttons to have equal width using the same approach as when you designed the UI for the TurtleMenu class:

```
float w = resumeButton.getWidth();
pauseOverlay.setBackground(pauseBackground);
pauseOverlay.add(pauseLabel).pad(20);
pauseOverlay.row();
pauseOverlay.add(resumeButton);
pauseOverlay.row();
pauseOverlay.add(quitButton).width(w);
pauseOverlay.row();
pauseOverlay.add(volumeLabel).padTop(100);
pauseOverlay.row();
pauseOverlay.add(audioSlider).width(400);
```

You initialize pauseOverlay to be invisible:

```
pauseOverlay.setVisible(false);
```

Finally, you add the following line of code to the handle method of the Pause button's EventListener, which will make pauseOverlay visible whenever the game is paused:

```
pauseOverlay.setVisible( isPaused() );
```

This completes the final layer for your user interface; the three layers are illustrated side by side in Figure 4-12.

Figure 4-12. *The three layers of content in Starfish Collector*

This brings you to the end of your refinements to the Starfish Collector game! To practice these techniques, I recommend that you rewrite the corresponding portions of the other previous games, Cheese, Please! and Balloon Buster, to incorporate this new approach to user-interface design.

Summary

In this chapter, you added quite a bit of polish to the Starfish Collector game. You started by adding sound effects and background music, using the audio object and the Sound and Music interfaces. Then you designed and implemented a sophisticated user interface, including a Start menu screen, a user interface for the main game screen, and a menu that overlays the main screen when the game is paused. You learned how to use the Table class to simplify the layout of user interfaces, and the Skin class to manage resources. You restructured your custom BaseScreen class and added a BaseGame class to incorporate these new classes. You also saw how to create a variety of user-interface elements using the classes Label, Button, TextButton, Image, and Slider, and their associated style objects. In the next chapter, you'll continue your focus on the user's experience, focusing on providing the user alternative forms of input to play the game.

CHAPTER 5

■ ■ ■

Alternative Sources of User Input

In previous chapters, your games have been controlled with traditional desktop computer hardware: a keyboard and a mouse. In this chapter, you'll explore two alternative sources of user input: gamepad controllers and touch-screen controls. If you do not have access to a gamepad with a USB connector (as discussed later in this chapter), you can still follow along; the code will still compile, and you'll leave keyboard controls as a feedback (a good practice to consider in general for the convenience of your game's players). Similarly, even if you don't have access to device that's touch-screen capable, learning about the associated design considerations is still worthwhile. Furthermore, touch events and mouse events are handled by the same methods in LibGDX; you can simulate single-touch input (but not multitouch input) with the mouse. On the other hand, if neither gamepad nor touch-based input is of interest to you, this entire chapter may be omitted without loss of continuity.

As a starting point, I've updated the code from the Cheese, Please! game (introduced in Chapter 3) to include the structural and design modifications introduced in Chapter 4: incorporating the new BaseGame class together with Skin and Table objects to organize the user interface. This revised code can be found in the CheesePleaseUpdate directory containing the source code for this chapter, and will serve as your starting point for both of the main sections that follow.

Gamepad Controllers

Gamepad controllers are specialized hardware devices that make it easier for the player to enter game-related input. They have been in existence as long as game consoles, and have included various configurations of components such as joysticks, buttons, directional pads, dials, triggers, and touch pads. With the increase in console-style gaming available on desktop computers, many gamepads that can be connected via USB ports are now available. In this section, you'll develop controls for an Xbox 360 gamepad, or one of the many alternative products that emulate it, such as the Logitech F310 gamepad, shown in Figure 5-1.

Figure 5-1. *Xbox 360 and Logitech F310 gamepad controllers*

Support for gamepad input is provided by the Controller and Controllers classes. These are not part of the core LibGDX libraries, and thus their code is contained in different JAR files, which must be included in your project. From the same download location where you obtained the file libgdx.jar, discussed in Chapter 1, locate the directory extensions/gdx-controllers/ and download the following files:

```
gdx-controllers.jar
gdx-controllers-desktop.jar
gdx-controllers-desktop-natives.jar
```

To begin, make a copy of the CheesePleaseUpdate project folder and rename it to CheesePleaseGamepad. Copy the JAR files you have downloaded into the +libs folder in your project directory. Once these files have been added, you will need to restart BlueJ for the newly added classes to be available. The first addition you need to make to your code is to import all the controller-related classes to your customized classes that will use them. To do so, add the following import statement to the BaseScreen, MenuScreen, and GameScreen classes:

```
import com.badlogic.gdx.controllers.*;
```

Recall that you can process user input in one of two ways. For continuous input (corresponding to actions such as walking), you poll the state of the hardware device in the update method, which typically runs 60 times per second. Later you will see that this process is analogous to polling for keyboard input: keyboard polling uses methods of the Gdx.input object such as isKeyPressed, while gamepad polling uses methods of a Controller object such as getAxis and getButton. For discrete input (corresponding to actions such as jumping), you previously configured the program to monitor (or "listen") for events, such as when a keyboard key is initially pressed down. Similarly, you will include additional code in the BaseScreen class to monitor for discrete gamepad events, such as when a gamepad button is initially pressed down. You will introduce code for both continuous and discrete gamepad input over the course of the next two sections.

Continuous Input

In this section, you will add code to the update method of the GameScreen class, which will determine the direction in which the joystick is being pressed, and move the player's character accordingly. First, you need to retrieve the instance of the active Controller object. The Controllers class provides the static utility method getControllers that retrieves an Array of active, connected Controller objects. Assuming that just a single gamepad is connected, you need only get the zeroth element of the Array, as follows:

```
Controller gamepad = Controllers.getControllers().get(0);
```

Once the Controller has been obtained, you can poll for the state of joysticks, buttons, directional pads, and trigger buttons by using one of four provided get-style methods. Many of these require a single parameter: a constant value that corresponds to a component of the gamepad. These values are gamepad specific, and a particular gamepad might even have different values for different operating systems. The most robust method for determining these values is to allow the player to configure the gamepad mapping at runtime, by looping through the different actions required by the game, asking the player to press the corresponding button, and storing the values for later use. For simplicity in this section, I have included a class called XBoxGamepad that stores the codes for an Xbox 360-style controller (which includes those such as the Logitech F310 controller mentioned earlier). This code for this class is presented here, and I'll explain how to use the values afterward:

```java
import com.badlogic.gdx.controllers.PovDirection;

public class XBoxGamepad
{
    /** button codes */
    public static final int BUTTON_A               = 0;
    public static final int BUTTON_B               = 1;
    public static final int BUTTON_X               = 2;
    public static final int BUTTON_Y               = 3;
    public static final int BUTTON_LEFT_SHOULDER   = 4;
    public static final int BUTTON_RIGHT_SHOULDER  = 5;
    public static final int BUTTON_BACK            = 6;
    public static final int BUTTON_START           = 7;
    public static final int BUTTON_LEFT_STICK      = 8;
    public static final int BUTTON_RIGHT_STICK     = 9;

    /** directional pad codes */
    public static final PovDirection DPAD_UP     = PovDirection.north;
    public static final PovDirection DPAD_DOWN   = PovDirection.south;
    public static final PovDirection DPAD_RIGHT  = PovDirection.east;
    public static final PovDirection DPAD_LEFT   = PovDirection.west;

    /** joystick axis codes */
    // X-axis: -1 = left, +1 = right
    // Y-axis: -1 = up  , +1 = down
    public static final int AXIS_LEFT_X  = 1;
    public static final int AXIS_LEFT_Y  = 0;
    public static final int AXIS_RIGHT_X = 3;
    public static final int AXIS_RIGHT_Y = 2;
```

```
/** trigger codes */
// Left & Right Trigger buttons treated as a single axis; same ID value
// Values - Left trigger: 0 to +1.  Right trigger: 0 to -1.
// Note: values are additive; they can cancel each other if both are pressed.
public static final int AXIS_LEFT_TRIGGER  = 4;
public static final int AXIS_RIGHT_TRIGGER = 4;
}
```

The following methods are available to poll the state of a gamepad component:

- To poll the state of the joystick, use getAxis(code), where code is an integer corresponding to either the left or right joystick, and either the x or y direction. The value returned is a float in the range from –1 to 1. On the x axis, –1 corresponds to left and +1 corresponds to right, while on the y axis, –1 corresponds to up and +1 corresponds to down. For example, consider the following line of code:

  ```
  float x = gamepad.getAxis(XBoxGamepad.AXIS_LEFT_X);
  ```

  If the value of x equals 0.5, then that means the left joystick of the gamepad is being pressed halfway to the right.

  I emphasize that the orientation of the y axis used by most controllers (negative values correspond to the "up" direction) is the opposite orientation assumed by the LibGDX libraries (positive values correspond to the "up" direction). This will need to be remembered when processing input in the update method.

- To poll the state of the triggers, you also use getAxis(code). On Xbox 360-style controllers, the left and right triggers are treated as a single axis. Pressing the left trigger generates the values in the range from 0 (not pressed) to +1 (fully pressed), while pressing the right trigger generates values in the range from 0 (not pressed) to –1 (fully pressed). If both triggers are pressed at once, the getAxis method will return the sum of their values; in particular, if both triggers are fully pressed, getAxis will return 0.

- To check the state of the gamepad buttons, use getButton(code), where code is an integer corresponding to a gamepad button. The value returned is a Boolean that indicates whether the corresponding button is currently being pressed down.

- To determine which direction is being pressed on the directional pad,[1] use getPov(num), where num is the index of the directional pad (typically 0). Directional pads are interesting, in that they yield return values more complex than a button (a boolean value) but less complex than a joystick axis (a float value). This "middle ground" level of input is handled by returning an enumerated type (an enum) defined in the imported PovDirection class. However, for convenience, I have defined alternative names (that may be more familiar to modern gamers) for these values in the XBoxGamepad class.

---

[1]The control element typically referred to as a directional pad was referred to as a *point-of-view* control in traditional flight simulators, which explains the use of the POV acronym in the LibGDX source code.

You are now ready to add gamepad-based controls to the update method of the GameScreen class. In particular, you enable the player to control Mousey with the gamepad left joystick, by incorporating the getAxis method. In the following code, you check to see whether a controller is connected by testing whether the Array of controllers contains at least one element. If so, then provided that the joystick has moved passed a certain threshold (called the *deadzone*, used to compensate for controller sensitivity, typically set to a value between 10 and 20 percent), you set the acceleration of your character accordingly. If not, you provide fallback keyboard controls for your game.

```
float accelerate = 100.0f;
if (Controllers.getControllers().size > 0)
{
    Controller gamepad = Controllers.getControllers().get(0);
    float xAxis =  gamepad.getAxis(XBoxGamepad.AXIS_LEFT_X);
    float yAxis = -gamepad.getAxis(XBoxGamepad.AXIS_LEFT_Y);
    float deadZone = 0.15f;
    if (Math.abs(xAxis) < deadZone)
        xAxis = 0;
    if (Math.abs(yAxis) < deadZone)
        yAxis = 0;
    mousey.setAccelerationXY( xAxis * accelerate, yAxis * accelerate);
}
else
{
    // keyboard fallback controls
    mousey.setAccelerationXY(0,0);
    if (Gdx.input.isKeyPressed(Keys.LEFT))
        mousey.addAccelerationXY(-accelerate,0);
    if (Gdx.input.isKeyPressed(Keys.RIGHT))
        mousey.addAccelerationXY(accelerate,0);
    if (Gdx.input.isKeyPressed(Keys.UP))
        mousey.addAccelerationXY(0,accelerate);
    if (Gdx.input.isKeyPressed(Keys.DOWN))
        mousey.addAccelerationXY(0,-accelerate);
}
```

Discrete Input

Next, you will introduce the code necessary to process discrete gamepad input events. First, you must declare that the BaseScreen class implements the ControllerListener interface. The first line of the class declaration should read as follows:

```
public abstract class BaseScreen implements Screen, InputProcessor, ControllerListener
```

You need to declare the methods required by the `ControllerListener` interface; these can be overridden if needed by the individual classes that extend `BaseScreen`. The methods you need to include are as follows:

```
public void connected(Controller controller)
{  }

public void disconnected(Controller controller)
{  }

public boolean xSliderMoved(Controller controller, int sliderCode, boolean value)
{  return false;  }

public boolean ySliderMoved(Controller controller, int sliderCode, boolean value)
{  return false;  }

public boolean accelerometerMoved(Controller controller, int accelerometerCode, Vector3 value)
{  return false;  }

public boolean povMoved(Controller controller, int povCode, PovDirection value)
{  return false;  }

public boolean axisMoved(Controller controller, int axisCode, float value)
{  return false;  }

public boolean buttonDown(Controller controller, int buttonCode)
{  return false;  }

public boolean buttonUp(Controller controller, int buttonCode)
{  return false;  }
```

Finally, you need to "activate" the listener. You will add the currently active Screen to the set of listeners managed by the `Controllers` class. You must also remove any previously added `ControllerListener` objects; you don't want other `Screen` objects that may be inactive (but still reside in memory) to respond to input, because this could cause unexpected problems. (For example, if the Start button were used to begin a new game from the menu screen, after switching to the game screen, you no longer want this action to be occur when clicking Start; therefore, you must stop the menu screen from "listening" and responding to these events.) You can perform this task in the `BaseScreen` constructor by adding the following lines of code:

```
Controllers.clearListeners();
Controllers.addListener(this);
```

Now that your modifications to the `BaseScreen` class are complete, you are ready to write game-specific code to respond to discrete gamepad input. For example, you want to enable the player to pause the game by pressing the X button on the Xbox gamepad. It would be inaccurate to poll for the state of the button in the update method, as this could result in toggling the pause state 60 times per second. Pausing the game is a *discrete* action, and thus you override one of the ControllerListener methods to listen for the event of pressing the X button. The following code, to be added to the GameScreen class, accomplishes this task:

```
public boolean buttonDown(Controller controller, int buttonCode)
{
    if (buttonCode == XBoxGamepad.BUTTON_X)
        togglePaused();

     return false;
}
```

Similarly, you would like to be able to start the game by clicking the Start button while the main menu screen is active. To this end, you add the following code to the MenuScreen class:

```
public boolean buttonDown(Controller controller, int buttonCode)
{
    if (buttonCode == XBoxGamepad.BUTTON_START)
        game.setScreen( new GameScreen(game) );

    return false;
}
```

This completes the controller-based additions to the Cheese, Please! game. The final version of the source code is contained within the CheesePleaseGamepad folder that contains the source code for this chapter.

Touch-Screen Controls

In this section, you'll learn how to implement gamepad-inspired onscreen touch controls. Again, as mentioned in the beginning of the chapter, access to a touch-screen device is not needed to test the code for this section, as LibGDX handles mouse events and touch events with the same methods; single-touch input is simulated by the mouse. Since you have already learned about the Button class in the previous chapter, you're well on your way. In what follows, you'll learn about another user-interface control provided by the LibGDX library, the Touchpad class, which was created to simulate a traditional arcade joystick. Figure 5-2 shows an example of a traditional arcade-style joystick, and a touch-pad control that can be created with LibGDX, which is rendered in a top-down perspective of the arcade-style joystick.

Figure 5-2. *A traditional arcade-style joystick, and a touch-pad control created in LibGDX*

The biggest challenge to successfully using these controls is not the creation of the object, but rather a design challenge: how should these elements be arranged and placed on the screen? One option is to overlay the elements on top of the game world itself, as you have with various Label objects in previous chapters. However, you rapidly discover the problem that having too many controls—which must typically be much larger than labels, for easy operation—can obscure the game world to the extent that it interferes with game play. If poorly placed, a touch pad could completely obscure the main character. Figure 5-3 illustrates this possible situation by placing the touch pad in the lower-left corner of the game screen. Notice how it could cover Mousey completely!

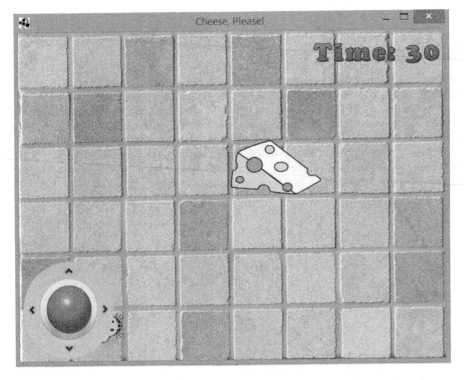

Figure 5-3. *A poorly placed touch-pad control obscuring the main character, Mousey*

Some games attempt to address this issue by making the controls on the user interface translucent, yet the core difficulty remains because the player's fingers will often be positioned over the region where the controls are, thus still obscuring the view of the game world. An alternative approach that you will implement in this section is to reserve a particular region of the screen for the controls, and render the game world in the remaining area, as illustrated in Figure 5-4.

Figure 5-4. Placing the game controls below the game world

Working with a Touch Pad

Touchpad objects are rendered using two images: one representing the background, and the other representing the knob. The user can touch (or click) the knob and drag it off-center; its movement is constrained to a circular area contained within the rectangular region defined by the background image.

These objects require two parameters to be initialized. First, you supply a value for the deadzone radius—the minimal distance (in pixels) the knob must be dragged in order for any change to register. This is useful for situations when the player wants to leave a finger on the touch pad and also for the character to remain still. Without a deadzone setting, the controls would be too sensitive for this to be possible. It is unlikely that the average player would have pixel-perfect finger positioning to keep the knob exactly centered, and the result would be unwanted (and possibly player-frustrating) drift of the character being controlled.

Second, the images used in a Touchpad object are stored in a TouchpadStyle object, which contains two images, both stored as Drawable objects, as is standard for UI elements in LibGDX. As usual, you will load each image into a Texture object and convert it into a Drawable by using the game's Skin object. Because only one screen in your game uses this style, you won't initialize the style in the class extending BaseGame, as you have with other style data objects.

To begin this project, start by making another local copy of the CheesePleaseUpdate project directory, renaming it to CheesePleaseTouchscreen. You'll also need to copy some images from this chapter's source code directory: from CheesePleaseTouchscreen/assets, copy all of the images into your local project's assets directory.

In the GameScreen class, you begin by adding the import statements:

```
import com.badlogic.gdx.scenes.scene2d.ui.Touchpad;
import com.badlogic.gdx.scenes.scene2d.ui.Touchpad.TouchpadStyle;
import com.badlogic.gdx.scenes.scene2d.ui.Button.ButtonStyle;
import com.badlogic.gdx.scenes.scene2d.InputListener;
import com.badlogic.gdx.scenes.scene2d.InputEvent;
```

You include the following code to declare the Touchpad object in the GameScreen class, so that both the create and update methods can access it:

```
private Touchpad touchPad;
```

Next, in the create method, you use the following code to initialize the Touchpad object as well as its corresponding TouchpadStyle. While it is possible to add an event listener to monitor and respond to changes in the state of the touch pad, instead you will poll for the state of the touch pad later, in the update method.

```
TouchpadStyle touchStyle = new TouchpadStyle();

Texture padKnobTex = new Texture(Gdx.files.internal("assets/joystick-knob.png"));
game.skin.add("padKnobImage", padKnobTex );
touchStyle.knob = game.skin.getDrawable("padKnobImage");

Texture padBackTex = new Texture(Gdx.files.internal("assets/joystick-bg.png"));
game.skin.add("padBackImage", padBackTex );
touchStyle.background = game.skin.getDrawable("padBackImage");

touchPad = new Touchpad(5, touchStyle);
```

In the update method, you can use the Touchpad object methods getKnobPercentX and getKnobPercentY to determine the current position of the knob. The returned values range from –1 to +1; you can multiply these values by the maximum desired acceleration for your character, which will give the player a great deal of control over the speed: the further the knob is dragged from the center of the touch pad, the greater the character's speed will be. You replace the code that polls the state of the keyboard arrow keys and sets Mousey's acceleration with the following:

```
float accelerate = 100;
mousey.setAccelerationXY(
    touchPad.getKnobPercentX() * accelerate, touchPad.getKnobPercentY() * accelerate );
```

For completeness, the code that you will use to create the Pause button displayed in the game screenshot in Figure 5-4 is given below; this code should be included in the create method. In this case, an event listener is attached to the Button object, since pausing the game is a discrete action.

```
Texture pauseTexture = new Texture(Gdx.files.internal("assets/pause.png"));
game.skin.add("pauseImage", pauseTexture );
ButtonStyle pauseStyle = new ButtonStyle();
pauseStyle.up = game.skin.getDrawable("pauseImage");

Button pauseButton = new Button( pauseStyle );

pauseButton.addListener(
    new InputListener()
    {
        public boolean touchDown (InputEvent event, float x, float y, int pointer,
        int button)
        {
            togglePaused();
            return true;
        }
    });
```

With these elements in place, you are ready to focus your attention on creating the user interface layout illustrated in Figure 5-4.

Redesigning the User Interface

As mentioned in the beginning of our discussion of touch-screen controls, you have to deal with the issue of control elements obstructing the user's view of the game world; we have elected to display the controls at the bottom of the screen and render the game world above them.

First, you'll set the configuration options in the Launcher class so that the window has width 600 and height 800; the main function becomes as follows:

```
public static void main (String[] args)
{
    LwjglApplicationConfiguration config = new LwjglApplicationConfiguration();
    config.width = 600;
    config.height = 800;
    config.title = "Cheese, Please!";

    CheeseGame myProgram = new CheeseGame();
    LwjglApplication launcher = new LwjglApplication( myProgram, config );
}
```

Next, you'll make some changes to the BaseScreen class. The user interface will still fill the entire window, but the game world (the contents of mainStage) will be rendered in the upper area of this window, as illustrated in Figure 5-4. Thus, you'll change the dimensions of mainStage to 600 by 600 pixels, and later you'll see how to render mainStage in a different location. The constants viewWidth and viewHeight will now exclusively refer to the dimensions of mainStage, and you'll declare the constants uiWidth and uiHeight to store the dimensions of uiStage.

The variable declarations in the BaseScreen class should now be as follows:

```
public final int viewWidth  = 600;
public final int viewHeight = 600;
public final int uiWidth    = 600;
public final int uiHeight   = 800;
```

In the constructor method, the initialization of mainStage remains the same, but the line of code initializing uiStage should be changed to the following:

```
uiStage = new Stage( new FitViewport(uiWidth, uiHeight) );
```

In the render method, you can change the rendering location of each stage by using the method glViewport of the Gdx.gl object, before the draw method of each stage is called. The parameters of glViewport define the rectangular region where the stage should be rendered: the x and y coordinates of the bottom-left corner, followed by the width and height of the rectangle. In the following code listing, the code to be added (to adjust the rendering locations as previously described) appears in bold:

```
Gdx.gl.glViewport(0, uiHeight-viewHeight, viewWidth, viewHeight );
mainStage.draw();
Gdx.gl.glViewport(0,0, uiWidth,uiHeight);
uiStage.draw();
```

In general, it is recommended to use the glViewport method sparingly, as it changes the rendering parameters, but not the coordinates of touch events generated by event listeners. This is why uiStage was kept at the same size as the window. Otherwise, the call to glViewport could result in a mismatch between where the controls are drawn and where the controls are activated.

Next, you plan the new layout of uiTable that incorporates the onscreen controls, as illustrated in Figure 5-4; an abstract diagram of this layout is presented in Figure 5-5.

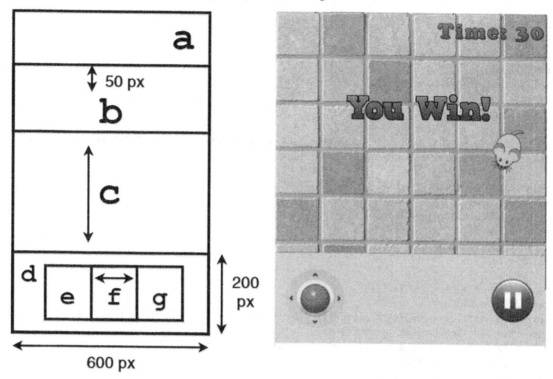

Figure 5-5. *Abstract diagram of the new user-interface layout, including control elements*

The contents of Figure 5-5 are as follows:

- Cell a contains a right-aligned label displaying the time elapsed.

- Cell b contains the You Win image (separated by 50 pixels of padding in between), as in the previous version of this game.

- Cell c is empty and set to expand in the y direction to fill any available space, to ensure that cell d will be positioned at the bottom of the screen.

- Cell d has a fixed size of 200 by 600 pixels, and contains another Table, which in turn contains the onscreen touch controls; the Table in cell d is padded by 25 pixels all around, has a background image that is repeated (or *tiled*) to fill the available space, and contains three cells in a single row: e, f, and g.

- Cell e contains the touchPad object.

- Cell f is empty and set to expand in the x direction to fill any available space, so that cell e is closer to the left side of the screen, and cell g is closer to the right side.

- Cell g contains the Button used to pause the game.

Before you implement this layout, you must remove the code for the previous version of the UI. In particular, *delete* the following lines from the `create` method:

```
uiTable.pad(10);
uiTable.add().expandX();
uiTable.add(timeLabel);
uiTable.row();
uiTable.add(winImage).colspan(2).padTop(50);
uiTable.row();
uiTable.add().colspan(2).expandY();
```

In its place, you add the following code, which uses the previously created `touchpad` and `pauseButton` elements and implements the table layout as described:

```
uiTable.add(timeLabel).right().pad(10);
uiTable.row();
uiTable.add(winImage).padTop(50);
uiTable.row();
uiTable.add().expandY();
uiTable.row();

Table controlTable = new Table();
controlTable.pad(25);
Texture controlTex = new Texture(Gdx.files.internal("assets/pixels-white.png"), true);
game.skin.add( "controlTex", controlTex );
controlTable.background( game.skin.getTiledDrawable("controlTex") );
controlTable.add(touchPad);
controlTable.add().expandX();
controlTable.add(pauseButton);

uiTable.add(controlTable).width(600).height(200);
```

With this code, the Cheese, Please! game should now render as illustrated in Figure 5-4. The source code that incorporates all of these changes is contained within the CheesePleaseTouchscreen directory. The touch-screen controls are best experienced when the program is run on a touch-screen device, such as a tablet running the Android OS; this topic is discussed briefly in Chapter 9.

Summary

In this chapter, you added two new ways for the player to interact with your game. First, you added gamepad controller support to the base game by using the controller extensions for the LibGDX libraries. This required the inclusion of some new JAR files in your project, as well as a class dedicated to storing the values corresponding to each of the joysticks, buttons, directional pads, and triggers on your particular gamepad. You learned how to poll for continuous input, as well as how to set up event listeners to monitor for discrete input. Afterward, you saw how to add touch-screen support to the base game, using Touchpad and Button objects. This chapter discussed at length the design issues that arise when adding onscreen controls, and showed one way to alleviate these issues, by repositioning the rendering locations of the stages using the glViewport method. With these new techniques at your disposal, you will be able to greatly improve the gameplay experience for your players.

CHAPTER 6

■ ■ ■

Additional Game Case Studies

This chapter introduces a series of games and focuses on how to implement a variety of game mechanics. Each of the examples is playable, but certainly not a polished product—for example, none has a Start menu or a user interface, and we won't implement win or lose conditions (these are left for the you to implement as recommended "Next Steps" at the end of each section). Nonetheless, the techniques covered should prove to be useful for many situations.

For each of the new games that is presented, you should begin by creating a new project in BlueJ. In each project, you should copy over the classes BaseGame, BaseScreen, BaseActor, AnimatedActor, and PhysicsActor. In the BaseScreen class, you should change the values of viewWidth and viewHeight to 800 and 600, respectively, as the games in this chapter require a larger window. You should also create a launcher-style class and a class that extends BaseGame, as in earlier projects. In each section, you will write a class called GameScreen that is initialized by the customized BaseGame-extending class of each project.

Space Rocks

This section introduces a game called *Space Rocks*, a space-themed shoot-'em-up game inspired by the classic arcade game Asteroids. The user controls a spaceship; the goal is to shoot lasers to destroy all the rocks floating around the screen. Figure 6-1 shows this game in action.

Figure 6-1. *The Space Rocks game*

The spaceship steers much like the turtle from the Starfish Collector game: it can rotate left and right, and move forward in whatever direction it is facing. The new mechanics and topics introduced with this game include the following:

- Creating a template instance of an object to be used as a basis for spawning later

- Using new methods for the BaseActor class to simplify centering objects

- Updating the BaseActor class so that groups of objects can move together

- Maintaining multiple lists of actor objects

- Using a new method to wrap the position of an actor around the screen (an object that moves past one edge of the screen reappears on the opposite side)

After creating a new project and including the classes as described at the beginning of this chapter, you should copy all the images from this chapter's source directory SpaceRocks/assets into your local project's assets folder. You then create the core of the GameScreen class, including the import statements and variable and method declarations you will need:

```
import com.badlogic.gdx.Gdx;
import com.badlogic.gdx.Input.Keys;
import com.badlogic.gdx.graphics.Texture;
import com.badlogic.gdx.scenes.scene2d.actions.Actions;
import com.badlogic.gdx.graphics.Texture.TextureFilter;
import com.badlogic.gdx.graphics.g2d.Animation;
import com.badlogic.gdx.graphics.g2d.Animation.PlayMode;
import com.badlogic.gdx.math.MathUtils;
import java.util.ArrayList;

public class GameScreen extends BaseScreen
{
    private BaseActor background;
    private PhysicsActor spaceship;
    private BaseActor rocketfire;

    // create "base" objects to clone later
    private PhysicsActor baseLaser;
    private AnimatedActor baseExplosion;

    private ArrayList<PhysicsActor> laserList;
    private ArrayList<PhysicsActor> rockList;
    private ArrayList<BaseActor> removeList;

    // game world dimensions
    final int mapWidth = 800;
    final int mapHeight = 600;

    public GameScreen(BaseGame g)
    {  super(g);  }

    public void create()
    {               }

    public void update(float dt)
    {               }

}
```

Next, you proceed to fill in the methods. In the create method, you initialize the background object:

```
background = new BaseActor();
background.setTexture( new Texture(Gdx.files.internal("assets/space.png")) );
background.setPosition( 0, 0 );
mainStage.addActor( background );
```

Each of the remaining objects to be initialized needs to have its origin set to the center of its associated image, for rotations to appear correct. To simplify the code that follows, add the following method to the BaseActor class, which automates this process for you:

```
public void setOriginCenter()
{
    if ( getWidth() == 0 )
        System.err.println("error: actor size not set");

    setOrigin( getWidth()/2, getHeight()/2 );
}
```

The Spaceship

Returning to the create method of the GameScreen class, you initialize the spaceship object as usual:

1. Load and store a Texture (which is automatically converted to an Animation for you).

2. Set the starting position.

3. Set the physics properties (a small deceleration value will provide a "drifting" effect).

4. Select a shape for collision-detection purposes.

5. Add the object to a Stage.

In contrast to the turtle object from the Starfish Collector game, you do not want to set the autoAngle parameter to true, because the spaceship should be able to face in a different direction than the one corresponding to its angle of motion. In fact, this is one of the distinguishing features of this game: to slow down quickly, the spaceship must turn around and accelerate in the opposite direction. Here's the code that accomplishes the features listed above:

```
spaceship = new PhysicsActor();
Texture shipTex = new Texture(Gdx.files.internal("assets/spaceship.png"));
shipTex.setFilter(TextureFilter.Linear, TextureFilter.Linear);
spaceship.storeAnimation( "default", shipTex );

spaceship.setPosition( 400,300 );
spaceship.setOriginCenter();
spaceship.setMaxSpeed(200);
spaceship.setDeceleration(20);
spaceship.setEllipseBoundary();

mainStage.addActor(spaceship);
```

Steering the spaceship in Space Rocks is slightly different from moving the turtle in Starfish Collector, in that you'd like to be able to change the spaceship's acceleration gradually in various directions. To this end, you need to add the following method to the PhysicsActor class, which will adjust an actor's acceleration by adding a given amount of acceleration in another direction:

```
public void addAccelerationAS(float angle, float amount)
{
    acceleration.add( amount * MathUtils.cosDeg(angle), amount * MathUtils.sinDeg(angle) );
}
```

With this new method in place, it is time to return to the GameScreen class. To steer the spaceship, you add the following code to the update method:

```
spaceship.setAccelerationXY(0,0);

if (Gdx.input.isKeyPressed(Keys.LEFT))
    spaceship.rotateBy(180 * dt);
if (Gdx.input.isKeyPressed(Keys.RIGHT))
    spaceship.rotateBy(-180 * dt);
if (Gdx.input.isKeyPressed(Keys.UP))
    spaceship.addAccelerationAS(spaceship.getRotation(), 100);
```

One of the interesting features of the Space Rocks game world is that there are no "boundaries": an object travelling past the right edge of the screen reappears on the left (and vice versa), and similarly for the bottom and top edges. This behavior is called *wraparound*, and can be implemented by including the following method in the GameScreen class:

```
public void wraparound(BaseActor ba)
{
    if ( ba.getX() + ba.getWidth() < 0 )
        ba.setX( mapWidth );
    if ( ba.getX() > mapWidth )
        ba.setX( -ba.getWidth() );
    if ( ba.getY() + ba.getHeight() < 0 )
        ba.setY( mapHeight );
    if ( ba.getY() > mapHeight )
        ba.setY( -ba.getHeight() );
}
```

Then in the update method, this method should be invoked on each of the moving entities in the game. To start, include the following line of code:

```
wraparound( spaceship );
```

This is a good point to compile your project and to test whether the ship moves across the screen as expected.

Your next goal is to create a visual special effect: a rocket-fire image, which appears to be coming from the back end of the spaceship, and should be visible when (and only when) the user is pressing the key that makes the spaceship accelerate forward. Ideally, you want to somehow "attach" this image to the spaceship, offset a bit from the spaceship's center, and move the rocket-fire image along with the spaceship image, taking into account the position and rotation of the spaceship, as illustrated in Figure 6-2.

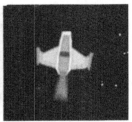

Figure 6-2. *Spaceship without and with rocket fire visible in different positions*

In LibGDX, the Group class was created for exactly this purpose: it is an extension of the Actor class, and also similar to a Stage in that you can add other Actor objects to it. The draw method of the Group class calculates the position and rotation of all attached Actor objects, and then calls their draw methods in turn. To adapt your BaseActor class to take advantage of this, you need to make a few changes. First, add the import statement:

```
import com.badlogic.gdx.scenes.scene2d.Group;
```

Next, change the declaration of the BaseActor class so that it extends the Group class instead of the Actor class:

```
public class BaseActor extends Group
```

At the end of the draw method of the BaseActor class, you need to include the following line of code; as discussed previously, this calls the draw method of the Group class, which in turn calls the draw methods of all the actors that have been attached to this object:

```
super.draw(batch, parentAlpha);
```

Then you initialize the rocketfire object in the create method of the GameScreen class as follows. Note in particular that the rocket fire's position should be thought of as offset from the spaceship's position, as illustrated by the dashed lines on the right side of Figure 6-3. Also note that the rocketfire object is added to spaceship, rather than mainStage.

```
rocketfire = new BaseActor();
rocketfire.setPosition(-28,24);
Texture fireTex = new Texture(Gdx.files.internal("assets/fire.png"));
fireTex.setFilter(TextureFilter.Linear, TextureFilter.Linear);
rocketfire.setTexture( fireTex );
spaceship.addActor(rocketfire);
```

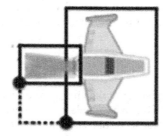

Figure 6-3. *The default position of the rocketfire object when added to the spaceship (left) and after setting the position relative to the spaceship (right)*

Recall that the rocketfire object should be visible only if the player is pressing the keyboard key that accelerates the spaceship. This is accomplished by adding the following line of code to the update method:

```
rocketfire.setVisible( Gdx.input.isKeyPressed(Keys.UP) );
```

This is a good time to compile the code and run the game to verify that everything is behaving as expected.

Lasers

Next, you set up the baseLaser object, from which additional lasers will be cloned for the spaceship to shoot at the rocks. As usual, this requires you to load and store a Texture, set physics properties and a collision shape, and in this case you *do* want the laser be oriented in the direction of motion, so you set autoAngle to true. To accomplish these tasks, add the following code to the create method of the GameScreen class:

```
baseLaser = new PhysicsActor();
Texture laserTex = new Texture(Gdx.files.internal("assets/laser.png"));
laserTex.setFilter(TextureFilter.Linear, TextureFilter.Linear);
baseLaser.storeAnimation( "default", laserTex );

baseLaser.setMaxSpeed(400);
baseLaser.setDeceleration(0);
baseLaser.setEllipseBoundary();
baseLaser.setOriginCenter();
baseLaser.setAutoAngle(true);
```

In addition, you need to initialize the list that will be used to store instances of laser objects, for later use in collision detection:

```
laserList = new ArrayList<PhysicsActor>();
```

Instances of lasers are stored by two objects in this game: a Stage object, which activates the updating and drawing of the actor, and an ArrayList object, which is used to organize the collision detection code. When one of these instances needs to be removed from the game, to do so completely requires that it be removed from both the Stage and the ArrayList that contains it. The Actor class contains a remove method to remove `itself` from the `Stage`. Inspired by this functionality, you will add some code to the `BaseActor` class to similarly manage removal from the associated `ArrayList`. First, in the `BaseActor` class, add the import statement:

```
import java.util.ArrayList;
```

Then add a new variable: an `ArrayList` called `parentList`, which can store a reference to an `ArrayList` the actor has been added to. The difficult part of declaring this variable is choosing the type of data that the `ArrayList` contains: in general, it could contain `BaseActor` objects, or `AnimatedActor` objects, or `PhysicsActor` objects—in short, any of the classes that extend the `BaseActor` class. To express this in the declaration, the Java syntax for the type declaration is `? extends BaseActor`. In the `BaseActor` class, add the following line of code to the variable declarations:

```
private ArrayList<? extends BaseActor> parentList;
```

Then add a method to the `BaseActor` class that can be used to set this data:

```
public void setParentList(ArrayList<? extends BaseActor> pl)
{   parentList = pl;   }
```

Initialize this data to `null` in the `BaseActor` constructor by adding the following line of code:

```
parentList = null;
```

And finally, add a method called `destroy` that will cause a `BaseActor` to remove itself from the `Stage` that contains it, as well as removing it from its `parentList` (if it exists):

```
public void destroy()
{
    remove(); // removes self from Stage

    if (parentList != null)
        parentList.remove(this);
}
```

Next, you will set up the code to fire a laser. Lasers should appear to be coming from the spaceship object. To align their origin coordinates correctly, you must take into account the position of the target, the origin of the target, and the origin of the object being centered. The results of taking these values into account, one step at a time, are illustrated in Figure 6-4.

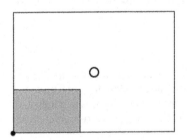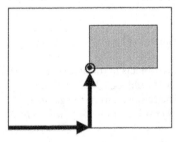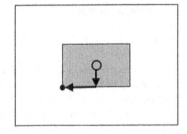

Figure 6-4. *An illustration of the effects of each step in the calculation for centering a small rectangle within a larger rectangle*

Since this is a commonly needed operation, add the following method, named moveToOrigin, to the BaseActor class:

```
public void moveToOrigin(BaseActor target)
{
    this.setPosition(
        target.getX() + target.getOriginX() - this.getOriginX(),
        target.getY() + target.getOriginY() - this.getOriginY() );
}
```

In addition, laser objects will need to be cloned so there need to be clone methods for the AnimatedActor and PhysicsActor classes. Previously, only BaseActor objects were cloned, so the analogous methods for the more sophisticated classes have not been introduced until now. In the AnimatedActor class, add the following methods. Note that in the copy method, the method call super.copy activates the copy method of the BaseActor class, which ensures that all the data defined in that class will also get copied into the new actor.

```
public void copy(AnimatedActor original)
{
    super.copy(original);
    this.elapsedTime = 0;
    this.animationStorage = original.animationStorage;
    this.activeName = new String(original.activeName);
    this.activeAnim = this.animationStorage.get( this.activeName );
}
```

```
public AnimatedActor clone()
{
    AnimatedActor newbie = new AnimatedActor();
    newbie.copy( this );
    return newbie;
}
```

In the PhysicsActor class, for similar purposes, add the following methods:

```
public void copy(PhysicsActor original)
{
    super.copy(original);
    this.velocity     = new Vector2(original.velocity);
    this.acceleration = new Vector2(original.acceleration);
    this.maxSpeed     = original.maxSpeed;
    this.deceleration = original.deceleration;
    this.autoAngle    = original.autoAngle;
}
```

```
public PhysicsActor clone()
{
    PhysicsActor newbie = new PhysicsActor();
    newbie.copy( this );
    return newbie;
}
```

Now you are ready to return to implementing game mechanics in the GameScreen class. Since firing a laser is a discrete event, you'll override the keyDown method in the GameScreen class to handle this action. If the space key is pressed, create a new PhysicsActor, called laser, by cloning baseLaser. Center the laser on the spaceship by using the newly created moveToOrigin method, set the velocity so that it is aligned with the angle of the spaceship, and add the laser to the appropriate Stage and ArrayList. Also, an Action sequence is added that will cause the laser to fade out quickly after an initial 2-second delay:

```
public boolean keyDown(int keycode)
{
    if (keycode == Keys.SPACE)
    {
        PhysicsActor laser = baseLaser.clone();
        laser.moveToOrigin( spaceship );
        laser.setVelocityAS( spaceship.getRotation(), 400 );
        laserList.add(laser);
        laser.setParentList(laserList);
        mainStage.addActor(laser);

        laser.addAction(
            Actions.sequence(Actions.delay(2), Actions.fadeOut(0.5f), Actions.visible(false)) );
    }

    return false;
}
```

In the update method of GameScreen, you can set up a loop to apply the wraparound method to each object in the laserList. You can also check whether any of the lasers are invisible, which is an indicator that they should be removed from the game. However, an object can't be removed from a list while iterating over the list (this would cause a "concurrent modification exception" error and crash the program). To work around this, in the GameScreen class, there is an ArrayList called removeList. In the create method, it is initialized:

```
removeList = new ArrayList<BaseActor>();
```

At the beginning of the update method, its contents are cleared:

```
removeList.clear();
```

Then, if an object in laserList is invisible, it is added to removeList. Later, you iterate over removeList and call the destroy method on each of its elements. This removes them from the game completely, while avoiding the previously described error:

```
for ( PhysicsActor laser : laserList )
{
    wraparound( laser );
    if ( !laser.isVisible() )
        removeList.add( laser );
}

for (BaseActor ba : removeList)
{
    ba.destroy();
}
```

Rocks and Explosions

Next, it is time to move on to the rocks of the Space Rocks game. There does not need to be a base version of the object to clone later, since rocks are destroyed when hit by lasers, and no new rocks spawn at a later time.[1] For simplicity, you could still create a base version and clone it repeatedly to produce the set of rocks drifting around the screen at the start of the game. However, you will instead attempt to make the individual rocks appear and act differently to add interest to the game. In particular, the rocks will use different images (the file names are rock0.png, rock1.png, rock2.png, and rock3.png), the initial positions will be random, and they will have different speeds and rates of rotation. Here, you must also initialize the ArrayList being used to keep track of the rocks for collision detection. The code that accomplishes this is given here:

```
rockList = new ArrayList<PhysicsActor>();
int numRocks = 6;
for (int n = 0; n < numRocks; n++)
{
    PhysicsActor rock = new PhysicsActor();

    String fileName = "assets/rock" + (n%4) + ".png";
    Texture rockTex = new Texture(Gdx.files.internal(fileName));
    rockTex.setFilter(TextureFilter.Linear, TextureFilter.Linear);
    rock.storeAnimation( "default", rockTex );

    rock.setPosition(800 * MathUtils.random(), 600 * MathUtils.random() );
    rock.setOriginCenter();
    rock.setEllipseBoundary();
    rock.setAutoAngle(false);

    float speedUp = MathUtils.random(0.0f, 1.0f);
    rock.setVelocityAS( 360 * MathUtils.random(), 75 + 50*speedUp );
    rock.addAction( Actions.forever( Actions.rotateBy(360, 2 - speedUp) ) );

    mainStage.addActor(rock);
    rockList.add(rock);
    rock.setParentList(rockList);
}
```

In the update method of the GameScreen class, some code must be added that causes the rocks to wrap around the screen in the same style as the spaceship:

```
for ( PhysicsActor rock : rockList )
{
    wraparound( rock );
}
```

This is another good point to compile your project and run the game to make sure that the rock objects are behaving as expected.

---

[1]This is in contrast to the original Asteroids game, in which larger rocks would typically spawn multiple smaller rocks after being hit by a laser. In this case, having a base object available to clone at a later point could be useful.

Next, you'll set up the AnimatedActor that stores an animated explosion that will appear when lasers collide with rocks. For animation sequences consisting of many images, it is common practice to combine all these images into a single image file called a *sprite sheet*, and this is the case for the image you will use, pictured in Figure 6-5.

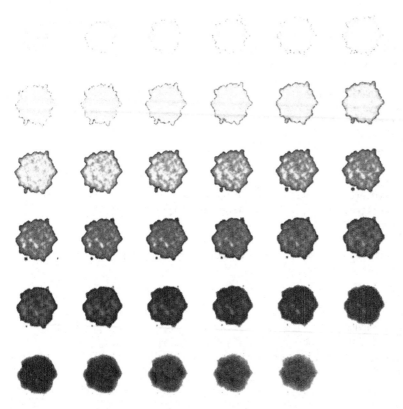

Figure 6-5. *A sprite sheet consisting of images for an animation of an explosion*

The TextureRegion class has a method called split that divides an image into rectangular sections, and returns the results in a two-dimensional array of TextureRegion objects, which you can convert into an Array and use in creating an Animation. For convenience, I have written a static method named parseSpriteSheet that performs these steps. In particular, this includes a nested for loop that transfers the contents of the two-dimensional array into a single-dimensional array before creating the animation. This method is in a new helper class called GameUtils; the code for this class is presented here:

```
import com.badlogic.gdx.Gdx;
import com.badlogic.gdx.graphics.Texture;
import com.badlogic.gdx.graphics.g2d.TextureRegion;
import com.badlogic.gdx.graphics.g2d.Animation;
import com.badlogic.gdx.graphics.g2d.Animation.PlayMode;
import com.badlogic.gdx.utils.Array;
import com.badlogic.gdx.graphics.Texture.TextureFilter;
```

```
public class GameUtils
{
    public static Animation parseSpriteSheet(String fileName, int frameCols, int frameRows,
        float frameDuration, PlayMode mode)
    {
        Texture t = new Texture(Gdx.files.internal(fileName), true);
        t.setFilter(TextureFilter.Linear, TextureFilter.Linear);

        int frameWidth = t.getWidth() / frameCols;
        int frameHeight = t.getHeight() / frameRows;

        TextureRegion[][] temp = TextureRegion.split(t, frameWidth, frameHeight);
        TextureRegion[] frames = new TextureRegion[frameCols * frameRows];

        int index = 0;
        for (int i = 0; i < frameRows; i++)
        {
            for (int j = 0; j < frameCols; j++)
            {
                frames[index] = temp[i][j];
                index++;
            }
        }

        Array<TextureRegion> framesArray = new Array<TextureRegion>(frames);
        return new Animation(frameDuration, framesArray, mode);
    }
}
```

Now, returning to the create method of the GameScreen class, this animation-generating method is used to create the base object from which all explosion effects will be cloned later:

```
baseExplosion = new AnimatedActor();
Animation explosionAnim = GameUtils.parseSpriteSheet(
    "assets/explosion.png", 6, 6, 0.03f, PlayMode.NORMAL);
baseExplosion.storeAnimation( "default", explosionAnim );
baseExplosion.setWidth(96);
baseExplosion.setHeight(96);
baseExplosion.setOriginCenter();
```

Finally, return to the update method of the GameScreen class. When a laser overlaps a rock, both the laser and rock should be removed from the game, and an explosion object should be cloned from baseExplosion and centered on the position of the rock. The explosion does not need to be added to any ArrayList; furthermore, an Action can be set up that causes the explosion to automatically remove itself from its Stage after its animation is complete (which requires 1.08 seconds, since each of the 36 animation images is displayed for 0.03 seconds). Since every possible pair of lasers and rocks needs to be checked for overlaps, the following code must be inserted within the loop that iterates through laserList:

```
for ( PhysicsActor rock : rockList )
{
    if ( laser.overlaps(rock, false) )
    {
        removeList.add( laser );
        removeList.add( rock );
        AnimatedActor explosion = baseExplosion.clone();
        explosion.moveToOrigin(rock);
        mainStage.addActor(explosion);
        explosion.addAction( Actions.sequence(Actions.delay(1.08f), Actions.removeActor()) );
    }
}
```

Next Steps

This completes our Space Rocks example; the complete source code can be found in the SpaceRocks directory for this chapter. As mentioned before, however, this is by no means a completed game. You should try your skill at adding various features, such as these:

- A menu screen that contains a button to start the game.

- Background music and sound effects (such as the sound of lasers firing or explosions).

- A user interface that lists how many rocks have been destroyed.

- The spaceship explodes when it collides with a rock.

- Limit the number of lasers that can be onscreen at once.

- A Congratulations message appears if all rocks are destroyed.

- A Game Over message appears if the spaceship is destroyed.

- Integrating game-pad controller support.

- Any other features you can think of!

Plane Dodger

This section introduces a game called *Plane Dodger*, inspired by modern touch-screen games such as Flappy Bird and Jetpack Joyride. In this game, the user controls a green plane that can maneuver up and down as it continuously flies through the game world. Stars periodically appear in the sky; the user's goal is to collect as many as possible. At the same time, "enemy" red planes also appear regularly; dodging these planes must be the user's first priority, as collision with them will end the game. This becomes more difficult as time progresses, as the speed of the red planes will increase. Figure 6-6 shows this game in action.

Figure 6-6. *The Plane Dodger game*

The new game-play mechanics featured by this game include the following:

- A side-view perspective
- Creating an illusion of rightward movement by scrolling backgrounds to the left
- Creating an illusion of depth by using *parallax*: scrolling distant objects more slowly
- Simulating gravity using constant acceleration
- Randomizing game features to produce different game-play experiences each time

As was the case last time, you should begin by creating a new project in BlueJ and copying over the classes BaseGame, BaseScreen, BaseActor, AnimatedActor, and PhysicsActor from the previous project, as well as the recently created class GameUtils. You should also create a launcher-style class and a class that extends BaseGame, as usual. In addition, you should copy all the images from this chapter's source directory PlaneDodger/assets into your local project's assets folder. As in the last project, you start off by creating a new GameScreen class, and declaring the variables you will need:

```
import com.badlogic.gdx.Gdx;
import com.badlogic.gdx.Input.Keys;
import com.badlogic.gdx.graphics.Texture;
import com.badlogic.gdx.graphics.Texture.TextureFilter;
import com.badlogic.gdx.graphics.g2d.Animation;
import com.badlogic.gdx.graphics.g2d.Animation.PlayMode;
import com.badlogic.gdx.scenes.scene2d.actions.Actions;
import com.badlogic.gdx.math.MathUtils;
import java.util.ArrayList;
```

```java
public class GameScreen extends BaseScreen
{
    private PhysicsActor[] background;
    private PhysicsActor[] ground;
    private PhysicsActor player;

    private PhysicsActor baseEnemy;
    private ArrayList<PhysicsActor> enemyList;
    private float enemyTimer;
    private float enemySpeed;

    private PhysicsActor baseStar;
    private ArrayList<PhysicsActor> starList;
    private float starTimer;

    private AnimatedActor baseSparkle;
    private AnimatedActor baseExplosion;

    private ArrayList<BaseActor> removeList;
    private boolean gameOver;

    // game world dimensions
    final int mapWidth = 800;
    final int mapHeight = 600;

    public GameScreen(BaseGame g)
    {  super(g);  }

    public void create()
    {    }

    public void update(float dt)
    {    }
}
```

Infinite Scrolling Effects

Next, background elements will be set up to provide an "infinite" scrolling effect. This purpose requires a *seamless texture*: an image that can be placed side by side with itself and does not create a noticeable boundary. Two copies of such an image will be used, each of which is at least as large as the screen. The setup is shown in Figure 6-7; the rectangles with dashed-line boundaries contain the seamless texture, while the rectangle with the solid-line boundary represents the game screen. The left edge of image 2 is adjacent to the right edge of image 1, and they both move to the left at the same rate. When the right edge of image 1 moves completely past the left edge of the screen, image 1 will be repositioned to the opposite side: the left edge of image 1 will become adjacent to the right edge of image 2. This process continues indefinitely.

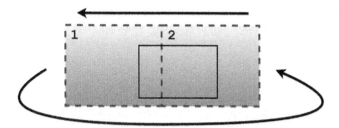

Figure 6-7. *Positioning seamless textures to create an infinite scrolling effect*

To set this up, in the create method you initialize an array called background that will contain two PhysicsActor objects. After creating the first of these, create a second instance by cloning the first and changing its x coordinate as described previously. Then, add both of these objects to background and also to mainStage. The code that accomplishes this is as follows:

```
background = new PhysicsActor[2];

PhysicsActor bg0 = new PhysicsActor();
bg0.storeAnimation( "default", new Texture(Gdx.files.internal("assets/sky.png")) );
bg0.setPosition( 0, 0 );
bg0.setVelocityXY(-50,0);
background[0] = bg0;
mainStage.addActor( bg0 );

PhysicsActor bg1 = bg0.clone();
bg1.setX( bg0.getWidth() );
background[1] = bg1;
mainStage.addActor(bg1);
```

Next, you must add the following code to the update method, to reposition these elements after they move past the left edge of the screen:

```
// manage background objects
for (int i = 0; i < 2; i++)
{
    PhysicsActor bg = background[i];
    if ( bg.getX() + bg.getWidth() < 0 )
        bg.setX( bg.getX() + 2 * bg.getWidth() );
}
```

To create an infinitely scrolling image of the ground, repeat the previous process that loaded the background images of the sky: initialize an array, set up the first object and clone it to get the second, and so forth. The only difference will be the velocity of the ground images. If you have ever watched the scenery go by while travelling in a car or a train, you may have noticed that the more distant objects appear to change position more slowly than closer objects. This effect, called *parallax*, provides an easy way to add an illusion of depth in a 2D game. Since the ground should appear closer to the player than the background images of the sky, the ground should be moving at a faster rate. To implement this, add the following code to the create method:

```
ground = new PhysicsActor[2];

PhysicsActor gr0 = new PhysicsActor();
gr0.storeAnimation( "default", new Texture(Gdx.files.internal("assets/ground.png")) );
gr0.setPosition( 0, 0 );
gr0.setVelocityXY(-200,0);
gr0.setRectangleBoundary();
ground[0] = gr0;
mainStage.addActor( gr0 );

PhysicsActor gr1 = gr0.clone();
gr1.setX( gr0.getWidth() );
ground[1] = gr1;
mainStage.addActor(gr1);
```

You also need to add the corresponding code to the update method, within the same loop you recently wrote to reposition the background images:

```
PhysicsActor gr = ground[i];
if ( gr.getX() + gr.getWidth() < 0 )
    gr.setX( gr.getX() + 2 * gr.getWidth() );
```

This is a good point to compile your project and run the code to check that everything appears okay.

Player Plane

Next, you'll set up the player object: a green plane that can maneuver vertically. This plane is constantly being pulled down by the force of gravity, but the player can move it upward by pressing a key on the keyboard to apply vertical thrust.

To simplify the creation of the Animation for this object (and others that will follow), at this point you will write another helper method in the new GameUtils class (introduced in the previous section). This method, called parseImageFiles, will create an Animation from a set of image files, provided they follow a specified naming convention: the file names should be identical except for a number used to specify the order in which they appear. This process, which you've seen in previous programs, is carried out by the following code:

```
// creates an Animation from a set of image files
// name format: fileNamePrefix + N + fileNameSuffix, where 0 <= N < frameCount

public static Animation parseImageFiles(String fileNamePrefix, String fileNameSuffix,
    int frameCount, float frameDuration, PlayMode mode)
{
    TextureRegion[] frames = new TextureRegion[frameCount];
```

```
for (int n = 0; n < frameCount; n++)
{
    String fileName = fileNamePrefix + n + fileNameSuffix;
    Texture tex = new Texture( Gdx.files.internal(fileName) );
    tex.setFilter(TextureFilter.Linear, TextureFilter.Linear);
    frames[n] = new TextureRegion( tex );
}

Array<TextureRegion> framesArray = new Array<TextureRegion>(frames);
return new Animation(frameDuration, framesArray, mode);
}
```

Returning to the GameScreen class, the code for the player object will now be added. First, initialize it in the create method using the following code. Note in particular that you set a negative y component for acceleration to simulate the pull of gravity; this value will remain unchanged throughout the program.

```
player = new PhysicsActor();
Animation anim = GameUtils.parseImageFiles(
    "assets/planeGreen", ".png", 3, 0.1f, Animation.PlayMode.LOOP_PINGPONG);
player.storeAnimation( "default", anim );
player.setPosition(200,300);
player.setAccelerationXY(0, -600); // gravity
player.setOriginCenter();
player.setEllipseBoundary();
mainStage.addActor( player );
```

Next, you add some code that enables the player to control the plane. The plane should be given an upward boost in speed whenever the player presses a key. This is implemented this as a discrete event (in the style of the game Flappy Bird), and thus the keyDown method must be overridden in the GameScreen class as follows:

```
public boolean keyDown(int keycode)
{
    if (keycode == Keys.SPACE)
        player.setVelocityXY(0,300);

    return false;
}
```

However, if desired, you could instead adjust the plane's velocity as a continuous event (in the style of the game Jetpack Joyride); instead of the preceding code, you could poll for keyboard input in the update method and increase upward velocity as follows:

```
if (Gdx.input.isKeyPressed(Keys.SPACE))
    player.addVelocityXY(0, 25);
```

Notice that the change in the y component of velocity is much smaller here than in the discrete variation of the event. This is because a continuous event will be processed 60 times per second (when possible), so the change in velocity must be smaller to compensate for this.

Finally, some collision-detection code will be included in the update method. In particular, if the player hits the top of the screen or the ground, the player's velocity should be set to zero, and the position of the player should be adjusted accordingly. For the top of the screen, you can calculate the new position easily;

143

for the ground objects, you can take advantage of the overlaps method, which will adjust the position of a BaseActor object when the second parameter is set to true.

```
if ( player.getY() > mapHeight - player.getHeight() )
{
    player.setVelocityXY(0,0);
    player.setY( mapHeight - player.getHeight() );
}

for (int i = 0; i < 2; i++)
{
    PhysicsActor gr = ground[i];
    if ( player.overlaps(gr, true) )
    {
        player.setVelocityXY(0,0);
    }
}
```

Once again, this is a good time to test your project and verify that everything is working as expected.

Stars and Sparkles

Next, you initialize baseStar, an object from which collectible star objects will be cloned later. The stars should appear stationary with respect to the ground, so the velocity of baseStar should be set equal to the velocity of the ground objects. It is also necessary to initialize the ArrayList used to store the stars for use in the update method later, and also to initialize a float named starTimer that will keep track of when new star objects should be created.

```
baseStar = new PhysicsActor();
Texture starTex = new Texture(Gdx.files.internal("assets/star.png"));
starTex.setFilter(TextureFilter.Linear, TextureFilter.Linear);
baseStar.storeAnimation( "default", starTex );
baseStar.setVelocityXY(-200,0);
baseStar.setOriginCenter();
baseStar.setEllipseBoundary();

starList = new ArrayList<PhysicsActor>();
starTimer = 0;
```

At this time, you also set up baseSparkle, an object from which a sparkling animation effect will be cloned whenever a star is collected. The images for the Animation are contained within a sprite sheet, so the corresponding method of the GameUtils class can be used here:

```
baseSparkle = new AnimatedActor();
Animation sparkleAnim = GameUtils.parseSpriteSheet(
    "assets/sparkle.png", 8,8, 0.01f, PlayMode.NORMAL);
baseSparkle.storeAnimation( "default", sparkleAnim );
baseSparkle.setWidth(64);
baseSparkle.setHeight(64);
baseSparkle.setOriginCenter();
```

While you're still working with the create method, the ArrayList used for removal must also be initialized:

```
removeList = new ArrayList<BaseActor>();
```

Next, in the update method, add the following code to increase starTimer according to the amount of time that has passed (dt). If more than 1 second has elapsed, reset the value of starTimer and create a new star via the clone method of the baseStar object. Also, the vertical position of the newly cloned star is randomized so that the game play will be different for each game.

```
starTimer += dt;
if (starTimer > 1)
{
    starTimer = 0;
    PhysicsActor star = baseStar.clone();
    star.setPosition( 900, MathUtils.random(100,500) );

    starList.add( star );
    star.setParentList( starList );
    mainStage.addActor( star );
}
```

Finally, you set the conditions under which a star should be removed from the game: if the star passes beyond the left edge of the screen, or if the player overlaps with the star. In both situations, the star is added to removeList, which will be used at a later point to call the destroy method. In the latter situation, you also spawn a new sparkle object by cloning baseSparkle, and a sequence of actions is added that will cause the sparkle to remove itself from its Stage after enough time has passed for the animation to complete (since there are 64 images in the sprite sheet, each of which is displayed for 0.01 seconds, the animation is complete after 0.64 seconds have passed). These tasks are accomplished with the following code:

```
removeList.clear();

for (PhysicsActor star : starList)
{
    if ( star.getX() + star.getWidth() < 0 )
        removeList.add(star);

    if ( player.overlaps(star, false) )
    {
        removeList.add(star);
        AnimatedActor sparkle = baseSparkle.clone();
        sparkle.moveToOrigin(star);
        sparkle.addAction( Actions.sequence( Actions.delay(0.64f), Actions.removeActor() ) );
        mainStage.addActor(sparkle);
    }
}

for (BaseActor ba : removeList)
{
    ba.destroy();
}
```

Enemy Planes

At this point, you add the enemy planes to your game. This process closely parallels the creation and management of the star objects discussed previously. First, in the create method, all the enemy-related variables are initialized: baseEnemy for later cloning, enemyList to store the enemy objects for use in the update method, enemyTimer to keep track of when enemies should be spawned, and enemySpeed to set the velocity of each newly created enemy. Also, the enemy objects will be made 25 percent larger than the original size of the image.

```
baseEnemy = new PhysicsActor();
Animation redAnim = GameUtils.parseImageFiles(
    "assets/planeRed", ".png", 3, 0.1f, Animation.PlayMode.LOOP_PINGPONG);
baseEnemy.storeAnimation( "default", redAnim );
baseEnemy.setWidth( baseEnemy.getWidth() * 1.25f );
baseEnemy.setHeight( baseEnemy.getHeight() * 1.25f );
baseEnemy.setOriginCenter();
baseEnemy.setEllipseBoundary();

enemyTimer = 0;
enemySpeed = -250;
enemyList = new ArrayList<PhysicsActor>();
```

Also, just as the special effect baseSparkle was created for use when the player collides with a star, the special effect baseExplosion must now be set up for use when the player collides with an enemy:

```
baseExplosion = new AnimatedActor();
Animation explosionAnim = GameUtils.parseSpriteSheet(
    "assets/explosion.png", 6, 6, 0.03f, PlayMode.NORMAL);
baseExplosion.storeAnimation( "default", explosionAnim );
baseExplosion.setWidth(96);
baseExplosion.setHeight(96);
baseExplosion.setOriginCenter();
```

Since enemies have the capability to end the game, now is a good time to initialize the Boolean variable gameOver, whose use will be explained in what follows. At the end of the create method, add this line:

```
gameOver = false;
```

Next, two major additions must be made to the update method. First, new enemy objects must be created at regular time intervals, and at random vertical positions. An Action will also be added to make the enemies more visually interesting, by slowly tilting them up and down. This is accomplished with the following code:

```
enemyTimer += dt;
if (enemyTimer > 3)
{
    enemyTimer = 0;
    if (enemySpeed > -800)
        enemySpeed -= 15;
```

```
PhysicsActor enemy = baseEnemy.clone();
enemy.setPosition( 900, MathUtils.random(100,500) );
enemy.setVelocityXY(enemySpeed, 0);

enemy.setRotation(10);
enemy.addAction( Actions.forever(
    Actions.sequence( Actions.rotateBy(-20,1), Actions.rotateBy(20,1) ) ));

enemyList.add( enemy );
enemy.setParentList( enemyList );
mainStage.addActor( enemy );
}
```

Next, each enemy must be processed, similar to the way the stars were processed earlier. If an enemy moves beyond the left edge of the screen, that enemy should be added to removeList. If the player overlaps an enemy, then create an explosion special effect centered on the player, add the player to removeList, and set gameOver to true. To accomplish these tasks, insert the following code after removeList is cleared, but before the loop that calls the destroy method of all elements of removeList:

```
for (PhysicsActor enemy : enemyList )
{
    if ( enemy.getX() + enemy.getWidth() < 0)
        removeList.add(enemy);

    if ( player.overlaps(enemy, false) )
    {
        AnimatedActor explosion = baseExplosion.clone();
        explosion.moveToOrigin(player);
        explosion.addAction( Actions.sequence( Actions.delay(1.08f), Actions.removeActor() ) );
        mainStage.addActor(explosion);
        removeList.add(player);
        gameOver = true;
    }
}
```

Finally, when gameOver becomes true, new stars and enemy planes should no longer be spawned, but the background should continue scrolling. To accomplish this, insert the following code in the update method, after the loop that manages the background objects, and before everything else. It will cause the update loop to terminate earlier than usual, skipping over the parts of code you no longer wish to run:

```
if ( gameOver )
    return;
```

Next Steps

This completes the new game mechanics for Plane Dodger. As usual, this program should be considered a work in progress, with plenty of features remaining to be added to create a quality game. Many of the suggestions from the Space Rocks game are applicable here: a menu screen, background music and sound effects, and a Game Over message at the end of the game. Other game-specific features you may wish to consider include the following:

- Keep track of the number of stars collected, and display it on the user interface.

- Keep track of the player's total progress; you could display one of the following:

  - The total number of enemy planes dodged

  - The total time the player has been playing

  - Some measure of the game world distance the player has travelled (perhaps 20 pixels per meter)

- Increase the challenge by slowly increasing the spawn frequency of the enemy planes as the game progresses, or by adding a small random amount to the vertical velocity of the enemy planes so that their paths are less predictable.

- Add enemy planes with different colors or sizes for variety.

- When the game is finished, calculate and display some type of performance rating for the player. Here are two possible methods:

  - Calculate a final score using a formula such as this:

    score = (100 × seconds survived) + (200 × stars collected)

  - Calculate a rank or rating (such as A/B/C/D/E). Let N be calculated as follows:

    N = seconds survived + stars collected

    Then assign a rank to each range of values. Perhaps rank E corresponds to $0 <= N <= 20$, rank D corresponds to $21 <= N <= 40$, and so forth.

Rectangle Destroyer

This section introduces a game called *Rectangle Destroyer*, inspired by the classic arcade game Breakout and later variations such as Arkanoid and Quester. In this game, using either mouse or touch controls, the player moves a paddle back and forth along the bottom of the screen in order to bounce a ball upward with the goal of colliding with (and thereby destroying) rectangular objects called *bricks*. Occasionally, a destroyed brick will spawn an item that typically changes the game play in some way, such as changing the size of the paddle or the speed of the ball; changes may increase or decrease the difficulty level. Figure 6-8 shows this game in action.

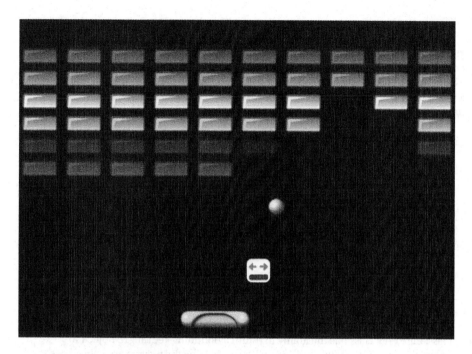

Figure 6-8. *The Rectangle Destroyer game*

The new game-play mechanics and topics introduced by this game include the following:

- Creating game-specific extensions of your custom actor classes

- Implementing circle-rectangle collision detection

- Overloading methods to provide various types of collision responses

- Creating new animated effects from the Action class

- Randomly spawning items that affect game play

As before, you begin by creating a new project containing the classes BaseGame, BaseScreen, BaseActor, AnimatedActor, PhysicsActor, and GameUtils. You should also create a launcher-style class and a class that extends BaseGame. You will need to copy all the images from this chapter's source directory RectangleDestroyer/assets into your local project's assets folder.

Unlike the previously discussed games in this chapter, you will begin by writing a new set of classes before working with the GameScreen class. In general, this is necessary whenever you have game-specific objects that require additional data or functionality beyond that provided by your custom Actor extensions.

The Paddle

The Paddle class is the first of the custom object classes. For the customized collision-detection code that will be introduced throughout this project, Rectangle and Circle objects will be used rather than Polygon objects. In this game, the paddle doesn't require any of the functionality of the AnimatedActor or PhysicsActor classes, so Paddle extends the BaseActor class. The main purpose of this class is to add a method that will return a bounding Rectangle object for this actor. The code for this class is presented here:

```
import com.badlogic.gdx.math.Rectangle;

public class Paddle extends BaseActor
{
    public Paddle()
    {  super();  }

    public Rectangle getRectangle()
    {  return new Rectangle( getX(), getY(), getWidth(), getHeight() );  }
}
```

The Brick

Similar to the Paddle class, the Brick class has the ability to return a bounding Rectangle object. In addition, since you're going to need to clone Brick objects when initializing the playing area, the clone method of BaseActor needs to be overridden so that it returns a Brick object rather than a BaseActor object. Finally, when a brick is destroyed, it is more visually interesting for it to fade out rather than just disappear from its stage, its destroy method will also be overridden in order to include a fading-out action before the actor is removed from the stage. This requires an adjustment to be made in the BaseActor class in the variable declaration for parentList: it needs to be changed from private to protected, so that the Brick class can access the variable. The code for the Brick class is as follows:

```
import com.badlogic.gdx.math.Rectangle;
import com.badlogic.gdx.scenes.scene2d.actions.Actions;

public class Brick extends BaseActor
{
    public Brick()
    {  super();  }

    public Rectangle getRectangle()
    {  return new Rectangle( getX(), getY(), getWidth(), getHeight() );  }

    public Brick clone()
    {
        Brick newbie = new Brick();
        newbie.copy( this );
        return newbie;
    }
```

```
public void destroy()
{
    addAction( Actions.sequence( Actions.fadeOut(0.5f), Actions.removeActor() ) );

    if (parentList != null)
        parentList.remove(this);
}
}
```

The Ball

Next, the Ball class will be introduced, which will be the most conceptually complicated of the classes in this game due to its unique collision-detection and response algorithms. Because the ball object will be moving around the screen, the Ball class should extend the PhysicsActor class. For collision detection, a Circle will be used as the bounding shape. To this end, there needs to be a getCircle method that returns a Circle object, whose parameters are the x and y coordinates of the center of the circle, and its radius. The code for the Ball class thus far is as follows:

```
import com.badlogic.gdx.math.Circle;
public class Ball extends PhysicsActor
{
    public Ball()
    {  super();  }

    public Circle getCircle()
    {  return new Circle( getX() + getWidth()/2, getY() + getHeight()/2, getWidth()/2 );  }
}
```

Collision detection and response, which is carried out by the overlaps method, will be considered next. In the BaseActor class, the overlaps method takes two parameters: another BaseActor, and a Boolean variable that indicates whether an overlap should be "resolved." In the BaseActor class, resolving a collision involves adjusting the position of the actor calling the method so that there is no longer any overlap, which is particularly useful for simulating collision with a solid object. In the Ball class, you will overload the overlaps method, creating two new versions: one to handle collision with a paddle, and the other to handle collision with a brick. In each of these situations, the velocity of the ball must be adjusted, and in different ways.

When a ball collides with a paddle, the speed of the ball remains the same, but the angle of motion changes depending on the location of the collision on the paddle. (The ball's angle of motion before the collision has no effect on the resulting angle of motion, in contrast to the laws of physics.) If the ball collides with the left side of the paddle, the ball bounces to the left; similarly, collision with the right side of the paddle causes the ball to bounce to the right. Collision with an intermediate position is interpolated accordingly; in particular, colliding with the exact center of the paddle causes the ball to bounce straight up. Sample collision locations on the paddle and the resulting angle of motion of the ball are illustrated in Figure 6-9.

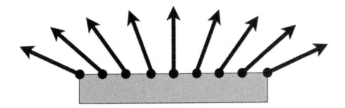

Figure 6-9. *Bounce angles resulting from ball-paddle collision at different positions*

The method that performs these tasks is presented next, and should be included in the Ball class. Note that, conveniently, the Intersector class contains an overloaded version of its overlaps method that checks whether a Circle and Rectangle overlap. For consistency with the earlier declaration of the overlaps method in the BaseActor class, a Boolean parameter is included that determines whether the velocity of the ball should be adjusted to simulate bouncing off the paddle, as described previously. This parameter is usually set to true. First, add the import statement:

```
import com.badlogic.gdx.math.Intersector;
```

Then, the code for the overlaps method is as follows:

```
public boolean overlaps(Paddle paddle, boolean bounceOff)
{
    if ( !Intersector.overlaps( this.getCircle(), paddle.getRectangle() ) )
        return false;

    if ( bounceOff )
    {
        float ballCenterX = this.getX() + this.getWidth()/2;
        float percent = (ballCenterX - paddle.getX()) / paddle.getWidth();
        // interpolate value between 150 and 30
        float bounceAngle = 150 - percent * 120;
        this.setVelocityAS( bounceAngle, this.getSpeed() );
    }

    return true;
}
```

Next, consider the situation of a ball colliding with a brick. The code used in the past to determine when two objects overlap does not provide enough information about the circumstances of the collision to calculate the desired reaction: realistic bouncing. In this game, the collision response more closely adheres to the laws of physics: the result of a collision is that the velocity of the ball will reverse in either the x or y direction (or possibly both), depending on which side or corner of the rectangle the ball first overlaps with. In order for the Ball class to be able to access the velocity variable of the PhysicsActor class, you must change its access modifier from private to protected. After this change is complete, add the following methods to the Ball class that allow you to multiply either the x or y component of the velocity by a constant (multiplying it by –1 reverses it in that direction):

```
public void multVelocityX(float m)
{  velocity.x *= m;  }

public void multVelocityY(float m)
{  velocity.y *= m;  }
```

The difficult part of the code is determining the side (or corner) of the rectangle that the ball first collided with. To help understand this, one particular case will be examined and discussed in detail: determining whether the circle collided with the bottom edge of the rectangle. In order for this to happen, two conditions must be met:

- The y component of the ball's velocity must be positive, indicating that it was moving up.

- While the circle was travelling from its previous position to its current position, the top point of the circle (the point directly above the center) must have crossed the bottom edge of the rectangle.

This scenario is illustrated in Figure 6-10; the circle with the dashed boundary represents its previous position, the circle with the solid boundary represents its current position, and the arrow indicates the direction of motion.

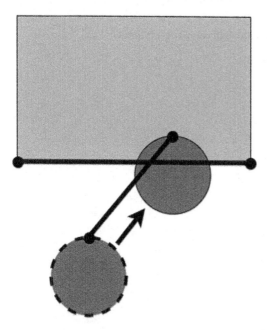

Figure 6-10. *The line-segment intersection corresponding to the collision of a circle with the bottom edge of a rectangle*

It is simple to check whether the y component of velocity is positive. More difficult is checking for the intersection of the top point of the circle with the bottom edge of the rectangle. To do this, the previous boundary circle and the current boundary circle must be known, and a line segment can be drawn connecting these two points; if this line segment crosses the line segment connecting the bottom two points of the rectangle, then the second condition listed is satisfied. When both conditions are true, the velocity is adjusted by multiplying the y component by –1.

Checking for collisions with the other sides are analogous. For example, say the ball collided with the left edge of the rectangle exactly when the x component of velocity is positive, and the rightmost point of the circle crossed the left edge of the rectangle as the ball moved from its previous to its current position. In this case, the x component of velocity should be multiplied by –1.

If the ball did not collide with one of the edges of the rectangle, but the two objects overlap, then by process of elimination the ball must have collided with one of the corners of the rectangle, in which case both the x and y coordinates should be multiplied by –1.

To implement this calculation in the Ball class, you do the following:

- Introduce two new variables to store the previous and current boundary circle.

- Override the act method to store these Circle objects before and after the act method of PhysicsActor is called.

- Create helper methods that return the top/bottom/left/right points of a Circle.

- Create helper methods that return the corner points of a Rectangle.

- Use the overlaps method of the Intersector class to check for any overlap between the boundary circle of the ball and the boundary rectangle of the brick.

- Use the intersectSegments method of the Intersector class to check the conditions described previously, involving a point on the circle crossing an edge of the rectangle.

- Based on the results of the collision tests, adjust the ball velocity accordingly.

Two import statements must be added to the Ball class:

```
import com.badlogic.gdx.math.Vector2;
import com.badlogic.gdx.math.Rectangle;
```

The code to add to the Ball class is as follows:

```
private Circle prevCircle;
private Circle currCircle;

public void act(float dt)
{
    // store previous position before and after updating
    prevCircle = getCircle();
    super.act(dt);
    currCircle = getCircle();
}

public Vector2 getTop(Circle c)
{   return new Vector2(c.x, c.y + c.radius);  }
public Vector2 getBottom(Circle c)
{   return new Vector2(c.x, c.y - c.radius);  }
public Vector2 getLeft(Circle c)
{   return new Vector2(c.x - c.radius, c.y);  }
public Vector2 getRight(Circle c)
{   return new Vector2(c.x + c.radius, c.y);  }

public Vector2 getBottomLeft(Rectangle r)
{   return new Vector2( r.getX(), r.getY() );  }
public Vector2 getBottomRight(Rectangle r)
{   return new Vector2( r.getX() + r.getWidth(), r.getY() );  }
public Vector2 getTopLeft(Rectangle r)
{   return new Vector2( r.getX(), r.getY() + r.getHeight() );  }
public Vector2 getTopRight(Rectangle r)
{   return new Vector2( r.getX() + r.getWidth(), r.getY() + r.getHeight() );  }
```

```
public boolean overlaps(Brick brick, boolean bounceOff)
{
    if ( !Intersector.overlaps( this.getCircle(), brick.getRectangle() ) )
        return false;

    if ( bounceOff )
    {
        Rectangle rect = brick.getRectangle();
        boolean sideHit = false;

        if (velocity.x > 0 && Intersector.intersectSegments(
            getRight(prevCircle), getRight(currCircle),
            getTopLeft(rect), getBottomLeft(rect), null) )
        {
            multVelocityX(-1);
            sideHit = true;
        }
        else if (velocity.x < 0 && Intersector.intersectSegments(
            getLeft(prevCircle), getLeft(currCircle),
            getTopRight(rect), getBottomRight(rect), null) )
        {
            multVelocityX(-1);
            sideHit = true;
        }

        if (velocity.y > 0 && Intersector.intersectSegments(
            getTop(prevCircle), getTop(currCircle),
            getBottomLeft(rect), getBottomRight(rect), null) )
        {
            multVelocityY(-1);
            sideHit = true;
        }
        else if (velocity.y < 0 && Intersector.intersectSegments(
            getBottom(prevCircle), getBottom(currCircle),
            getTopLeft(rect), getTopRight(rect), null) )
        {
            multVelocityY(-1);
            sideHit = true;
        }

        if (!sideHit) // by process of elimination, corner was hit first
        {
            multVelocityX(-1);
            multVelocityY(-1);
        }
    }

    return true;
}
```

With this addition, the Ball class is now complete.

The Power-up

When a brick is destroyed, it may occasionally spawn a random item that falls toward the bottom of the screen. If the player collects the item (by touching it with the paddle), some feature of the game will be changed, such as the size of the paddle. We'll refer to these items as *power-ups*, even though their effect may increase the difficulty of the game.

The Powerup class has some of the same features as the Brick class: it uses a Rectangle for collision detection, and because a base object will be used for spawning power-ups later, the clone method must be overridden to return a Powerup object. The Powerup class requires some of the functionality of AnimatedActor (because it stores multiple images— one for each kind of power-up), as well as some of the functionality of PhysicsActor (because power-ups, once spawned, constantly move downward). Therefore, the Powerup class will extend the PhysicsActor class. An overlaps method must be written to check for when a power-up overlaps the paddle. A randomize method will also be created to randomly select one of the stored animations; to be able to do this, you must make an alteration to the AnimatedActor class: the access modifier of animationStorage must be changed from private to protected, so that the Powerup class can access that data. The complete code for the class is presented here:

```
import com.badlogic.gdx.math.Rectangle;
import com.badlogic.gdx.math.MathUtils;
import com.badlogic.gdx.math.Intersector;
import java.util.ArrayList;

public class Powerup extends PhysicsActor
{
    public Powerup()
    {  super();  }

    public Rectangle getRectangle()
    {  return new Rectangle( getX(), getY(), getWidth(), getHeight() );  }

    public Powerup clone()
    {
        Powerup newbie = new Powerup();
        newbie.copy( this );
        return newbie;
    }

    public boolean overlaps(Paddle other)
    {
        return Intersector.overlaps( this.getRectangle(), other.getRectangle() );
    }

    // randomly select one of the stored animations
    public void randomize()
    {
        ArrayList<String> names = new ArrayList<String>( animationStorage.keySet() );
        int n = MathUtils.random( names.size() - 1 );
        setActiveAnimation( names.get(n) );
    }
}
```

Setting Up the Game

Now that you have defined all the game entities that you need for the Rectangle Destroyer game, you are ready to begin writing the GameScreen class. First, you add the core code for the class, which declares all the variables that will eventually be needed:

```
import com.badlogic.gdx.Gdx;
import com.badlogic.gdx.graphics.Color;
import com.badlogic.gdx.graphics.Texture;
import com.badlogic.gdx.graphics.Texture.TextureFilter;
import com.badlogic.gdx.scenes.scene2d.actions.Actions;
import java.util.ArrayList;

public class GameScreen extends BaseScreen
{
    private Paddle paddle;
    private Ball ball;

    private Brick baseBrick;
    private ArrayList<Brick> brickList;

    private Powerup basePowerup;
    private ArrayList<Powerup> powerupList;

    private ArrayList<BaseActor> removeList;

    // game world dimensions
    final int mapWidth = 800;
    final int mapHeight = 600;

    public GameScreen(BaseGame g)
    {  super(g);  }

    public void create()
    {    }

    public void update(float dt)
    {    }

}
```

In the create method, the various objects needed will be initialized: paddle, baseBrick, ball, and basePowerup. All the various lists must also be initialized:

```
paddle = new Paddle();
Texture paddleTex = new Texture(Gdx.files.internal("assets/paddle.png"));
paddleTex.setFilter( TextureFilter.Linear, TextureFilter.Linear );
paddle.setTexture( paddleTex );
mainStage.addActor(paddle);
```

```
baseBrick = new Brick();
Texture brickTex = new Texture(Gdx.files.internal("assets/brick-gray.png"));
baseBrick.setTexture( brickTex );
baseBrick.setOriginCenter();

brickList = new ArrayList<Brick>();

ball = new Ball();
Texture ballTex = new Texture(Gdx.files.internal("assets/ball.png"));
ball.storeAnimation( "default", ballTex );
ball.setPosition( 400, 200 );
ball.setVelocityAS( 30, 300 );
ball.setAccelerationXY( 0, -10 );
mainStage.addActor( ball );

basePowerup = new Powerup();
basePowerup.setVelocityXY(0, -100);
basePowerup.storeAnimation("paddle-expand",
    new Texture(Gdx.files.internal("assets/paddle-expand.png")) );
basePowerup.storeAnimation("paddle-shrink",
    new Texture(Gdx.files.internal("assets/paddle-shrink.png")) );
basePowerup.setOriginCenter();

powerupList = new ArrayList<Powerup>();

removeList = new ArrayList<BaseActor>();
```

The final task to accomplish in the create method is to initialize a rectangular grid of bricks by cloning the baseBrick object created earlier. To make the game more aesthetically pleasing, each row of bricks will be tinted using a different Color, as follows:

```
Color[] colorArray = { Color.RED, Color.ORANGE, Color.YELLOW,
                       Color.GREEN, Color.BLUE, Color.PURPLE };

for (int j = 0; j < 6; j++)
{
    for (int i = 0; i < 10; i++)
    {
        Brick brick = baseBrick.clone();
        brick.setPosition( 8 + 80*i,  500 - (24 + 16)*j );
        brick.setColor( colorArray[j] );
        brickList.add( brick );
        brick.setParentList( brickList );
        mainStage.addActor( brick );
    }
}
```

Next, interactivity will be added to the update method. First, the horizontal position of the paddle must be continuously adjusted to center on the x coordinate of the mouse, and the paddle object should be bound to the screen:

```
paddle.setPosition( Gdx.input.getX() - paddle.getWidth()/2, 32 );

if ( paddle.getX() < 0 )
    paddle.setX(0);

if ( paddle.getX() + paddle.getWidth() > mapWidth )
    paddle.setX(mapWidth - paddle.getWidth());
```

Next, code will be added to bounce the ball off the edges of the screen. For testing purposes, the ball will also bounce off the bottom edge of the screen. (In a finished version of this game, this does not happen; if the ball passes below the bottom edge, the player loses the game.)

```
if (ball.getX() < 0)
{
    ball.setX(0);
    ball.multVelocityX(-1);
}

if (ball.getX() + ball.getWidth() > mapWidth)
{
    ball.setX( mapWidth - ball.getWidth() );
    ball.multVelocityX(-1);
}

if (ball.getY() < 0)
{
    ball.setY(0);
    ball.multVelocityY(-1);
}

if (ball.getY() + ball.getHeight() > mapHeight)
{
    ball.setY( mapHeight - ball.getHeight() );
    ball.multVelocityY(-1);
}
```

To bounce the ball off the paddle, call the overlaps method of the ball with the following line of code. (Although this method returns a Boolean value, we do not have a use for this value at this time. It could be useful later when adding polish to your game: for example, if the ball overlaps the paddle, then a sound effect could be played.)

```
ball.overlaps(paddle, true);
```

Next, check whether the ball has collided with any of the bricks. If so, add the brick to removeList, which will later call the destroy method of the brick (which activates the previously discussed fading-out effect). Also, in the event of a brick being hit, there will be a 20 percent chance that a randomized power-up will be spawned. Using an Action, an animated scaling effect will be added that will make the power-up appear to grow from a single pixel to its full size over the course of half a second.

```
removeList.clear();

for (Brick br : brickList)
{
    if ( ball.overlaps(br, true) ) // bounces off bricks
    {
        removeList.add(br);
        if (Math.random() < 0.20)
        {
            Powerup pow = basePowerup.clone();
            pow.randomize();
            pow.moveToOrigin(br);

            pow.setScale(0,0);
            pow.addAction( Actions.scaleTo(1,1, 0.5f) );

            powerupList.add(pow);
            pow.setParentList(powerupList);
            mainStage.addActor(pow);
        }
    }
}
```

You also need to check whether any of the power-ups have collided with the paddle. If so, determine the name of the animation and carry out the associated effect. In this version of the game, the only power-up effects are to change the size of the paddle. Reasonable constraints will be set on the maximum and minimum size the paddle can attain, and the change in size is animated using an Action:

```
for (Powerup pow : powerupList)
{
    if ( pow.overlaps(paddle) )
    {
        String powName = pow.getAnimationName();
        if ( powName.equals("paddle-expand") && paddle.getWidth() < 256)
        {
            paddle.addAction( Actions.sizeBy(32,0, 0.5f) );
        }
        else if ( powName.equals("paddle-shrink") && paddle.getWidth() > 64)
        {
            paddle.addAction( Actions.sizeBy(-32,0, 0.5f) );
        }

        removeList.add(pow);
    }
}
```

Finally, after all the collision detection is complete, iterate over removeList, to destroy any objects that should be removed from the game:

```
for (BaseActor b : removeList)
{
    b.destroy();
}
```

Next Steps

As usual, I recommend adding a Start menu screen, sound effects, and end-of-game messages to this program. Additional specific ideas for this game include the following:

- When the game loads, stop the ball from automatically moving (set the speed of the ball to zero) until the user clicks a mouse button to start the game; then launch the ball upward.

- Disable collision detection and response for the bottom edge of the screen; when the ball passes below the bottom edge, the game is over.

- Gain a set number of points for each brick that is destroyed, and display the score in the user interface. As a slight variation, bricks could be worth different amounts of points depending on either their color or height on the screen (bricks that are higher up are more difficult to hit and could be worth more points).

- For increased difficulty, gradually increase the speed of the ball as the game progresses.

- Add new power-ups that change properties of the ball such as its size or speed.

- Add a fireball power-up. When the power-up is collected, tint the ball orange. When it collides with a brick, a moderately sized explosion effect is spawned; if the effect overlaps any other bricks, destroy them as well.

- Add a thru-ball power-up. When this power-up is collected, tint the ball green. When checking for the collision of the ball with the bricks using the overlaps method, let the Boolean parameter be false, so that the velocity is not adjusted; the ball will be able to pass through groups of bricks.

- Add multiball capabilities, enabling multiple balls to be on the screen at a time. This requires numerous small changes throughout the program: most code involving the ball object (such as collision detection) will need to be iterated over a list of ball objects. Add a corresponding multiball power-up that spawns a new ball (typically from the position of the paddle) when it is collected.

52-Card Pickup

In this section, you'll create the card game *52-Card Pickup*. In this game, the 52 cards from a standard deck of playing cards are randomly scattered around a playing area, and the goal is to pick up the cards and arrange them in piles according to matching suit (clubs, hearts, spades, diamonds) and ascending rank (Ace, 2, 3, 4, 5, 6, 7, 8, 9, 10, Jack, Queen, King). Figure 6-11 shows this game in action.

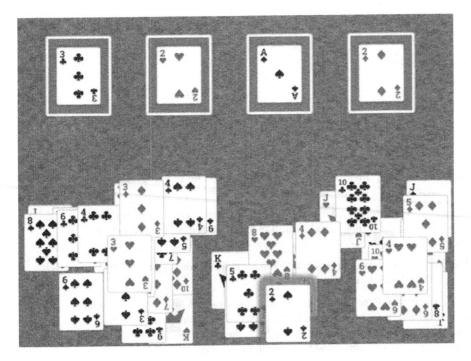

Figure 6-11. *The 52-Card Pickup game*

The main purpose of this example is to demonstrate how to implement two new mechanics: drag-and-drop interactions, and objects that provide visual hints. These techniques are useful in all manner of card games, as well as tile-matching games such as Bejeweled.

As usual, you begin by creating a new project containing the classes BaseGame, BaseScreen, BaseActor, AnimatedActor, PhysicsActor, and GameUtils. You should create a launcher-style class and a class that extends BaseGame, and you will need to copy the images from this chapter's source directory 52Pickup/assets into your local project's assets folder.

Cards and Piles

In addition to the functionality provided by the BaseActor class, the objects in this game need to store additional data, and so you begin by writing two extensions of this class.

First, create a Card class. This class contains two String variables that store the rank and suit of the card. The remaining variables are related to movement of the card: offsetX and offsetY store the coordinates of the point where the player first touches a card, originalX and originalY store the original position of the card on the stage before it is dragged, and dragable indicates whether the card can be dragged by the player. In addition to the constructor, there are also accessor methods for the private variables rank and suit, and a method getRankIndex that associates a numerical value to the rank of the card.

```
public class Card extends BaseActor
{
    private String rank;
    private String suit;
    public float offsetX;
    public float offsetY;
```

```java
    public float originalX;
    public float originalY;
    public boolean dragable;

    public Card(String r, String s)
    {
        super();
        rank = r;
        suit = s;
        dragable = true;
    }

    public String getRank()
    {   return rank;   }
    public String getSuit()
    {   return suit;   }

    public int getRankIndex()
    {
        String[] rankNames = {"A", "2", "3", "4", "5", "6", "7", "8", "9", "10", "J", "Q", "K"};
        for (int i = 0; i < rankNames.length; i++)
        {
            if ( rank.equals( rankNames[i] ) )
                return i;
        }
        return -1;
    }
}
```

Second, create a class called Pile that stores a list of Card objects by using the ArrayList class. Pile extends the BaseActor class because it will be a visible object in the game and serve as a drop target for Card objects. The various methods check whether the list is empty, add a Card to the list, retrieve the top (most recently added) Card, and for convenience check the rank, suit, and rank index of the top Card.

```java
import java.util.ArrayList;

public class Pile extends BaseActor
{
    private ArrayList<Card> list;

    public Pile()
    {
        super();
        list = new ArrayList<Card>();
    }

    public boolean isEmpty()
    {   return list.isEmpty();   }
```

```
    public void addCard(Card c)
    {  list.add(c);  }

    public Card getTopCard()
    {
        if ( list.isEmpty() )
            return null;
        else
            return list.get( list.size()-1 );
    }

    public String getRank()
    {  return getTopCard().getRank();  }
    public String getSuit()
    {  return getTopCard().getSuit();  }
    public int getRankIndex()
    {  return getTopCard().getRankIndex();  }
}
```

Setting Up the Game

Next, you will set up the core of the GameScreen class, declaring all the variables you will require later. The ArrayList named cardList keeps track of all 52 Card objects that will be created, and the ArrayList named pileList keeps track of the four Pile objects, to which the player will be dragging the Card objects. The variables glowEffect and hintTimer will be used to provide hints to the player, and are discussed in a later section.

```
import com.badlogic.gdx.Gdx;
import com.badlogic.gdx.Input.Keys;
import com.badlogic.gdx.graphics.Texture;
import com.badlogic.gdx.math.MathUtils;
import com.badlogic.gdx.scenes.scene2d.InputEvent;
import com.badlogic.gdx.scenes.scene2d.InputListener;
import com.badlogic.gdx.scenes.scene2d.actions.Actions;
import java.util.ArrayList;

public class GameScreen extends BaseScreen
{
    private BaseActor background;

    private ArrayList<Card> cardList;
    private ArrayList<Pile> pileList;

    private BaseActor glowEffect;
    private float hintTimer;

    // game world dimensions
    final int mapWidth = 800;
    final int mapHeight = 600;
```

```
    public GameScreen(BaseGame g)
    {   super(g);   }

    public void create()
    {     }

    public void update(float dt)
    {     }
}
```

First, background texture should be initialized; at the start of the create method, insert the code:

```
background = new BaseActor();
background.setTexture( new Texture(Gdx.files.internal("assets/felt.jpg")) );
mainStage.addActor(background);
```

After this, the Pile objects will be initialized. An image of the back of a playing card will be used to indicate where each Pile is located, and its size will be set to be slightly larger than the images used for the cards themselves, so that piles can be clearly identified even when cards are on top. The positions of the piles are set so that they are equally spaced along the top of the screen, and a rectangular boundary is set for the purpose of collision detection later.

```
pileList = new ArrayList<Pile>();
Texture pileTex = new Texture(Gdx.files.internal("assets/cardBack.png"));
for (int n = 0; n < 4; n++)
{
    Pile pile = new Pile();
    pile.setTexture( pileTex );
    pile.setWidth(120);
    pile.setHeight(140);
    pile.setOriginCenter();
    pile.setPosition(70 + 180*n, 400);
    pile.setRectangleBoundary();
    pileList.add( pile );
    mainStage.addActor( pile );
}
```

Next, the Card objects will be initialized. Arrays will be used to contain the names of the various ranks and suits, for use in initializing the Card data as well as constructing the file name of the associated image. The most subtle part of this code is setting the z-index of each card, which controls the order in which they are rendered, and can be done only after an Actor is added to a Stage. Actors with lower z-index values render before actors with higher values, and thus appear "beneath" them on the screen. In 52-Card Pickup, you want the cards that the player needs first to appear on top of the other randomly scattered cards. Therefore, the cards with higher rank must render earlier (moving them to the "bottom"), so their z-index must be set to a small number, which also advances all the cards previously added (those with smaller ranks) to a later rendering position (moving them to the "top"). The reason you set the z-index to the particular value 5 is so that all of the Card objects will render after the background object and the four piles, which have z-indices 0 through 4, because they were the first five objects added to this stage.

```
String[] rankNames = {"A", "2", "3", "4", "5", "6", "7", "8", "9", "10", "J", "Q", "K"};
String[] suitNames = {"Clubs", "Hearts", "Spades", "Diamonds"};

cardList = new ArrayList<Card>();
for (int r = 0; r < rankNames.length; r++)
{
    for (int s = 0; s < suitNames.length; s++)
    {
        Card card = new Card( rankNames[r], suitNames[s] );
        String fileName = "assets/card" + suitNames[s] + rankNames[r] + ".png";
        card.setTexture( new Texture(Gdx.files.internal(fileName)) );
        card.setWidth(80);
        card.setHeight(100);
        card.setOriginCenter();
        card.setRectangleBoundary();

        cardList.add(card);
        mainStage.addActor(card);
        card.setZIndex(5); // cards created later should render earlier (on bottom)
    }
}
```

At this point, interactivity can be added to the Card objects. This is accomplished by adding an InputListener to each card, similar to the approach used for the Balloon objects in the Balloon Buster game from Chapter 3, but with much greater complexity. Three different input actions must be processed:

- When the player first touches a Card (handled by the touchDown method), if the card is not draggable, then exit the method and do not process any other input actions for this card. Otherwise, move the card to the top of the rendering order and store the related movement data: the position on the Card that was touched, as well as the original location of the Card on the Stage.

- When the player drags a Card (handled by the touchDragged method), move the card to a new position. However, you don't want to move the lower-left corner of the card to the touch position; you want to move the position on the card that was initially touched (stored in offsetX and offsetY) to this position. Therefore, you take these values into account when using the moveBy method of the card.

- When the player releases a Card (handled by the touchUp method), a variety of actions could take place. First, you check whether the card is overlapping any of the Pile objects. If the card is overlapping a pile, and it is the next card in sequence (same suit, next greater rank index), then you'll add an Action that slides the card to the center of the pile, update the pile data, and lock the card in place by setting dragable to false. If the card is overlapping one or more piles but is not the next card in sequence for any of them, then you'll add an Action that slides the card back to its original position (since you don't want the card to obstruct any part of the piles in this case). If the card is not overlapping any Pile objects when it is released, you just leave it at that position, adjusting the position only if part of the card is off-screen.

These tasks are implemented with the following code, which should be added in the loop that initializes all the Card objects, directly before the line of code that adds card to cardList:

```
card.addListener(
    new InputListener()
    {
        public boolean touchDown(InputEvent event, float x, float y,
                                  int pointer, int button)
        {
            if (!card.dragable)
                return false;

            card.setZIndex(1000); // render currently dragged card on top
            card.offsetX = x;
            card.offsetY = y;
            card.originalX = event.getStageX();
            card.originalY = event.getStageY();
            return true;
        }

        public void touchDragged(InputEvent event, float x, float y, int pointer)
        {
            if (!card.dragable)
                return;

            card.moveBy(x - card.offsetX, y - card.offsetY);
        }

        public void touchUp(InputEvent event, float x, float y, int pointer, int button)
        {
            boolean overPile = false;
            for (Pile pile : pileList)
            {
                if ( card.overlaps(pile, false) )
                {
                    overPile = true;
                    if ( card.getRankIndex() == pile.getRankIndex() + 1
                        && card.getSuit().equals( pile.getSuit() ) )
                    {
                        float targetX = pile.getX() + pile.getOriginX() - card.getOriginX();
                        float targetY = pile.getY() + pile.getOriginY() - card.getOriginY();
                        card.dragable = false;
                        card.addAction( Actions.moveTo( targetX, targetY, 0.5f ) );
                        pile.addCard(card);
                        return;
                    }
                }
            }
```

```
            if (overPile) // overlapping piles but not the right one; move off the pile
                card.addAction( Actions.moveTo(
                    card.originalX - card.offsetX, card.originalY - card.offsetY, 0.5f ) );

            // make sure card is completely visible on screen
            if ( card.getX() < 0 )
                card.setX(0);
            if ( card.getX() + card.getWidth() > mapWidth )
                card.setX(mapWidth - card.getWidth());
            if ( card.getY() < 0 )
                card.setY(0);
            if ( card.getY() + card.getHeight() > mapHeight )
                card.setY(mapHeight - card.getHeight());
        }
    });
```

When the game starts, the Aces should be positioned on top of the four piles, and all other cards scattered about the screen. To do this, iterate over cardList, and when the card has rank A, locate the first empty pile and move the card to that pile. If the card has any other rank, randomize its position on the lower half of the screen. This is accomplished with the following code, which should be added in the create method, after the loops that initialize the Card and Pile objects:

```
// move Aces to piles; randomize positions of all other cards
for (Card card : cardList)
{
    if ( card.getRank().equals("A")  )
    {
        for (Pile pile : pileList)
        {
            if ( pile.isEmpty() )
            {
                card.moveToOrigin( pile );
                pile.addCard( card );
                card.dragable = false;
                break;
            }
        }
    }
    else
    {
        card.setPosition( MathUtils.random(720), MathUtils.random(200) );
    }
}
```

At this point, the game is completely playable! However, in the interest of providing a better player experience and making the game accommodating to a variety of skill levels, one additional feature will be included: hints that assist the player by indicating a possible course of action.

Providing Visual Hints

Sometimes players might have difficulty finding an object or figuring out the next step in a game. Rather than allowing frustration to build, you will introduce a game mechanic that provides a visual hint after a certain amount of time has elapsed. The visual indicator in this game is provided by an object named glowEffect which, as the name suggests, creates a glowing effect around the border of one of the cards that could currently be moved to one of the piles. You'll add a pulsing effect by fading glowEffect in and out, to more easily draw the player's attention. The float variable hintTimer keeps track of how much time has passed since the player touches a card, and if its value becomes large enough, then the hint mechanic becomes activated and glowEffect becomes visible. Conversely, whenever the player touches a card, the hint timer will be reset and glowEffect will be made invisible.

The first step in this process is to initialize glowEffect and hintTimer, which is accomplished by including the following code in the create method, after cardList has been created and the card objects have been added to it:

```
glowEffect = new BaseActor();
Texture glowTex = new Texture(Gdx.files.internal("assets/glowBlue.png"));
glowEffect.setTexture( glowTex );
glowEffect.setWidth( cardList.get(0).getWidth() * 1.5f );
glowEffect.setHeight( cardList.get(0).getHeight() * 1.5f );
glowEffect.setOriginCenter();
glowEffect.addAction(
    Actions.forever( Actions.sequence( Actions.fadeOut(0.5f), Actions.fadeIn(0.5f) ) ) );
glowEffect.setVisible( false );
mainStage.addActor( glowEffect );

hintTimer = 0;
```

Then in the update method, include the following code that updates the hint timer. When the hint mechanic is activated, the glowing effect and the selected card have their z-index adjusted (via the toFront method) so that they render above everything else, just in case the selected card had been previously obscured by other cards as the player dragged them around the screen.

```
hintTimer += dt;

if ( Gdx.input.isTouched() )
{
    hintTimer = 0;
    glowEffect.setVisible(false);
}

// activate hint mechanic
if ( hintTimer > 3 && !glowEffect.isVisible() )
{
    for (Card hintCard : cardList)
    {
        if ( hintCard.dragable )
        {
            glowEffect.setVisible(true);
            glowEffect.moveToOrigin( hintCard );
            glowEffect.toFront();
```

```
            hintCard.toFront();
            break; // exits loop at first chance
        }
    }
}
```

That completes the implementation of the hint mechanic, as well as the code for 52-Card Pickup.

Next Steps

The standard advice for improving the sample games in this chapter applies here (adding a Start menu, sound effects, and a Congratulations message when game is finished). Here are some suggestions specific to this game:

- Instead of having the cards appear in a random position when GameScreen is loaded, create an Action for each card that moves it into its random starting position from an off-screen location.

- Give the player the option to enable/disable hints completely, or add a Button that will activate the glowing hint effect only when pressed.

- Keep track of the time elapsed and display it in the user interface.

- When the game is over, celebrate the player's victory by adding some fun visual effects, such as AnimatedActor objects that contain firework animations, or have the cards move around the screen in interesting patterns using the Action class.

An alternative to polishing this game is to create a completely new game by using the mechanics introduced here. One recommended project is to create a single-player version of the card game Crazy Eights (which is similar to the popular commercial game Uno). The setup and rules are as follows:

- There are two piles: *draw*, which initially contains all 52 cards, and *discard*, which initially contains no cards.

- At the start of the game, remove seven cards from the draw pile and arrange them on the screen; this becomes your *hand*. Also, remove one card from the draw pile and add it to the discard pile.

- At any time, you may move any card from your hand to the top of the discard pile, provided that your card has the same rank or suit as the top card of the discard pile, or has rank 8 (such a card, which can be played at any time, is often called a *wild* card).

- At any point, you may remove the top card from the draw pile and add it to your hand.

- Your goal is to move all the cards from your hand to the discard pile while drawing as few cards from the draw pile as possible.

Creating this game will require many additions and modifications to the code given in this example (for example, adding a removeCard method to the Pile class), but completing this project will give your game programming skills an excellent workout!

Summary

In this chapter, you've learned how to implement a great variety of game mechanics by creating four new games: Space Rocks, Plane Dodger, Rectangle Destroyer, and 52-Card Pickup. Along the way, you gained practical experience with the following material:

- Creating base objects for later spawning using `clone` methods

- Simplifying the creation of `Animation` objects with static utility methods

- Managing lists of different types of actors to check for and handle various interactions

- Adding new methods to your custom `Actor` extensions

- Further extending your custom `Actor` extensions to incorporate additional game-specific data or functionality

- Implementing advanced collision detection and response

- Incorporating randomness into games to provide new game-play experiences

In the next chapter, you'll investigate how to implement even more advanced visual effects and game mechanics by incorporating third-party software, libraries, and extensions.

■ ■ ■

CHAPTER 7

Integrating Third-Party Software

This chapter covers how to use third-party software and libraries to simplify your workflow and increase the sophistication of your games. In particular, you will use the following:

- The LibGDX Particle Editor, to create visual effects

- Tiled, a general-purpose map editor, to simplify the level design process

- Box2D, a physics engine, to simulate realistic physics-based interactions

You'll use each of these in developing new LibGDX projects. The chapter concludes with a project that incorporates features from all three of these tools.

Working with Particle Systems in LibGDX

A *particle system* is a collection of many small images that can be used to create a variety of graphical special effects. Some effects that can be well replicated by this technique include fire, smoke, explosions, fireworks, electric sparks, water fountains, rain, snow, and star fields. Each of the small images in a particle system is called a *particle*. Every particle has many properties (such as velocity, size, color, and transparency) that can be initialized to a random value within a given range, and these property values may be configured to change over time. Particles are produced at a set rate by an object called an *emitter*, which may be configured to spawn particles either for a limited time or continuously, depending on the visual effect being created.

LibGDX provides classes that support the display of particle systems. Furthermore, the Particle Editor tool provided with LibGDX can be used to design and preview particle effects, and export them to a file format that can be easily imported within the LibGDX framework.

The LibGDX Particle Editor

The LibGDX Particle Editor can be run directly from the source code, as explained on the LibGDX wiki.[1] However, for simplicity, I recommend that you use the executable JAR file I have created to run the Particle Editor: `ParticleEditor.jar`, available in the `ParticleEditor` folder in the source code directory for this chapter. Figure 7-1 shows this program when it is first started.

---

[1]`https://github.com/libgdx/libgdx/wiki/2D-Particle-Editor`

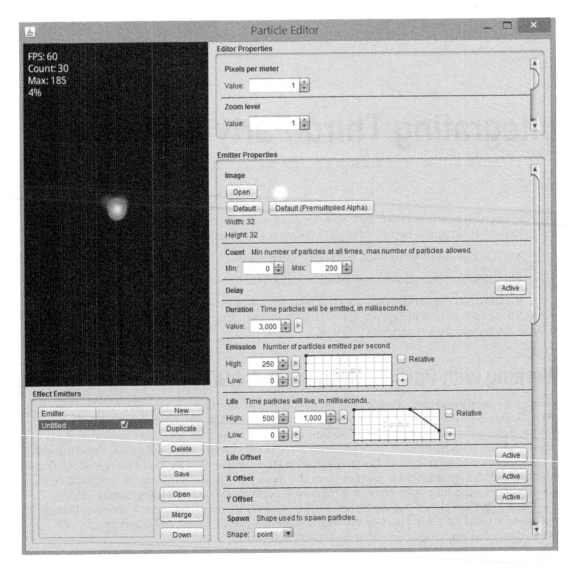

Figure 7-1. *The LibGDX Particle Editor program at startup*

A fire effect appears in the preview region in the upper-left panel of the Particle Editor window. The parameters that produce this effect are in the Emitter Properties panel that occupies the majority of the right-hand side of the window. This panel has so many properties, each with corresponding values and graphs, that it can be somewhat overwhelming at first. This section discusses only the emitter properties that have the greatest impact on the final visual effect; for more thorough coverage, please consult the LibGDX wiki (previously referenced) for details.

- *Image*: From this area, you can select the image used for each particle. Particles are often tinted with a color; grayscale images work best for this purpose.

- *Count*: This area can be used to set the minimum and maximum number of particles that should appear onscreen at any time.

- *Duration*: This is how long the emitter will produce particles. (When creating a continuous effect, this value will be ignored.)

- *Emission*: This is how many particles will be emitted per second.

- *Life*: This is how long each particle will be active in the particle system.

- *Size*: This is the size of the image, in pixels.

- *Velocity*: This is the particle speed, in pixels per second.

- *Angle*: This is the particle direction, in degrees.

- *Tint*: This displays the color(s) used to tint the particle image.

- *Transparency*: This controls the transparency of the images over time.

- *Additive*: When active, this blends colors by adding together the color components, resulting in brighter areas where many particles are present.

- *Continuous*: When active, this causes the emitters to continue emitting particles (ignoring the preceding Duration value).

Next to some of the parameters, you'll see text boxes and a graph, as shown in Figure 7-2, which can be used for fine-tuning the initial values and changes in values over time. (For some parameters, you will need to click the Active button to the right of the parameter name to make these elements appear.)

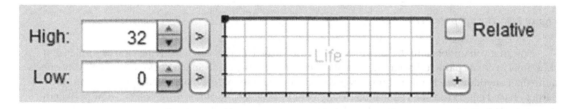

Figure 7-2. *Particle Editor interface for fine-tuning parameter values*

The numeric values in the High and Low boxes refer to the values of the top and bottom edges on the graph to the right. The blue line on the graph indicates how the parameter value will change during the lifetime of the particle. In the graph pictured in Figure 7-2, the blue line remains straight across the top, indicating that the parameter value will remain constant at the High value. Figure 7-3 illustrates two more possible graphs; the graph on the left represents a continuous decrease from the High value to the Low value, while the graph on the right represents a parameter that remains at the High value for the majority of the lifetime of the particle, and then suddenly decreases to the Low value. I refer to these two graphs as the Gradual Decrease and the Sudden Decrease graphs later in this section.

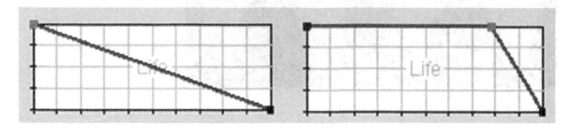

Figure 7-3. *Variations on the parameter change graph*

To modify one of these graphs, you can click anywhere to add a point, click and drag to move a point around, and double-click a point to remove it.

In addition, next to the High and Low values are small buttons labelled with > or <; these can be used to toggle between one or two values appearing in the corresponding row. When two values are displayed, they represent a range of values from which the High or Low value will be randomly selected for each particle. This can be used to great effect, as you will see later.

Finally, let's discuss how to set the parameters for the Tint property. If desired, the color of a particle can change over time; the progression of the color is displayed from the left to the right in the topmost rectangle. For example, Figure 7-4 represents a particle that will begin tinted red, shift to blue, and finally end tinted green. As with the parameter change graphs discussed previously, additional points (represented by triangles) can be added by clicking within the rectangle. Triangles can be selected by clicking them, and their colors can be adjusted by using the sliders underneath, which control the hue, saturation, and brightness of the color. The triangles can be moved by clicking and dragging, and they can be deleted by double-clicking.

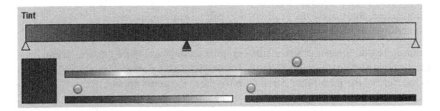

Figure 7-4. *The tint parameter graph*

Now that you understand the user interface of the Particle Editor, you'll work through examples that show how to create particle-based versions of the effects from the game Space Rocks. Creating lots of effects, more than anything, is what will ultimately give you a feel for the role each parameter plays in crafting a particle-based effect. You need a location to save your final effects, so at this time, create a new project in BlueJ called Starscape; within the project directory, create an assets folder, where you will store the effect files created with the LibGDX Particle Editor.

Rocket-Thruster Effect

Your first goal is to create a rocket-thruster effect, pictured in Figure 7-5.

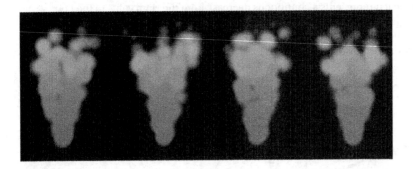

Figure 7-5. *The rocket-thruster particle effect*

After starting the Particle Editor program, in the Effect Emitters panel in the lower left, click the New button and rename the newly created list entry **thruster**. Click the list item named Untitled (which corresponds to the default fire-like example), and click the Delete button to remove it.

In the set of options at the bottom of the Emitter Properties panel, deselect the Additive check box, and select the Continuous check box. You should now see a single red dot in the middle of the preview panel.

First, you will adjust the number of particles that will be active at any given moment. Change the Count property Max value to 100. To achieve this amount, you also must change the Emission property High value to 200. (Changing this value to 100 would be insufficient, as each particle lasts for only 0.5 seconds, since 500 milliseconds is the default value for the Life property. An emission rate of 100 would result in only 50 active particles at any given time.)

Next, click the Active buttons next to the Velocity and Angle properties. For Velocity, click the ➤ button next to High, and enter the values 300 and 400. For Angle, again click the ➤ button next to High, and enter the values 70 and 110. You should now see red particles spraying upward in a wobbly, cone-shaped pattern.

Now change the Tint parameter graph so that the tint color changes from red at the start, to orange in the middle, and yellow at the end. After completing this step, the particles in the preview panel should appear red at the base of the emitter, and gradually change colors until they become yellow at the top.

Finally, you'd like particles to shrink and fade out of existence at the end of their lifetime. To accomplish this, modify the parameter change graphs for both *Size* and Transparency so that they both resemble the Sudden Decrease graph from Figure 7-3.

When this step is finished, click the Save button and save your file to your local `Starscape/assets` directory using the file name `thruster.pfx`. Although the particle effect data is stored in a text file, you will use the extension `pfx` as a mnemonic to indicate the type of data in the file. In addition, you will need to copy the image file `particle.png` from the Particle Editor directory to your local project's `assets` directory as well.

Explosion Effect

A classic effect that you will now create is an explosion effect, as illustrated in Figure 7-6. This effect is composed of two emitters, one controlling the fire that appears initially, and the other controlling the smoke that appears afterward.

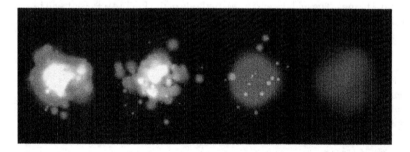

Figure 7-6. *The explosion particle effect*

Restart the Particle Editor. As before, create a new emitter. Name it **fire**, and then delete the default emitter. You'll keep the default option settings: the Additive check box should be selected, and the Continuous check box should not.

Adjust the Count property Max value to 100. Change the Duration value to 250. To attain the maximum number of particles, change the Emission property High value to 400. Set the Size property High value to range from 0 to 100, and modify the graph so that it resemble the Gradual Decrease graph. Set the Velocity property to Active, set its High value to range from 0 to 160, and modify its graph so that it resembles the Sudden Decrease graph. Set the Angle property to Active, and set its High value to range from 0 to 360. Finally, set the Tint property so that the color changes from red to orange over the course of the particle lifetime.

At this point, the preview panel should be displaying the following effect repeatedly: a globule shape appears, red at the borders and yellow in the center, which then expels fragments that shrink as they move away from the center.

Once you are pleased with this effect, create another emitter and name it **smoke**. (Do *not* delete the fire emitter!) Select the smoke emitter from the list, and click the Up button; this moves it higher up in the rendering order. This is important, because you want the smoke particles to appear behind the fire particles, and so the smoke particles must be rendered first. Before continuing, make sure that in the emitter list, the smoke emitter is both selected (so it is visible) and highlighted (so that the parameters that will be changed are those of the smoke emitter).

Now you'll change the smoke emitter properties. Set the Count Max value to 20, the Duration value to 200, and the Emission High value to 100. Set the Delay property to Active, and set its value to 400; this will cause the smoke emitter to begin 400 milliseconds after the fire emitter has started. Next, change the Size High value to 64. Activate the Velocity property, set the High value to 100, and modify the graph so that it is gradually decreasing. Also activate the Angle property, and set the High value to range from 0 to 360. Change the Tint color to a medium shade of gray, by dragging the knob on the lower-left color slider all the way to the right, and then dragging the knob on the lower-right color slider to the middle. Modify the Transparency graph so that it is slowly decreasing. Last of all, uncheck the Additive option.

This completes the explosion effect! Save your file to the `Starscape/assets` directory with the file name `explosion.pfx`.

The ParticleActor Class

At this point, you are ready to begin writing code for the Starscape project. First, from your most recent project, copy the usual classes: BaseGame, BaseScreen, BaseActor, AnimatedActor, PhysicsActor, and GameUtils. You should create a launcher-style class and a class that extends BaseGame, and you will need to copy the images from this chapter's source directory `Starscape/assets` into your local project's `assets` folder.

To integrate particle effects into your projects, you will once again create an extension of the Actor class, called ParticleActor. This class stores a ParticleEffect object, which is used to update and draw the effect. Most of the methods in this class simply activate the methods of the corresponding ParticleEffect object, with somewhat more intuitive names. The update and draw methods of the ParticleEffect will be activated by the standard act and draw methods common to all Actor objects, and a clone method will be included for convenience. The code for the ParticleActor class is as follows:

```
import com.badlogic.gdx.Gdx;
import com.badlogic.gdx.scenes.scene2d.Actor;
import com.badlogic.gdx.graphics.g2d.Batch;
import com.badlogic.gdx.graphics.g2d.ParticleEffect;
import com.badlogic.gdx.graphics.g2d.ParticleEmitter;

public class ParticleActor extends Actor
{
    private ParticleEffect pe;

    public ParticleActor()
    {
        super();
        pe = new ParticleEffect();
    }
```

```java
public void load(String pfxFile, String imageDirectory)
{  pe.load(Gdx.files.internal(pfxFile), Gdx.files.internal(imageDirectory));  }

public void start()
{  pe.start();  }

// pauses continuous emitters
public void stop()
{  pe.allowCompletion();  }

public boolean isRunning()
{  return !pe.isComplete();  }
public void setPosition(float px, float py)
{
    for (ParticleEmitter e : pe.getEmitters() )
        e.setPosition(px, py);
}

public void act(float dt)
{
    super.act( dt );
    pe.update( dt );
    if ( pe.isComplete() && !pe.getEmitters().first().isContinuous() )
    {
        pe.dispose();
        this.remove();
    }
}

public void draw(Batch batch, float parentAlpha)
{  pe.draw(batch);  }

public ParticleActor clone()
{
    ParticleActor newbie = new ParticleActor();
    newbie.pe = new ParticleEffect(this.pe);
    return newbie;
}
}
```

With this class ready for action, you can use it, together with the particle effects you recently generated, in a demo program called Starscape.

Starscape: An Interactive Visual Demo

Starscape, which appears visually similar to the game Space Rocks, is more accurately classified as a demo than a fully functional game. In this demo, the player controls a spaceship as in the Space Rocks game: the left and right arrow keys rotate the spaceship, and the up arrow key accelerates the spaceship forward. While the up arrow key is pressed, the thruster particle effect is visible. However, pressing the space key in this demo doesn't shoot lasers as it did in Space Rocks; instead, it generates an explosion effect at a random location on the screen. Figure 7-7 contains a screenshot of this demo.

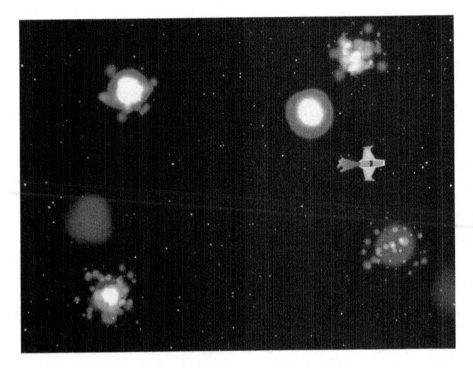

Figure 7-7. The demo Starscape

Next, you will include the code for the GameScreen class, which carries out the tasks previously described. The only tricky part of this code pertains to rotating and scaling a ParticleActor, which is necessary to align and resize the thruster effect before attaching it to the spaceship object. Unfortunately, the draw method of a ParticleEffect does not have this functionality. To remedy this situation, you'll create an auxiliary BaseActor object named thrusterAdjuster, add the thruster effect to it, and make the necessary adjustments to thrusterAdjuster. Since the auxiliary object should not be visible, its texture will be an image consisting of a single transparent pixel, from the image file blank.png.

```
import com.badlogic.gdx.Gdx;
import com.badlogic.gdx.Input.Keys;
import com.badlogic.gdx.graphics.Texture;
import com.badlogic.gdx.graphics.Texture.TextureFilter;
import com.badlogic.gdx.math.MathUtils;
import java.util.ArrayList;

public class GameScreen extends BaseScreen
{
    private PhysicsActor spaceship;
    private ParticleActor thruster;
    private ParticleActor baseExplosion;

    public GameScreen(BaseGame g)
    {  super(g);  }
```

```java
public void create()
{
    BaseActor background = new BaseActor();
    background.setTexture( new Texture(Gdx.files.internal("assets/space.png")) );
    background.setPosition(0, 0);
    mainStage.addActor(background);

    spaceship = new PhysicsActor();
    Texture shipTex = new Texture(Gdx.files.internal("assets/spaceship.png"));
    shipTex.setFilter(TextureFilter.Linear, TextureFilter.Linear);
    spaceship.storeAnimation( "default", shipTex );
    spaceship.setPosition(400, 300);
    spaceship.setOriginCenter();
    spaceship.setMaxSpeed(200);
    spaceship.setDeceleration(20);
    mainStage.addActor(spaceship);

    thruster = new ParticleActor();
    thruster.load("assets/thruster.pfx", "assets/");
    BaseActor thrusterAdjuster = new BaseActor();
    thrusterAdjuster.setTexture( new Texture(Gdx.files.internal("assets/blank.png")) );
    thrusterAdjuster.addActor(thruster);
    thrusterAdjuster.setPosition(0,32);
    thrusterAdjuster.setRotation(90);
    thrusterAdjuster.setScale(0.25f);
    thruster.start();
    spaceship.addActor(thrusterAdjuster);
    baseExplosion = new ParticleActor();
    baseExplosion.load("assets/explosion.pfx", "assets/");
}

public void update(float dt)
{
    spaceship.setAccelerationXY(0,0);

    if (Gdx.input.isKeyPressed(Keys.LEFT))
        spaceship.rotateBy(180 * dt);
    if (Gdx.input.isKeyPressed(Keys.RIGHT))
        spaceship.rotateBy(-180 * dt);
    if (Gdx.input.isKeyPressed(Keys.UP))
    {
        spaceship.addAccelerationAS(spaceship.getRotation(), 100);
        thruster.start();
    }
    else
    {
        thruster.stop();
    }
}
```

```java
public boolean keyDown(int keycode)
{
    if (keycode == Keys.P)
        togglePaused();

    if (keycode == Keys.R)
        game.setScreen( new GameScreen(game) );

    if (keycode == Keys.SPACE)
    {
        ParticleActor explosion = baseExplosion.clone();
        explosion.setPosition( MathUtils.random(800), MathUtils.random(600) );
        explosion.start();
        mainStage.addActor(explosion);
    }

    return false;
    }
}
```

This completes the code for Starscape. Try out the project, soar across space, and enjoy the sights of harmless explosions against the starry background.

Using Tiled for Level Design

In many of the previous games developed in this book, one challenging aspect has been the placement of objects; you often had to figure out or calculate the positions where actors will appear on the main stage. This section introduces Tiled, which greatly simplifies and accelerates this process. At this point, you should create a new project in BlueJ called TreasureQuest, and in the project directory, create a folder named assets to store the file you will produce using Tiled.

Tiled is a general-purpose map editor that can be used for multiple aspects of the level design process. Its primary feature is to take a *tileset* (a sprite sheet consisting of rectangular images, or *tiles*, that represent possible features of the game-world terrain) and enable the user to create a *tilemap* (a selection and arrangement of tiles that corresponds to an image of the game world). In addition, Tiled can also be used to store geometric data (such as the location, size, and shape of game entities). Levels can be designed for games with a top-down perspective or a side-view perspective, depending on the tileset being used.

The Tiled software can be downloaded from http://mapeditor.org. It is both free and open source, and is available for Windows, OS X, and Linux platforms. The sections that follow demonstrate how to create a tilemap using Tiled, and then import it into a new game that you will create called *Treasure Quest*. A screenshot of this game appears in Figure 7-8. The images used are in the TreasureQuest/assets folder in the source code directory for this chapter, which you will need for this process; the images should be copied into your local project's assets folder. The final version of the map file is saved as game-map.tmx in the aforementioned directory.

Figure 7-8. *The game Treasure Quest*

Creating Tilemaps

You'll be using a tileset created by Kenney Veugels, part of his excellent collection of freely available game art assets, available at http://kenney.nl. In your assets directory, the tileset image you will be using is called rpg-tiles-64.png (since each tile is 64 pixels by 64 pixels), and is pictured in Figure 7-9.

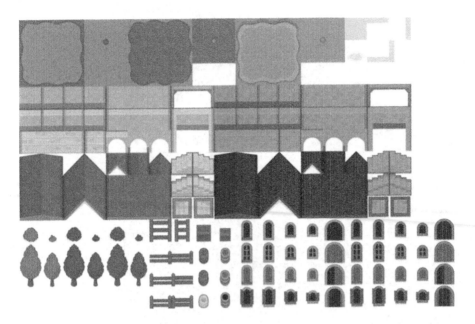

Figure 7-9. *The tileset used for the Treasure Quest game*

Start the Tiled software, and from the menu bar, choose File ➤ New. For the Map Size, set the Width and Height both to 20 tiles. For the Tile Size, set the Width and Height both to 64 pixels. These settings are illustrated in Figure 7-10.

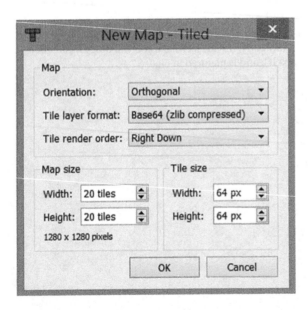

Figure 7-10. *Configuring settings for a new map in Tiled*

Next, from the menu bar, choose Map ➤ New Tileset. In the pop-up window that appears, click the Browse button, locate and select the image file rpg-tiles-64.png from your assets directory, and click the Open button. After returning to the New Tileset window, make sure that the tile width and tile height are both set to 64 px, and then click the OK button. The tileset should be visible in the lower-right panel of the Tiled window, similar to Figure 7-11.

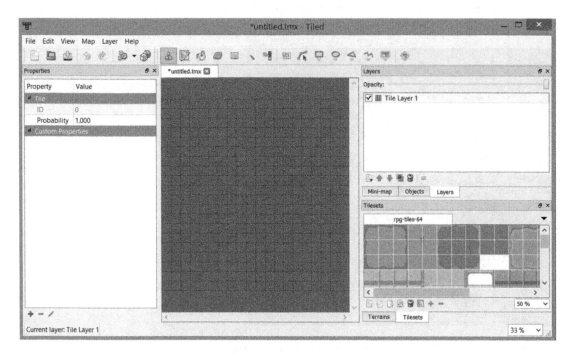

Figure 7-11. *The Tiled window after loading a tileset*

Next, you'll add a few layers to help keep your project organized, before you begin drawing. In the Layers panel in the upper-right area of the Tiled window, double-click Tile Layer 1 and change the name to **Background**. Then, in the menu bar, choose Layer ➤ Add Tile Layer, and after it appears in the Layers panel, change its name to **Scenery**. Repeat this process one more time, adding a tile layer named **Overlay**.

Next, you'll begin drawing the tilemap. You'll start with the Background layer; this will be used for the tiles that depict ground-level elements: grass, dirt, water, and so forth.

If the Background layer is not highlighted in the Layers panel, click it so that it becomes the active layer. Next, click the icon containing an image of a stamp; this selects the Stamp Brush tool, which is the tool you will use most frequently. In the Tilesets panel in the lower-right area of the Tiled window, click one of the rectangles containing a grass-like pattern. The tile becomes tinted blue to show that it has been selected. Click anywhere in the currently empty grid that represents your tilemap, and the tile image you previously selected appears in that square. (The Fill tool, represented by the icon containing an image of a bucket, can be used to fill large areas faster with the currently selected tile.) Continue this process, adding a variety of tiles, until all tiles are filled and you are satisfied with the layout.

Figure 7-12 shows one such possible design, but feel free to create your own; experiment with the different ways the tiles can be arranged to create continuous borders and visually interesting arrangements. (The grid lines that appear in the image are there as guides and will not appear later when the tilemap is rendered.) If you want to change the tile that has been placed in a given location, you can select the Eraser tool icon at the top of the window, or you can select a different tile and use the Stamp Brush tool to replace the tile at a given location. The only restriction you should consider at this stage is to limit yourself to the tiles whose image fills the entire square. In other words, while working on this layer, avoid using tiles with transparent areas (such as bushes, trees, or fences). Otherwise, the color used for clearing the screen (defined in the render method of the BaseScreen class) will appear at the transparent locations.

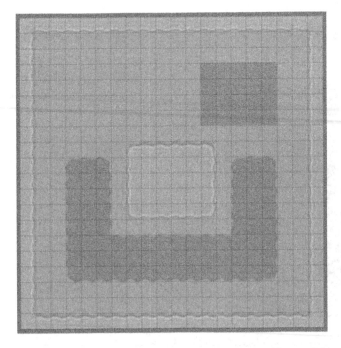

Figure 7-12. *One possible layout for the Background layer of the tilemap*

Next, you'll add visually interesting elements that render on top of the background, like the bushes, trees, and fences that you avoided in the Background layer. Click the Scenery layer in the Layers panel, and then click grid squares in the tilemap to add these images. Notice that they don't replace the tiles previously added to the Background layer; instead, they appear on top. This is particularly useful in keeping the size of tilesets small while allowing for a great variety of combinations. For example, you could create an image of a bush on grass or an image of a bush on dirt, without requiring these specific combinations to be available in the tileset; only the individual components need to be available.

Once again, I recommend a restriction when selecting objects to add to this layer: there may be some tiles that should be rendered above the game characters, such as roofs of buildings or the tops of trees. This creates an illusion of depth: the characters will appear to underneath the roofs, or behind the trees. Thus, after adding elements to the Scenery layer, select the layer named Overlay, and add any tiles that should be rendered above the player.

Figure 7-13 shows the result of adding various bushes, tree trunks, and building walls to the Scenery layer, followed by the result of adding treetops to the Overlay layer.

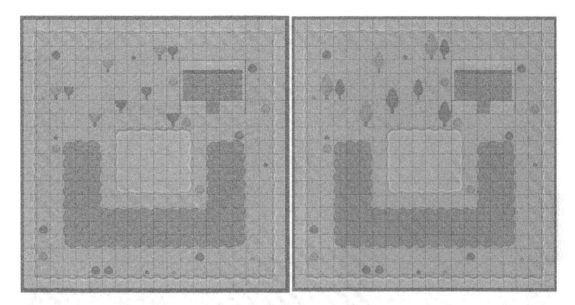

Figure 7-13. *Results of adding detail to the Scenery and Overlay layers of the tilemap*

Finally, you'll add some nonvisual data to this map: the positions and sizes of various in-game objects, such as the starting position of the player and various items the player can interact with. These objects aren't represented by tiles, but rather by images that will be loaded by the accompanying program you will write later. This data can be added by creating object layers; you'll create two of these, to keep the data organized.

To begin, choose Layer ➤ Add Object Layer from the menu bar, and name the newly added layer **ObjectData**. Repeat this process to add another object layer named **PhysicsData**.

Select the layer named ObjectData, and you'll notice that some of the tool icons in the menu bar (those involving image manipulation, such as the Stamp Brush and Eraser) are dimmed and are no longer accessible. Meanwhile, some of the previously unavailable tools (those involving creating geometric shapes) can now be selected, since you're working on an object layer.

Select the icon for the Insert Rectangle tool, and you'll be able to click and drag on the tilemap to add rectangles of any size at any position. The first click sets the upper-left corner of the rectangle; drag the mouse downward and to the right to set the rectangle's size. In the Treasure Quest game, the in-game entities the player can interact with include the player, a key, a door, and three coins. You should add rectangles (using the Insert Rectangle tool) to store the position of each item; one possible arrangement is illustrated in Figure 7-14.

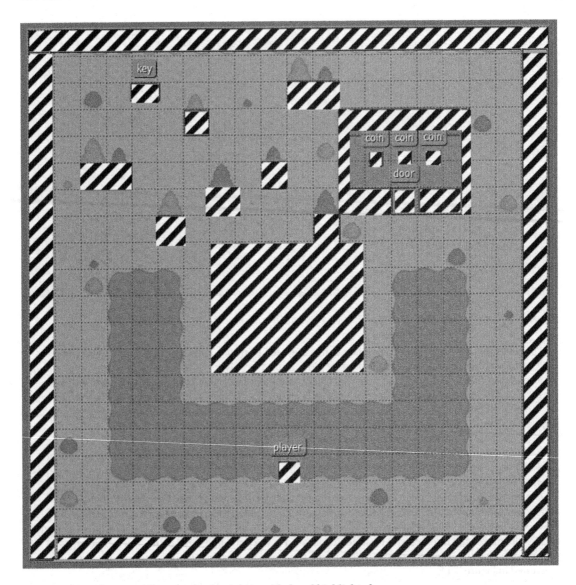

Figure 7-14. *Tilemap with rectangle object data added and highlighted*

To tell these types of objects apart, properties need to be set for each rectangle. To do so, click a rectangle to select it, and in the Properties panel on the left side of the Tiled window, enter a name in the Name field.. Names entered then appear above the corresponding rectangles on the tilemap. I recommend the obvious names (player, key, door, and coin). The names will be important later, because they will be used when importing the corresponding data into the program. If desired, you can also adjust the position and size of each rectangle numerically by using the Properties panel, or by using the Select Objects tool from the toolbar and clicking the rectangle that you want to reposition or resize.

Now select the layer named PhysicsData, and you'll add a series of rectangles to represent solid or impassible objects. For this example, you should place the rectangles over the water tiles, tree trunks, and building walls. In this case, you won't add names to these objects, as they all are used for the same purpose and it is not necessary to distinguish between them.

Figure 7-14 shows the placement of the rectangles on the object layers as discussed previously. Since rectangles in Tiled are displayed with light gray borders, for clarity, I have highlighted the rectangles in the screenshot using diagonal lines. (Rectangles do *not* appear this way when using the Tiled software.)

Once your map is complete, save it with the file name game-map.tmx in the assets folder of your BlueJ project. In the next section, you'll see how the built-in LibGDX classes can use this file format to render images and retrieve geometric data.

Treasure Quest: An Adventure-Style Exploration Game

This section demonstrates how to process the information store in Tiled map files in the context of making a new game called Treasure Quest. Inspired by classic top-down adventure games such as The Legend of Zelda, in this game the player controls a character who is searching the countryside for a key that will unlock the door to a building filled with gold coins.

Return to the TreasureQuest project in BlueJ, and as usual, copy the classes BaseGame, BaseScreen, BaseActor, AnimatedActor, PhysicsActor, and GameUtils. You can also copy a launcher-style class and a BaseGame-extending class from a previous project, and modify their code as needed. The only new class you need to code from scratch is the GameScreen class (which extends the BaseScreen class), discussed next.

You'll start with the core code for the GameScreen class, including the import statements you will eventually need (of which there are many!), variable declarations, and method declarations (which will be filled in later). You need various types of actor variables for the player, key, door, and a base coin instance from which additional coins will be cloned later. Lists are needed to keep track of the coins and walls for collision checking later in the update method. The variables tileSize, tileCountWidth, and tileCountHeight are used to calculate the values of mapWidth and mapHeight. The integer arrays backgroundLayers and foregroundLayers store the indices of the tilemap layers to be rendered before and after the main stage, respectively. Most interesting are the instances of the newly imported classes, which accomplish the following tasks:

- The TiledMap object is used to store the data from the tilemap file, which is loaded using a static method from the TmxMapLoader class.

- The OrthogonalTileMapRenderer object is used to draw the contents of the various layers of the tilemap; the layers to be rendered are specified by an array of integers.

- The OrthographicCamera is used to determine which region of a tilemap layer should be rendered, analogous to the role of the Camera object that belongs to each Stage.

Without further ado, here is the core code for the BaseScreen class:

```
import com.badlogic.gdx.Gdx;
import com.badlogic.gdx.Input.Keys;
import com.badlogic.gdx.graphics.Texture;
import com.badlogic.gdx.graphics.Texture.TextureFilter;
import com.badlogic.gdx.graphics.g2d.Animation;
import com.badlogic.gdx.graphics.g2d.Animation.PlayMode;
import com.badlogic.gdx.graphics.Camera;
import com.badlogic.gdx.math.MathUtils;
import com.badlogic.gdx.math.Rectangle;
import com.badlogic.gdx.graphics.GL20;

import com.badlogic.gdx.maps.MapObject;
import com.badlogic.gdx.maps.MapObjects;
import com.badlogic.gdx.maps.objects.RectangleMapObject;
import com.badlogic.gdx.maps.tiled.TiledMap;
```

```java
import com.badlogic.gdx.maps.tiled.TmxMapLoader;
import com.badlogic.gdx.maps.tiled.renderers.OrthogonalTiledMapRenderer;
import com.badlogic.gdx.graphics.OrthographicCamera;

import java.util.ArrayList;

public class GameScreen extends BaseScreen
{
    private PhysicsActor player;
    private BaseActor door;
    private BaseActor key;
    private boolean hasKey;

    private BaseActor baseCoin;
    private ArrayList<BaseActor> coinList;

    private ArrayList<BaseActor> wallList;
    private ArrayList<BaseActor> removeList;

    private int tileSize = 64;
    private int tileCountWidth = 20;
    private int tileCountHeight = 20;

    // calculate game world dimensions
    final int mapWidth  = tileSize * tileCountWidth;
    final int mapHeight = tileSize * tileCountHeight;

    private TiledMap tiledMap;
    private OrthographicCamera tiledCamera;
    private OrthogonalTiledMapRenderer tiledMapRenderer;
    private int[] backgroundLayers = {0,1};
    private int[] foregroundLayers = {2};

    public GameScreen(BaseGame g)
    {   super(g);    }

    public void create()
    {    }

    public void update(float dt)
    {    }

    public void render(float dt)
    {    }
}
```

Now let's turn our attention to the create method. The following code initializes the player, key, door, and a base coin instance. Note, however, that the positions of these objects are not set at this time; this data will be set later after retrieving it from the tilemap. In addition, the code initializes all the needed lists.

```
player = new PhysicsActor();
Texture playerTex = new Texture( Gdx.files.internal("assets/general-single.png") );
player.storeAnimation("default", playerTex);
player.setEllipseBoundary();
mainStage.addActor(player);

key = new BaseActor();
key.setTexture( new Texture(Gdx.files.internal("assets/key.png")) );
key.setSize(36,24);
key.setEllipseBoundary();
mainStage.addActor( key );

door = new BaseActor();
door.setTexture( new Texture(Gdx.files.internal("assets/door.png")) );
door.setRectangleBoundary();
mainStage.addActor( door );

baseCoin = new BaseActor();
baseCoin.setTexture( new Texture(Gdx.files.internal("assets/coin.png")) );
baseCoin.setEllipseBoundary();

coinList = new ArrayList<BaseActor>();
wallList = new ArrayList<BaseActor>();
removeList = new ArrayList<BaseActor>();
```

Next, you initialize the objects from the new classes:

```
// set up tile map, renderer, and camera
tiledMap = new TmxMapLoader().load("assets/game-map.tmx");
tiledMapRenderer = new OrthogonalTiledMapRenderer(tiledMap);
tiledCamera = new OrthographicCamera();
tiledCamera.setToOrtho(false, viewWidth, viewHeight);
tiledCamera.update();
```

Now you will write the code that retrieves geometric data from the tilemap. From the tilemap object, you can retrieve the list of layers, followed by a specific layer (by name), followed by a list of MapObjects contained in that layer. While iterating over this list, you can retrieve the name of each object (which you entered when using the Tiled program). Since only rectangles were used in the object data layers, each MapObject can be safely cast into a RectangleMapObject in order to retrieve its position. Then, with a sequence of conditional statements that check the name of the object, the position of the corresponding game entity can be set. If the MapObject represents a coin, the base coin instance must be cloned and this new actor added to the main stage.

```
MapObjects objects = tiledMap.getLayers().get("ObjectData").getObjects();
for (MapObject object : objects)
{
    String name = object.getName();

    RectangleMapObject rectangleObject = (RectangleMapObject)object;
    Rectangle r = rectangleObject.getRectangle();
```

```
switch (name)
{
    case "player":
        player.setPosition( r.x, r.y );
        break;
    case "coin":
        BaseActor coin = baseCoin.clone();
        coin.setPosition(r.x, r.y);
        mainStage.addActor(coin);
        coinList.add(coin);
        break;
    case "door":
        door.setPosition( r.x, r.y );
        break;
    case "key":
        key.setPosition( r.x, r.y );
        break;
    default:
        System.err.println("Unknown tilemap object: " + name);
}
}
```

You repeat this process to gather the geometric data that represents solid walls. First, retrieve the list of map objects from the layer named PhysicsData. The names of these objects don't need to be retrieved; you didn't set their names when using Tiled, because all objects in this layer serve the same purpose and it is not necessary to distinguish between them. Note in particular that no texture is set for these objects, nor are they added to any stage. This is because the graphics are already represented by the tilemap; the only purposes these actors serve is for collision detection, and so they only need to be added to the appropriate ArrayList for later checking in the update method.

```
objects = tiledMap.getLayers().get("PhysicsData").getObjects();
for (MapObject object : objects)
{
    RectangleMapObject rectangleObject = (RectangleMapObject)object;
    Rectangle r = rectangleObject.getRectangle();

    BaseActor solid = new BaseActor();
    solid.setPosition(r.x, r.y);
    solid.setSize(r.width, r.height);
    solid.setRectangleBoundary();
    wallList.add(solid);
}
```

This completes the code for the create method; the next area of focus is the contents of the update method.

The first part of the update method contains standard game logic code that you have seen in previous games, such as player movement when the arrow keys are pressed, and collision detection with walls and other objects. The main difference in the code for this game is that the key and door objects should be removed from the game at various points during game play, but it is needlessly complex to create an

ArrayList to hold a single instance of each object. Instead, you can check whether each object still "exists" in the game by checking whether it is still part of any stage with its getStage method. If this method returns null, the object is not part of any stage; this indicates that the object has been removed from the game, and thus the corresponding code does not need to be processed.

```
float playerSpeed = 100;
player.setVelocityXY(0,0);

if (Gdx.input.isKeyPressed(Keys.LEFT))
    player.setVelocityXY(-playerSpeed,0);
if (Gdx.input.isKeyPressed(Keys.RIGHT))
    player.setVelocityXY(playerSpeed,0);
if (Gdx.input.isKeyPressed(Keys.UP))
    player.setVelocityXY(0,playerSpeed);
if (Gdx.input.isKeyPressed(Keys.DOWN))
    player.setVelocityXY(0,-playerSpeed);

for (BaseActor wall : wallList)
{
    player.overlaps(wall, true);
}

if ( key.getStage() != null && player.overlaps(key, false) )
{
    hasKey = true;
    removeList.add(key);
}

if ( door.getStage() != null && player.overlaps(door, true) )
{
    if (hasKey)
        removeList.add(door);
}

for (BaseActor coin : coinList)
{
    if ( player.overlaps(coin, false) )
        removeList.add(coin);
}

for (BaseActor ba : removeList)
{
    ba.destroy();
}
```

In the update method, you need to adjust the Camera objects used to render the graphics. This situation has arisen before: in the Cheese, Please! game, since the game world was larger than the window size, you had to adjust the position of the camera so that it stayed centered on the player (and then also make sure that the camera's field of view stayed bounded within the game world). The main difference here is that there are two cameras to adjust: one corresponding to the main stage and the other corresponding to the tilemap. (The positions of both cameras will stay in sync.)

```
// camera adjustment
Camera mainCamera = mainStage.getCamera();

// center camera on player
mainCamera.position.x = player.getX() + player.getOriginX();
mainCamera.position.y = player.getY() + player.getOriginY();

// bound camera to layout
mainCamera.position.x = MathUtils.clamp(
    mainCamera.position.x, viewWidth/2,  mapWidth - viewWidth/2);
mainCamera.position.y = MathUtils.clamp(
    mainCamera.position.y, viewHeight/2, mapHeight - viewHeight/2);

mainCamera.update();

// adjust tilemap camera to stay in sync with main camera
tiledCamera.position.x = mainCamera.position.x;
tiledCamera.position.y = mainCamera.position.y;
tiledCamera.update();
tiledMapRenderer.setView(tiledCamera);
```

This completes the contents of the update method!

In past projects, after finishing the create and update methods (and occasionally some InputProcessor methods such as keyDown for processing discrete input), the project has been considered complete. However, there is one final step in this class: you *must* override the render method from the BaseScreen class. The render method draws the contents of the main stage and user-interface stage, but in this program the contents of the tilemap must also be rendered, using the TiledMapRenderer object. Furthermore, different layers need to be rendered at different times: the Background and Scenery layers (indexed by 0 and 1) must be rendered first, followed by the main stage (which contains the player), followed by the Overlay layer of the tilemap (since these objects should appear above the player), and finally, the user-interface stage. This is accomplished with the following code, to be inserted into the render method of the GameScreen class:

```
// override the render method to interleave tilemap rendering
public void render(float dt)
{
    uiStage.act(dt);

    // pause only gameplay events, not UI events
    if ( !isPaused() )
    {
        mainStage.act(dt);
        update(dt);
    }
```

```
// render
Gdx.gl.glClearColor(0,0,0,1);
Gdx.gl.glClear(GL20.GL_COLOR_BUFFER_BIT);
tiledMapRenderer.render(backgroundLayers);
mainStage.draw();
tiledMapRenderer.render(foregroundLayers);
uiStage.draw();
}
```

Finally, if desired, you could also add a keyDown method to the GameScreen class that enables the player to pause or restart the game with the following code:

```
public boolean keyDown(int keycode)
{
    if (keycode == Keys.P)
        togglePaused();

    if (keycode == Keys.R)
        game.setScreen( new GameScreen(game) );
    return false;
}
```

This completes the GameScreen class. Now is a good time to test the game: find the key and collect the treasure!

Creating Four-Directional Character Animations

Although the finished GameScreen class from the previous section results in a playable game, one feature is virtually begging to be added: four-directional movement animation for the player character. (At present, the player graphics consists of only a single image.) Many top-down perspective games give their characters four animations, representing walking in the directions north, south, east, and west on the tilemap. You will implement this feature in this section, but this process requires a few steps to do well.

First, observe that many sprite sheets containing top-down character walking animations typically contain the animation frames for all four directions in a single sprite sheet, one direction per row, as illustrated in Figure 7-15.[2] This layout standard has been popularized in particular by the game engine software RPG Maker.

---

[2]Thanks to Andrew Viola for creating this character sprite sheet that we will be using in our game.

Figure 7-15. *A sprite sheet containing walking animations in four directions*

In order to process this kind of sprite sheet more efficiently, extracting a subset of the images to create an animation, you'll write a new method for the GameUtils class. In particular, you will overload the parseSpriteSheet method; this version will enable the user to also provide an array of integers containing the indices of the images to be used in the resulting Animation. It will be assumed that the images are numbered starting with 0 in the upper-left corner, increasing first from left to right, and then from top to bottom. The code for this method is presented here, and should be added to the GameUtils class:

```
// creates an Animation from a single sprite sheet
//  with a subset of the frames, specified by an array
public static Animation parseSpriteSheet(String fileName, int frameCols, int frameRows,
    int[] frameIndices, float frameDuration, PlayMode mode)
{
    Texture t = new Texture(Gdx.files.internal(fileName), true);
    t.setFilter(TextureFilter.Linear, TextureFilter.Linear);

    int frameWidth = t.getWidth() / frameCols;
    int frameHeight = t.getHeight() / frameRows;

    TextureRegion[][] temp = TextureRegion.split(t, frameWidth, frameHeight);
    TextureRegion[] frames = new TextureRegion[frameCols * frameRows];

    int index = 0;
    for (int i = 0; i < frameRows; i++)
    {
        for (int j = 0; j < frameCols; j++)
```

```
        {
            frames[index] = temp[i][j];
            index++;
        }
    }

    Array<TextureRegion> framesArray = new Array<TextureRegion>();
    for (int n = 0; n < frameIndices.length; n++)
    {
        int i = frameIndices[n];
        framesArray.add( frames[i] );
    }

    return new Animation(frameDuration, framesArray, mode);
}
```

The next bit of functionality will need to be added to the AnimatedActor class. It is helpful to be able to stop an animation from playing, and also to be able set a particular frame to display (which will be useful only when the animation is paused). In Treasure Quest, the walking animation should stop whenever your character stops moving, and animation frame 1 should be displayed, which shows the character standing rather than striding. (These frames appear in the center column of Figure 7-15.) The changes indicated next should all be applied to the AnimatedActor class.

First, add a variable that keeps track of whether the animation is currently paused:

```
private boolean pauseAnim;
```

Then, initialize it in the constructor method:

```
pauseAnim = false;
```

Add a pair of methods that toggle the pause state of the animation:

```
public void pauseAnimation()
{   pauseAnim = true;   }
public void startAnimation()
{   pauseAnim = false;   }
```

In the act method, the pause state is used to determine whether the elapsed time should be increased (which results in subsequent frames being displayed by the draw method):

```
public void act(float dt)
{
    super.act( dt );
    if (!pauseAnim)
        elapsedTime += dt;
}
```

Code also needs to be added to the already existing `setActiveAnimation` method in the `AnimatedActor` class. First, if an animation is already playing, the `elapsedTime` variable should not be reset, and so it is necessary to return from the method immediately in this case. Second, the width and the height of the actor should only be updated if these values have not been set (which is indicated when either value is currently zero). The complete method is given here, with the additions to be made appearing in bold font:

```java
public void setActiveAnimation(String name)
{
    if ( !animationStorage.containsKey(name) )
    {
        System.out.println("No animation: " + name);
        return;
    }

    if ( name.equals(activeName) )
        return;

    activeName = name;
    activeAnim = animationStorage.get(name);
    elapsedTime = 0;

    if ( getWidth() == 0 || getHeight() == 0 )
    {
        Texture tex = activeAnim.getKeyFrame(0).getTexture();
        setWidth( tex.getWidth() );
        setHeight( tex.getHeight() );
    }
}
```

Finally, to set a particular frame of the animation to display, a method is needed that adjusts the elapsed time of the animation to the value corresponding to when that particular frame is displayed:

```java
public void setAnimationFrame(int n)
{   elapsedTime = n * activeAnim.getFrameDuration();   }
```

Now, taking advantage of this new functionality, add the following code to the GameScreen class. In the create method, remove the line of code that sets the player animation (named `default` and consisting of a single texture) and replace it with the following code:

```java
float t = 0.15f;
player.storeAnimation("down",
    GameUtils.parseSpriteSheet("assets/general-48.png", 3, 4,
        new int[] {0, 1, 2}, t, PlayMode.LOOP_PINGPONG));

player.storeAnimation("left",
    GameUtils.parseSpriteSheet("assets/general-48.png", 3, 4,
        new int[] {3, 4, 5}, t, PlayMode.LOOP_PINGPONG));

player.storeAnimation("right",
    GameUtils.parseSpriteSheet("assets/general-48.png", 3, 4,
        new int[] {6, 7, 8}, t, PlayMode.LOOP_PINGPONG));
```

```
player.storeAnimation("up",
    GameUtils.parseSpriteSheet("assets/general-48.png", 3, 4,
        new int[] {9, 10, 11}, t, PlayMode.LOOP_PINGPONG));
player.setSize(48,48);
```

Next, in the section of the update method that processes user input, add the following code that sets the corresponding animation whenever an arrow key is pressed. Also, the animation is either paused or started, depending on the speed of the player (which determines whether the player should appear to be walking). Here is the code that accomplishes these tasks:

```
if (Gdx.input.isKeyPressed(Keys.LEFT))
{
    player.setVelocityXY(-playerSpeed,0);
    player.setActiveAnimation("left");
}
if (Gdx.input.isKeyPressed(Keys.RIGHT))
{
    player.setVelocityXY(playerSpeed,0);
    player.setActiveAnimation("right");
}
if (Gdx.input.isKeyPressed(Keys.UP))
{
    player.setVelocityXY(0,playerSpeed);
    player.setActiveAnimation("up");
}
if (Gdx.input.isKeyPressed(Keys.DOWN))
{
    player.setVelocityXY(0,-playerSpeed);
    player.setActiveAnimation("down");
}
if ( player.getSpeed() < 1 )
{
    player.pauseAnimation();
    player.setAnimationFrame(1);
}
else
    player.startAnimation();
```

With these changes, try out the Treasure Quest game once more, and enjoy the improved animation as you guide your character around the map.

Simulating Advanced Physics with Box2D

Another challenging aspect you've encountered in previous projects is implementing realistic physics, and in particular, collision detection and response. LibGDX provides classes for circle, rectangle, and polygon shapes, and via methods provided by the Intersector class, you can check for two rectangles overlapping, a rectangle and a circle overlapping, two circles overlapping, or two polygons overlapping (but no other combinations can be checked with this class). Responding to collisions is even more difficult. Again, the Intersector class provides limited functionality: in the case of overlapping polygons, LibGDX can calculate the minimum translation vector, which represents the smallest distance one of the polygons must move so that the two shapes are no longer overlapping. This functionality was used in the BaseActor class, which allowed you to simulate collisions with solid objects (stopping one such BaseActor from passing through another).

In the game Rectangle Destroyer from the previous chapter, the topic of collision response was explored even further, and some code was presented to simulate a ball bouncing off a flat surface (such as a wall or a brick). In the game Plane Dodger, gravity was simulated by setting a constant negative acceleration in the y direction, and there were explanations about how to simulate upward momentum for the plane object, either continuously or discretely.

This section covers how to use a third-party software library called *Box2D*: a "physics engine" that is capable of handling all of the simulations described previously, and much, much more. Box2D is freely available and open source, originally written by Erin Catto in the C++ programming language and released in 2007. Since then, it has been ported to multiple programming languages (including Java), and has been incorporated into many game development frameworks (such as LibGDX).

In this section, you will learn how to use the basic features of Box2D in LibGDX while creating a new project called *Jumping Jack*. This project falls into the category of *sandbox games*, in which the user controls a character that can interact with the environment in a variety of ways, but there is neither a well-defined end goal nor a series of challenges to overcome (as is the case when playing in a real-life sandbox). Jumping Jack features platformer-style game play, in which the player controls Jack the Koala. Jack can jump around the screen and interact with a soccer ball and a crate, both of which have realistic physics behaviors. A screenshot of this game appears in Figure 7-16.

Figure 7-16. The sandbox game Jumping Jack

Physics Primer

Before you create your new project, it is important to understand some terms from physics and the corresponding objects from the Box2D library.

The first object you need to create when simulating physics is an instance of the World class; it manages all the physics entities, performs the calculations for the simulation, and reports all the collision events. The world constructor requires a Vector2 object representing the strength and direction of gravity, and a Boolean variable typically set to true to improve performance. Since the Box2D engine is optimized for realistic physics simulations, you will need to scale onscreen, pixel-based dimensions into a range more suitable for physics calculations; you will use a scaling factor of 1/100 for this purpose. This means that, for example, a 100-by-100 square displayed on the screen would be represented by a 1-by-1 square object in the physics simulation. Similarly, an onscreen rectangle with width 75 and height 250 would be represented in the simulation by a rectangle with width 0.75 and height 2.50. In accordance with these values, you set the World gravity to be the vector Vector2(0, -9.8f).

Each physics entity managed by the world object is a Body, whose overall properties are set using a BodyDef object, and whose individual parts are represented using Fixture objects. The BodyDef can be used to store the following:

- The initial position and angle of the body

- The initial linear velocity (which represents a change in position) and angular velocity (which represents the rate of rotation)

- Damping values (which, if set, will gradually decrease the linear velocity and angular velocity over time)

- The type of object: if the body should not be affected by forces or collisions, and does not move, then the type should be set to static (typically used for objects corresponding to ground and walls); otherwise, the type should be set to dynamic

- A Boolean value that indicates whether the body can rotate (which defaults to true, but is typically set to false for player objects and other types of objects that should not tip over or spin)

A Fixture, which represents a physical part of the associated Body, is initialized using a FixtureDef object that stores the following information:

- The physical *shape* of the object, which can be a circle (via the CircleShape class), a polygon (via the PolygonShape class), or a rectangle (which is implemented via the setAsBox method of the PolygonShape class).

- The *density* of the object, which is used to calculate the mass of the object (equal to the product of the area, calculated from the shape, and the density). Typically, the greater the density, the greater the mass, and the less of an effect forces will have when applied to this object. Generally, a density value of 1.0 should be used as a baseline, and thought of as having the same density as water. Heavier objects will have a greater density; lighter objects will have a lesser density.

- The *friction* of the object, which is used to calculate an opposing force when two objects slide across each other. A value of 0 represents a perfectly slippery surface with no friction; the velocity of the two objects sliding across each other will not be affected at all. A value of 1 represents high friction; the speed of the two objects will be greatly decreased while they are in contact.

- The *restitution* of the object, which is used to measure the "bounciness" of an object in response to a collision. A value of 0 indicates that there will be no bounce at all after a collision, while a value of 1 indicates that the object will bounce all the way back up to the original height from which the object initially fell.

A Fixture can also be set to act as a *sensor*, which means that it will correspond to a region of the Body but will have no physical effect on the simulation; such an object can be used to determine when different areas overlap in the simulation.

After the physics simulation begins, the position and velocity of a Body can be accessed by a number of get and set style methods, but if you want to move a body in the simulation, the proper way to do this is by applying forces and impulses. A *force* can be thought of as a continuous pushing or pulling action applied to an object, which may cause its velocity to change (and may also cause the object to rotate, if the force is not applied to the center of the object). An *impulse* is like a discrete version of a force, applied at a single instant in time (such as the effect of hitting a nail with a hammer, or the effect of a person jumping in the air). The strength and direction of a force or impulse is indicated by a Vector2 object, and may be applied to any point of a Body (you will typically choose the center of the body to avoid unwanted rotation).

Finally, every time that two bodies collide in the physics simulation, a Contact object is generated, which stores references to the two particular fixtures of the bodies involved in the collision. When two objects collide, that may have an effect on the game state (such as when the player collects an item). To access this information, you can create a ContactListener to process and handle these events; this is discussed in greater detail later.

The Box2DActor Class

To integrate the functionality of the Box2D objects into your LibGDX framework, you'll create another custom extension of the Actor class (in particular, the AnimatedActor class) that can effectively replace the PhysicsActor class. This extension will be called Box2DActor.

You begin by creating a new project in BlueJ, called JumpingJack, which needs to contain the classes BaseGame, BaseScreen, BaseActor, AnimatedActor, PhysicsActor, and GameUtils. As usual, you should create a launcher-style class and a class that extends BaseGame. You will also need to copy the images from this chapter's source directory JumpingJack/assets into your local project's assets folder. In addition, you will need to add two JAR files to your project's +libs folder: gdx-box2d.jar and gdx-box2d-natives.jar. These can be downloaded from the LibGDX web site as earlier chapters have discussed, or the files may be copied from this chapter's source directory JumpingJack/+libs.

Next follows the basics of the Box2DActor class: the import statements, variable declarations, and the constructor, which initializes the variables. In addition to storing a Body and the various objects used to define its properties, some Float variables are added that can be used to set a cap on the maximum overall speed, or the maximum speed in either the x or y direction. The main difference between a Float and a float (besides the capitalization) is that Float extends the basic Object class (whereas float is a primitive data type), and thus a Float can be set to null. Later, you'll use this to check whether the user has chosen to set any of these values (and act accordingly if they have).

```
import com.badlogic.gdx.physics.box2d.World;
import com.badlogic.gdx.physics.box2d.Body;
import com.badlogic.gdx.physics.box2d.BodyDef;
import com.badlogic.gdx.physics.box2d.BodyDef.BodyType;
```

```
import com.badlogic.gdx.physics.box2d.Fixture;
import com.badlogic.gdx.physics.box2d.FixtureDef;
import com.badlogic.gdx.physics.box2d.CircleShape;
import com.badlogic.gdx.physics.box2d.PolygonShape;
import com.badlogic.gdx.math.Vector2;
import com.badlogic.gdx.math.MathUtils;

public class Box2DActor extends AnimatedActor
{
    protected BodyDef bodyDef;
    protected Body body;
    protected FixtureDef fixtureDef;

    protected Float maxSpeed;
    protected Float maxSpeedX;
    protected Float maxSpeedY;

    public Box2DActor()
    {
        body       = null;
        bodyDef    = new BodyDef();
        fixtureDef = new FixtureDef();

        maxSpeed  = null;
        maxSpeedX = null;
        maxSpeedY = null;
    }
}
```

Next, are the methods that set the type of the body to be static or dynamic, and a method that can be used stop the body from rotating (by default, bodies are able to rotate):

```
public void setStatic()
{  bodyDef.type = BodyType.StaticBody;  }

public void setDynamic()
{  bodyDef.type = BodyType.DynamicBody;  }

public void setFixedRotation()
{  bodyDef.fixedRotation = true;  }
```

Following this are methods relating to the body's fixture: methods that set the shape to a circle or a rectangle, and a method to set the density, friction, and restitution all at once. When setting the shape, recall that the pixel dimensions must be scaled to the physics dimensions. Also note that the body positions are set to be the center of the shape. The dimensions of a rectangle are specified using distances from the center:

half the total width and half the total length, similar to how the radius of a circle indicates distance from the center to the boundary.

```
public void setShapeRectangle()
{
    setOriginCenter();
    bodyDef.position.set( (getX() + getOriginX()) / 100, (getY() + getOriginY())/100 );
    PolygonShape rect = new PolygonShape();
    rect.setAsBox( getWidth()/200, getHeight()/200 );
    fixtureDef.shape = rect;
}

public void setShapeCircle()
{
    setOriginCenter();
    bodyDef.position.set( (getX() + getOriginX()) / 100, (getY() + getOriginY())/100 );
    CircleShape circ = new CircleShape();
    circ.setRadius( getWidth()/200 );
    fixtureDef.shape = circ;
}

public void setPhysicsProperties(float density, float friction, float restitution)
{
    fixtureDef.density     = density;
    fixtureDef.friction    = friction;
    fixtureDef.restitution = restitution;
}
```

Next are have a trio of methods that enable the user to set the variables corresponding to maximum speeds:

```
public void setMaxSpeed(float f)
{   maxSpeed = f;   }

public void setMaxSpeedX(float f)
{   maxSpeedX = f;   }

public void setMaxSpeedY(float f)
{   maxSpeedY = f;   }
```

After using these methods to set the various properties of the object, the following method can be used to initialize the Body based on the BodyDef (it will be automatically added to the World), and initialize the Fixture (it will be automatically added to the Body). You can store additional data in the fixture, which may be any type of object; storing a String containing a name for the fixture will be useful in the future when creating bodies with multiple fixtures that need to be identified. You can also store additional data in the body, and here you should store a reference to this Box2DActor, which contains the Body. (This will prove useful later, in the collision-detection code in the main program.)

```
public void initializePhysics(World w)
{
    body = w.createBody(bodyDef);
    Fixture f = body.createFixture(fixtureDef);
    f.setUserData("main");
    body.setUserData(this);
}
```

An accessor method is needed to retrieve the Body of this actor, if it will be necessary to remove the actor from the game later, as this process must include removing the body from the physics simulation.

```
public Body getBody()
{   return body;   }
```

As previously discussed, once the simulation is in progress, the movement of the body can be affected by applying either a force (for a continuous action) or an impulse (for a discrete action). In either case, it should be applied to the center of the body to avoid spinning the object. This is accomplished using the following methods:

```
public void applyForce(Vector2 force)
{   body.applyForceToCenter(force, true);   }

public void applyImpulse(Vector2 impulse)
{   body.applyLinearImpulse(impulse, body.getPosition(), true);   }
```

Next, are a series of methods used to get and set the velocity and speed of the body, used internally when enforcing the maximum speed values (if previously set):

```
public Vector2 getVelocity()
{   return body.getLinearVelocity();   }

public float getSpeed()
{   return getVelocity().len();   }

public void setVelocity(float vx, float vy)
{   body.setLinearVelocity(vx,vy);   }

public void setVelocity(Vector2 v)
{   body.setLinearVelocity(v);   }

public void setSpeed(float s)
{   setVelocity( getVelocity().setLength(s) );   }
```

Following this is the act method, which serves two purposes. First, it will adjust the velocity of the body if it exceeds any of the set maximum values. Second, it will update the actor properties—position and angle—based on the properties of the body. In this process, physics units must be scaled back to pixel units, and the angle of rotation must be converted from radians (used by the body) to degrees (used by the actor).

```
public void act(float dt)
{
    super.act(dt);

    // cap max speeds, if they have been set

    if (maxSpeedX != null)
    {
        Vector2 v = getVelocity();
        v.x = MathUtils.clamp(v.x, -maxSpeedX, maxSpeedX);
        setVelocity(v);
    }
    if (maxSpeedY != null)
    {
        Vector2 v = getVelocity();
        v.y = MathUtils.clamp(v.y, -maxSpeedY, maxSpeedY);
        setVelocity(v);
    }
    if (maxSpeed != null)
    {
        float s = getSpeed();
        if (s > maxSpeed)
            setSpeed(maxSpeed);
    }

    // update image data - position and rotation - based on physics data

    Vector2 center = body.getWorldCenter();
    setPosition( 100*center.x - getOriginX(), 100*center.y - getOriginY() );

    float a = body.getAngle();                      // angle in radians
    setRotation( a * MathUtils.radiansToDegrees );  // convert from radians to degrees
}
```

Finally, a clone method is included that produces a new Box2DActor. However, only the information from the AnimatedActor class is duplicated, because copies of a given object will likely have different starting positions, which affects the initialization of the Body.

```
public Box2DActor clone()
{
    Box2DActor newbie = new Box2DActor();
    newbie.copy( this ); // only copies AnimatedActor data
    return newbie;
}
```

With this new class at your disposal, you are ready to create your physics-based sandbox game!

Jumping Jack: A Physics-Based Sandbox Game

The *Jumping Jack* game will contain a variety of Box2DActor objects: static objects for the ground, walls, and platforms, dynamic objects for the crate and ball, and sensors for the coin objects. Since there are multiple coins in this game, you'll create a Coin class extending the Box2DActor class to simplify the creation and cloning of these objects, as follows:

```java
import com.badlogic.gdx.physics.box2d.World;
public class Coin extends Box2DActor
{
    public Coin()
    {  super();  }

    public void initializePhysics(World world)
    {
        setStatic();
        setShapeCircle();
        fixtureDef.isSensor = true;
        super.initializePhysics(world);
    }

    public Coin clone()
    {
        Coin newbie = new Coin();
        newbie.copy( this );
        return newbie;
    }
}
```

The final, and most complicated object needed in this class is the player, which requires additional functionality beyond that provided by the Box2DActor class, motivating the creation of a class called Player that also extends the Box2DActor class. Platformer-style characters have two basic types of movement: moving to the left and right, and jumping. While moving is relatively straightforward to implement using forces, jumping is surprisingly complicated, since the player can jump only when standing on top of a solid object. The Player class will include a method named isOnGround that indicates when this is the case. To implement this, you'll start by adding a fixture to the player body, set as a sensor and positioned beneath the main fixture. Contact events will be used to keep track of how many solid objects the sensor is overlapping, stored in a variable named groundCount. Provided this number is greater than 0, the bottom of the player is touching a solid object, and isOnGround will return true. The code for the Player class is as follows:

```java
import com.badlogic.gdx.physics.box2d.World;
import com.badlogic.gdx.physics.box2d.Fixture;
import com.badlogic.gdx.physics.box2d.FixtureDef;
import com.badlogic.gdx.physics.box2d.PolygonShape;
import com.badlogic.gdx.math.Vector2;
```

```java
public class Player extends Box2DActor
{
    public int groundCount;
    public Player()
    {
        super();
        groundCount = 0;
    }

    public void adjustGroundCount(int i)
    {  groundCount += i;   }

    public boolean isOnGround()
    {  return (groundCount > 0);   }

    // uses data to initialize object and add to world
    public void initializePhysics(World world)
    {
        // first, perform initialization tasks from Box2DActor class
        super.initializePhysics(world);

        // create additional player-specific fixture
        FixtureDef bottomSensor = new FixtureDef();
        bottomSensor.isSensor = true;
        PolygonShape sensorShape = new PolygonShape();

        // center coordinates of sensor box - offset from body center
        float x = 0;
        float y = -20;
        // dimensions of sensor box
        float w = getWidth() - 8;
        float h = getHeight();
        sensorShape.setAsBox( w/200, h/200, new Vector2(x/200, y/200), 0 );
        bottomSensor.shape = sensorShape;

        // create and attach this new fixture
        Fixture bottomFixture = body.createFixture(bottomSensor);
        bottomFixture.setUserData("bottom");
    }
}
```

Now, you're ready to begin creating the GameScreen class for this project! As usual, you begin with the basics: import statements, and variable and method declarations.

```java
import com.badlogic.gdx.Gdx;
import com.badlogic.gdx.Input.Keys;
import com.badlogic.gdx.graphics.Texture;
import com.badlogic.gdx.graphics.Texture.TextureFilter;
import com.badlogic.gdx.graphics.g2d.Animation;
import com.badlogic.gdx.graphics.g2d.Animation.PlayMode;
import com.badlogic.gdx.math.Vector2;
import java.util.ArrayList;
```

```
import com.badlogic.gdx.physics.box2d.World;
import com.badlogic.gdx.physics.box2d.ContactListener;
import com.badlogic.gdx.physics.box2d.Contact;
import com.badlogic.gdx.physics.box2d.Manifold;
import com.badlogic.gdx.physics.box2d.ContactImpulse;

public class GameScreen extends BaseScreen
{
    private Player player;
    private World world;
    private int coins = 0;
    private ArrayList<Box2DActor> removeList;
    // game world dimensions
    final int mapWidth = 800;
    final int mapHeight = 600;

    public GameScreen(BaseGame g)
    {  super(g);  }

    public void create()
    {     }

    public void update(float dt)
    {     }

}
```

Some of the objects that need be to created repeatedly are the solid objects (ground, walls, and platforms), which motivates another method for the GameScreen class, called addSolid, that largely automates this process:

```
public void addSolid (Texture t, float x, float y, float w, float h)
{
    Box2DActor solid = new Box2DActor();
    t.setFilter(TextureFilter.Linear, TextureFilter.Linear);
    solid.storeAnimation( "default", t );
    solid.setPosition(x,y);
    solid.setSize(w,h);
    mainStage.addActor( solid );
    solid.setStatic();
    solid.setShapeRectangle();
    solid.initializePhysics(world);
}
```

Now let's begin listing the contents of the create method, starting with initializing the World and an ArrayList for removing objects later. You'll also set up a background image and use the addSolid method to create and add the stationary solid objects in the game:

```
world = new World(new Vector2(0, -9.8f), true);
removeList = new ArrayList<Box2DActor>();

// background image
BaseActor bg = new BaseActor();
Texture t = new Texture(Gdx.files.internal("assets/sky.png"));
```

```
bg.setTexture( t );
mainStage.addActor( bg );

// solid objects
Texture groundTex = new Texture(Gdx.files.internal("assets/ground.png"));
Texture dirtTex = new Texture(Gdx.files.internal("assets/dirt.png"));

addSolid( groundTex, 0,0, 800,32 );
addSolid( groundTex, 150,250, 100,32 );
addSolid( groundTex, 282,250, 100,32 );

addSolid( dirtTex, 0,0, 32,600 );
addSolid( dirtTex, 768,0, 32,600 );
```

Next, add the dynamic objects of the game: the (rectangular) crate and the (circular) ball.

```
Box2DActor crate = new Box2DActor();
Texture crateTex = new Texture(Gdx.files.internal("assets/crate.png"));
crateTex.setFilter(TextureFilter.Linear, TextureFilter.Linear);
crate.storeAnimation( "default", crateTex );
crate.setPosition(500, 100);
mainStage.addActor(crate);
crate.setDynamic();
crate.setShapeRectangle();
// set standard density, average friction, small restitution
crate.setPhysicsProperties(1, 0.5f, 0.1f);
crate.initializePhysics(world);

Box2DActor ball = new Box2DActor();
Texture ballTex = new Texture(Gdx.files.internal("assets/ball.png"));
ballTex.setFilter(TextureFilter.Linear, TextureFilter.Linear);
ball.storeAnimation( "default", ballTex );
ball.setPosition(300, 320);
mainStage.addActor(ball);
ball.setDynamic();
ball.setShapeCircle();
// set standard density, small friction, average restitution
ball.setPhysicsProperties(1, 0.1f, 0.5f);
ball.initializePhysics(world);
```

Then create the coin objects: a base coin object, cloned repeatedly for each instance that will be added to the game.

```
Coin baseCoin = new Coin();
Texture coinTex = new Texture(Gdx.files.internal("assets/coin.png"));
coinTex.setFilter(TextureFilter.Linear, TextureFilter.Linear);
baseCoin.storeAnimation( "default", coinTex );

Coin coin1 = baseCoin.clone();
coin1.setPosition(500, 250);
mainStage.addActor(coin1);
coin1.initializePhysics(world);
```

```
Coin coin2 = baseCoin.clone();
coin2.setPosition(550, 250);
mainStage.addActor(coin2);
coin2.initializePhysics(world);

Coin coin3 = baseCoin.clone();
coin3.setPosition(600, 250);
mainStage.addActor(coin3);
coin3.initializePhysics(world);
```

The next step is to initialize the Player object, which includes setting up animations for standing, walking, and jumping. To simplify the creation of an animation from multiple image files, first add the following convenience method to the GameUtils class that will load a series of files (named according to a given convention). This method, called parseImageFiles, is presented here:

```
// creates an Animation from a set of image files
// assumes file name format: fileNamePrefix + N + fileNameSuffix, where 0 <= N < frameCount
public static Animation parseImageFiles(String fileNamePrefix, String fileNameSuffix,
        int frameCount, float frameDuration, PlayMode mode)
{
    TextureRegion[] frames = new TextureRegion[frameCount];

    for (int n = 0; n < frameCount; n++)
    {
        String fileName = fileNamePrefix + n + fileNameSuffix;
        Texture tex = new Texture(Gdx.files.internal(fileName));
        tex.setFilter(TextureFilter.Linear, TextureFilter.Linear);
        frames[n] = new TextureRegion( tex );
    }

    Array<TextureRegion> framesArray = new Array<TextureRegion>(frames);
    return new Animation(frameDuration, framesArray, mode);
}
```

Next, let's return to the GameScreen class to initialize the player and its animations; a plethora of physics properties must be set for the player as well.

```
player = new Player();

Animation walkAnim = GameUtils.parseImageFiles(
        "assets/walk-", ".png", 3, 0.15f, Animation.PlayMode.LOOP_PINGPONG);
player.storeAnimation( "walk", walkAnim );

Texture standTex = new Texture(Gdx.files.internal("assets/stand.png"));
standTex.setFilter(TextureFilter.Linear, TextureFilter.Linear);
player.storeAnimation( "stand", standTex );

Texture jumpTex = new Texture(Gdx.files.internal("assets/jump.png"));
jumpTex.setFilter(TextureFilter.Linear, TextureFilter.Linear);
player.storeAnimation( "jump", jumpTex );
```

```
player.setPosition( 164, 300 );
player.setSize(60,90);
mainStage.addActor(player);
player.setDynamic();
player.setShapeRectangle();
// set standard density, average friction, small restitution
player.setPhysicsProperties(1, 0.5f, 0.1f);
player.setFixedRotation();
player.setMaxSpeedX(2);
player.initializePhysics(world);
```

The final step in the create method is to set up a ContactListener, which will be added to the World object and is used to respond to all collision events (much like an InputListener object is used to respond to user input events). While the World object is running the physics simulation in the update method, if any two fixtures collide, then the ContactListener will handle what should happen next in the game logic.

As it turns out, Contact objects are a little tricky to work with. They store the references to the two Fixture objects that came into contact; these can be retrieved with the Contact class methods getFixtureA and getFixtureB. However, for the purposes of game logic, you want to determine whether these fixtures belong to a certain type of object, and if so, return that object (and if not, return null). This task will be accomplished by a utility method called getContactObject that takes as parameters the Contact object being examined, as well as the Class of the object type being searched for. (Every class in Java has a static field named class that can be used to identify the type of object it is, such as Coin.class or Player.class. For an object whose class is unknown, you can use the getClass method to determine the correct class.) If the Contact object contains a Fixture of a Body corresponding to an Object with the specified class, then the getContactObject method will return a reference to that object.

There will also be an overloaded version of the getContactObject method that additionally has a String parameter corresponding to a name, and returns an Object only when the associated class has the given type *and* the associated fixture has the given name. For these methods to work correctly, the Body user data must store a reference to the associated object, and the Fixture user data must store the name of the fixture. The code that accomplishes these tasks is given next, and should be included in the GameUtils class. First, add the import statement:

```
import com.badlogic.gdx.physics.box2d.Contact;
```

Then add the following methods:

```
public static Object getContactObject(Contact theContact, Class theClass)
{
    Object objA = theContact.getFixtureA().getBody().getUserData();
    Object objB = theContact.getFixtureB().getBody().getUserData();

    if (objA.getClass().equals(theClass) )
        return objA;
    else if (objB.getClass().equals(theClass) )
        return objB;
    else
        return null;
}
```

```
public static Object getContactObject(Contact theContact, Class theClass, String fixtureName)
{
    Object objA = theContact.getFixtureA().getBody().getUserData();
    String nameA = (String)theContact.getFixtureA().getUserData();
    Object objB = theContact.getFixtureB().getBody().getUserData();
    String nameB = (String)theContact.getFixtureB().getUserData();

    if ( objA.getClass().equals(theClass) && nameA.equals(fixtureName) )
        return objA;
    else if ( objB.getClass().equals(theClass) && nameB.equals(fixtureName))
        return objB;
    else
        return null;
}
```

With these utility methods now available, you can now return to the GameScreen class and write an anonymous inner class that implements the ContactListener interface. The methods that must be written are called beginContact, endContact, preSolve, and postSolve. The latter two are not needed for this game, and so aren't covered here. The other two, beginContact and endContact, are quite useful; they are called when a pair of fixtures first come into contact with each other, and when a pair of fixtures cease being in contact with each other, respectively.

The types of contact events that are important to the game are as follows:

- When a Coin object and the "main" fixture of a Player object first make contact, the coin should be added to the removeList. This is handled in the beginContact method.

- If any solid (that is, non-Coin) object and the "bottom" fixture of a Player first make contact, add 1 to the player's ground-counting variable, and set the player's animation to stand. This is also handled in the beginContact method.

- If any solid (that is, non-Coin) object and the "bottom" fixture of a Player leave contact, subtract 1 from the player's ground-counting variable. This is handled in the endContact method.

These tasks are implemented by the following code:

```
world.setContactListener(
    new ContactListener()
    {
        public void beginContact(Contact contact)
        {
            Object objC = GameUtils.getContactObject(contact, Coin.class);
            if (objC != null)
            {
                Object p = GameUtils.getContactObject(contact, Player.class, "main");
                if (p != null)
                {
                    Coin c = (Coin)objC;
                    removeList.add( c );
                }

                return; // avoid possible jumps
            }
```

```
            Object objP = GameUtils.getContactObject(contact, Player.class, "bottom");
            if ( objP != null )
            {
                Player p = (Player)objP;
                p.adjustGroundCount(1);
                p.setActiveAnimation("stand");
            }
        }

        public void endContact(Contact contact)
        {
            Object objC = GameUtils.getContactObject(contact, Coin.class);
            if (objC != null)
                return;
            Object objP = GameUtils.getContactObject(contact, Player.class, "bottom");
            if ( objP != null )
            {
                Player p = (Player)objP;
                p.adjustGroundCount(-1);
            }
        }

        public void preSolve(Contact contact, Manifold oldManifold) { }

        public void postSolve(Contact contact, ContactImpulse impulse) { }

    });
```

At this point, the create method is finished. Because of all the game logic code that is contained in the preceding ContactListener object, the update method is quite short. To start, clear the contents of removeList. Then activate the physics simulation using the step method of the World object, assuming the game is running at 60 frames per second. During the simulation, the ContactListener may be activated and objects may be added to removeList; if so, remove them from their Stage and remove the corresponding Body from the World.[3] Then continuous user input is processed: if the user is pressing the left or right arrow key, a force is applied to move the player in that corresponding direction. The stand and walk animations are set depending on the speed of the player. (Note that if the player's jump animation is playing, the only way to switch to the stand animation is when the player lands on the ground, which was handled by the preceding ContactListener code.)

```
public void update(float dt)
{
    removeList.clear();
    world.step(1/60f, 6, 2);
    for (Box2DActor ba : removeList)
    {
        ba.destroy();
        world.destroyBody( ba.getBody() );
    }
```

---

[3]Similar to previous projects, in which you couldn't remove an object from a list while iterating through the list (necessitating the introduction of removeList), you can't remove a body from a world while the physics simulation is taking place (again necessitating the use of removeList).

```
    if( Gdx.input.isKeyPressed(Keys.LEFT) )
    {
        player.setScale(-1,1);
        player.applyForce( new Vector2(-3.0f, 0) );
    }

    if( Gdx.input.isKeyPressed(Keys.RIGHT) )
    {
        player.setScale(1,1);
        player.applyForce( new Vector2(3.0f, 0) );
    }

    if ( player.getSpeed() > 0.1 && player.getAnimationName().equals("stand") )
        player.setActiveAnimation("walk");
    if ( player.getSpeed() < 0.1 && player.getAnimationName().equals("walk") )
        player.setActiveAnimation("stand");
}
```

Finally, discrete user input—pausing the game, resetting the game, and making the player jump—is processed using the keyDown method:

```
public boolean keyDown(int keycode)
{
    if (keycode == Keys.P)
        togglePaused();

    if (keycode == Keys.R)
        game.setScreen( new GameScreen(game) );

    if (keycode == Keys.SPACE && player.isOnGround() )
    {
        Vector2 jumpVec = new Vector2(0,3);
        player.applyImpulse(jumpVec);
        player.setActiveAnimation("jump");
    }

    return false;
}
```

This completes the code for Jumping Jack. Try out the game—push the crate, kick the ball, and of course, jump around! Note in particular the subtle physics features being simulated: the ball rolls around the screen and bounces off objects, Jack can move both the crate and the ball by pushing one of them when they are next to each other, and Jack can jump extra high from the top of the ball (due to the ball's large restitution value).

Integrating Multiple Components

For the grand finale of this chapter, you will create a project that integrates all of the topics covered: a platformer-style game with particle effects and realistic physics, based on level data stored in a tilemap. In particular, due to the high critical acclaim we anticipate for the release of the previous project, Jumping Jack, in this section, you'll create a sequel called *Jumping Jack 2: Even More Coins*, pictured in Figure 7-17.

Figure 7-17. *The game Jumping Jack 2: Even More Coins*

In BlueJ, you'll start a new project called JumpingJack2. From the original Jumping Jack game, copy over *all* classes except GameScreen, which will be different enough that it will be easier to start from scratch (although *some* parts of the code will be identical, so you may want to keep the code from the previous GameScreen class handy for some copying and pasting later). You also need to copy the ParticleActor class from the Starscape demo. In addition, download the images from the chapter's JumpingJack2/assets folder to your local project assets folder.

Preliminary Setup

First, you'll create a sparkling special effect using the LibGDX Particle Editor, illustrated in Figure 7-18, which will appear every time Jack the Koala collects a coin.

Figure 7-18. *The sparkle particle effect*

To create this effect, start the LibGDX Particle Editor and create a new emitter named **sparkler** (and delete the preloaded example emitter). For variety, in the Image property section, click the Open button and select the file sparkle.png. Set Count Max to 25, Duration to 500, and Emission High to 50. Modify the Size graph to re-create the Sudden Decrease shape. Set Velocity to Active, and set its High range from 20 to 50. Set Angle to Active, and set its High range from 0 to 360. Finally, set the Tint color to orange. Save this emitter to your assets directory with the file name sparkle.pfx (and don't forget to add the pfx suffix, as the editor doesn't automatically add it for you).

Next, you'll set up a tilemap using Tiled. Create a new tilemap that is 20 tiles wide and 10 tiles high; the tiles have width and length 64 pixels. Then load the tileset platform-tiles-64.png (whose tiles are also 64 by 64 pixels). To organize your project into layers, first name the existing layer **Tiles**. Then from the menu bar, choose Layer ➤ Add Image Layer, and name it **Background**. (As you may have guessed, this layer can be used to display an image, and that image will be of the background.) In the Layers panel, right-click the Background layer and select Lower Layer; this moves the Background layer under the Tiles layer, which will be important when you render the tilemap. Finally, add two Object layers; name the first of these **ObjectData** and the second **PhysicsData**.

Now it is time to design and construct the level. First, click the Background layer, and in the Properties panel to the left, an Image field appears, where you can load an image. Instead of typing in a name, you can use the ellipsis button that appears when the field is selected. Select the image named background.png from the assets folder. Next, switch to the Tiles layer, and use the Stamp Brush to design your level. Figure 7-19 illustrates one design, but feel free to modify the layout to your liking.

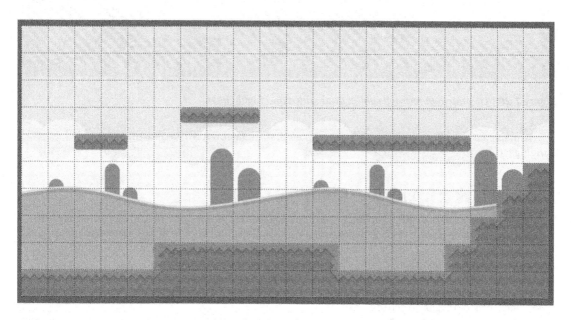

Figure 7-19. *Tilemap layout for Jumping Jack 2*

Next, geometric data needs to be added to the object layers. On the ObjectData layer, add a rectangle to indicate the starting position of the player, and in the Properties panel, name the rectangle **player**. Also on the ObjectData layer, add many rectangles indicating the position of the coin objects, and be sure to name each one of these rectangles **coin**. For convenience, the rectangle objects can be duplicated by right-clicking and selecting Duplicate Object; the new copy will appear directly on top of the original object, and can be dragged to a new position. Finally, on the PhysicsData layer, add rectangles that cover all of the parts of tiles that represent solid surfaces, and add some rectangles around the borders of the tilemap so that the player will not be able to walk past the boundaries of the map (you may need to zoom out to access the region beyond the borders of the tilemap). The addition of these rectangles is illustrated in Figure 7-20, and as before, I have highlighted the rectangles with diagonal stripes in the diagram to make them more visible. When you are finished, save your work to the assets directory with the file name platform-map.tmx.

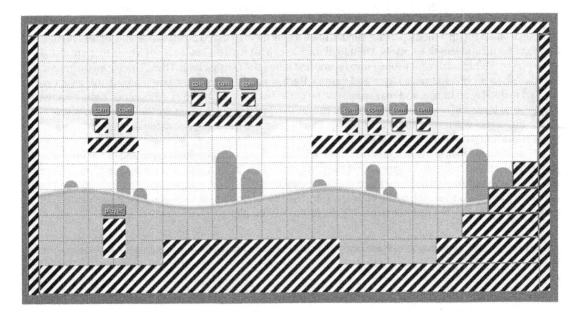

Figure 7-20. *Tilemap with rectangle object data added and highlighted*

With the particle effect and tilemap data completed, you can now move on to writing the code for Jumping Jack 2.

Jumping Jack 2: Even More Coins

With all the foundation laid by the ParticleActor and Box2DActor classes, you're ready to jump right into the code for the GameScreen class. You begin with an astounding number of import statements:

```
import com.badlogic.gdx.Gdx;
import com.badlogic.gdx.Input.Keys;
import com.badlogic.gdx.graphics.Texture;
import com.badlogic.gdx.graphics.GL20;
import com.badlogic.gdx.graphics.Texture.TextureFilter;
import com.badlogic.gdx.graphics.g2d.Animation;
import com.badlogic.gdx.graphics.g2d.Animation.PlayMode;
import com.badlogic.gdx.math.MathUtils;
import com.badlogic.gdx.math.Vector2;
import com.badlogic.gdx.math.Rectangle;
import java.util.ArrayList;
```

```
// box2d imports
import com.badlogic.gdx.physics.box2d.World;
import com.badlogic.gdx.physics.box2d.ContactListener;
import com.badlogic.gdx.physics.box2d.Contact;
import com.badlogic.gdx.physics.box2d.Manifold;
import com.badlogic.gdx.physics.box2d.ContactImpulse;


// tilemap imports
import com.badlogic.gdx.maps.MapObject;
import com.badlogic.gdx.maps.MapObjects;
import com.badlogic.gdx.maps.objects.RectangleMapObject;
import com.badlogic.gdx.maps.objects.PolygonMapObject;
import com.badlogic.gdx.maps.tiled.TiledMap;
import com.badlogic.gdx.maps.tiled.TiledMapRenderer;
import com.badlogic.gdx.maps.tiled.TmxMapLoader;
import com.badlogic.gdx.maps.tiled.renderers.OrthogonalTiledMapRenderer;
import com.badlogic.gdx.graphics.Camera;
import com.badlogic.gdx.graphics.OrthographicCamera;
```

Next are the variable declarations and the necessary methods. There is a Player object and a World to simulate the physics. An ArrayList will store actors to be removed from the game, and a base instance of a ParticleActor will be available for cloning when necessary. There is also a variable to store the tilemap, and objects used for rendering the tilemap.

```
public class GameScreen extends BaseScreen
{
    private Player player;
    private World world;
    private ArrayList<Box2DActor> removeList;
    private ParticleActor baseSparkle;

    TiledMap tiledMap;
    OrthographicCamera tiledCamera;
    TiledMapRenderer tiledMapRenderer;
    int[] backgroundLayer = {0};
    int[] tileLayer       = {1};

    // game world dimensions
    final int mapWidth = 1280; // bigger than before!
    final int mapHeight = 600;

    public GameScreen(BaseGame g)
    {  super(g);  }

    public void create()
    {    }

    public void update(float dt)
    {    }

}
```

There will also be a method named addSolid to generate Box2DActors corresponding to solid objects. However, unlike the version from the original Jumping Jack game, where positions and dimensions had to be calculated by hand, this method is designed to extra the necessary information from a RectangleMapObject from the tilemap data.

```java
public void addSolid(RectangleMapObject rmo)
{
    Rectangle r = rmo.getRectangle();
    Box2DActor solid = new Box2DActor();
    solid.setPosition(r.x, r.y);
    solid.setSize(r.width, r.height);
    solid.setStatic();
    solid.setShapeRectangle();
    solid.initializePhysics(world);
}
```

Next is the code for the create method. First, world and removeList are initialized as usual. A BaseActor is not needed to display the background image, because the tilemap will handle that. The player's animations are initialized immediately, but the player's physics data will not be initialized until after the player's position has been retrieved from the tilemap. Also initialized in this section are the base instance of a Coin object and the sparkle effect for later use.

```java
world = new World(new Vector2(0, -9.8f), true);
removeList = new ArrayList<Box2DActor>();

// background image provided by tilemap

// player
player = new Player();

Animation walkAnim = GameUtils.parseImageFiles(
        "assets/walk-", ".png", 3, 0.15f, Animation.PlayMode.LOOP_PINGPONG);
player.storeAnimation( "walk", walkAnim );

Texture standTex = new Texture(Gdx.files.internal("assets/stand.png"));
standTex.setFilter(TextureFilter.Linear, TextureFilter.Linear);
player.storeAnimation( "stand", standTex );

Texture jumpTex = new Texture(Gdx.files.internal("assets/jump.png"));
jumpTex.setFilter(TextureFilter.Linear, TextureFilter.Linear);
player.storeAnimation( "jump", jumpTex );

player.setSize(60,90);
mainStage.addActor(player);
// set other player properties later...
```

```
// coin
Coin baseCoin = new Coin();
Texture coinTex = new Texture(Gdx.files.internal("assets/coin.png"));
coinTex.setFilter(TextureFilter.Linear, TextureFilter.Linear);
baseCoin.storeAnimation( "default", coinTex );

baseSparkle = new ParticleActor();
baseSparkle.load("assets/sparkler.pfx", "assets/");
```

Next, load the tilemap and initialize the related objects, in the same way as in the Treasure Quest game:

```
// load tilemap
tiledMap = new TmxMapLoader().load("assets/platform-map.tmx");
tiledMapRenderer = new OrthogonalTiledMapRenderer(tiledMap);
tiledCamera = new OrthographicCamera();
tiledCamera.setToOrtho(false,viewWidth,viewHeight);
tiledCamera.update();
```

Iterate over the ObjectData layer of the tilemap to get data pertaining to the player and coin objects:

```
MapObjects objects = tiledMap.getLayers().get("ObjectData").getObjects();
for (MapObject object : objects)
{
    String name = object.getName();
    // all object data assumed to be stored as rectangles
    RectangleMapObject rectangleObject = (RectangleMapObject)object;
    Rectangle r = rectangleObject.getRectangle();

    if ( name.equals("player") )
    {
        player.setPosition( r.x, r.y );
    }
    else if ( name.equals("coin") )
    {
        Coin coin = baseCoin.clone();
        coin.setPosition(r.x, r.y);
        mainStage.addActor(coin);
        coin.initializePhysics(world);
    }
    else
        System.err.println("Unknown tilemap object: " + name);
}
```

Now that the player's position is known, the player's physics-related data can be initialized:

```
player.setDynamic();
player.setShapeRectangle();
player.setPhysicsProperties(1, 0.5f, 0.1f);
player.setMaxSpeedX(2);
player.setFixedRotation();
player.initializePhysics(world);
```

Next, iterate over the PhysicsData layer of the tilemap, and using the preceding addSolid method, initialize the solid objects:

```
objects = tiledMap.getLayers().get("PhysicsData").getObjects();
for (MapObject object : objects)
{
    if (object instanceof RectangleMapObject)
        addSolid( (RectangleMapObject)object );
    else
        System.err.println("Unknown PhysicsData object.");
}
```

Finally, in the create method, the ContactListener needs to be initialized. This code is nearly identical to the corresponding code from the original Jumping Jack game. The only difference is some additional code that spawns a new sparkling particle effect whenever the player makes contact with a coin.

```
world.setContactListener(
    new ContactListener()
    {
        public void beginContact(Contact contact)
        {
            Object objC = GameUtils.getContactObject(contact, Coin.class);
            if (objC != null)
            {
                Object objP = GameUtils.getContactObject(contact, Player.class, "main");
                if (objP != null)
                {
                    Coin c = (Coin)objC;
                    removeList.add( c );
                    ParticleActor sparkle = baseSparkle.clone();
                    sparkle.setPosition(
                        c.getX() + c.getOriginX(), c.getY() + c.getOriginY() );
                    sparkle.start();
                    mainStage.addActor(sparkle);
                }
                return; // avoid possible jumps
            }

            Object objP = GameUtils.getContactObject(contact, Player.class, "bottom");
            if ( objP != null )
            {
                Player p = (Player)objP;
                p.adjustGroundCount(1);
                p.setActiveAnimation("stand");
            }
        }
```

```
        public void endContact(Contact contact)
        {
            Object objC = GameUtils.getContactObject(contact, Coin.class);
            if (objC != null)
                return;

            Object objP = GameUtils.getContactObject(contact, Player.class, "bottom");
            if ( objP != null )
            {
                Player p = (Player)objP;
                p.adjustGroundCount(-1);
            }
        }

        public void preSolve(Contact contact, Manifold oldManifold) { }

        public void postSolve(Contact contact, ContactImpulse impulse) { }
    });
```

The update method and keyDown method are *exactly* the same as they were for the Jumping Jack game, but their code is included again here for the sake of completeness:

```
public void update(float dt)
{
    removeList.clear();
    world.step(1/60f, 6, 2);

    for (Box2DActor ba : removeList)
    {
        ba.destroy();
        world.destroyBody( ba.getBody() );
    }

    if ( Gdx.input.isKeyPressed(Keys.LEFT) )
    {
        player.setScale(-1,1);
        player.applyForce( new Vector2(-3.0f, 0) );
    }

    if ( Gdx.input.isKeyPressed(Keys.RIGHT) )
    {
        player.setScale(1,1);
        player.applyForce( new Vector2(3.0f, 0) );
    }

    if ( player.getSpeed() > 0.1 && player.getAnimationName().equals("stand") )
        player.setActiveAnimation("walk");
    if ( player.getSpeed() < 0.1 && player.getAnimationName().equals("walk") )
        player.setActiveAnimation("stand");
}
```

```java
public boolean keyDown(int keycode)
{
    if (keycode == Keys.P)
        togglePaused();

    if (keycode == Keys.R)
        game.setScreen( new GameScreen(game) );

    if (keycode == Keys.SPACE && player.isOnGround() )
    {
        Vector2 jumpVec = new Vector2(0,3);
        player.applyImpulse(jumpVec);
        player.setActiveAnimation("jump");
    }

    return false;
}
```

Finally, as was the case previously when working with tilemaps, the render method of the BaseScreen class needs to be overridden in order to render the layers of the tilemap in the correct order with respect to the stages. As a final finishing touch, a parallax effect is added to create the illusion of depth (as in the Plane Dodger game): when calculating the x coordinate of the camera for the background layer of the tilemap, reduce its value by a factor of 4, so that as the player walks across the level, the background layer will appear to scroll at one-fourth the speed of the tile layer.

```java
public void render(float dt)
{
    uiStage.act(dt);

    // only pause gameplay events, not UI events
    if ( !isPaused() )
    {
        mainStage.act(dt);
        update(dt);
    }

    // render
    Gdx.gl.glClearColor(0,0,0,1);
    Gdx.gl.glClear(GL20.GL_COLOR_BUFFER_BIT);

    Camera mainCamera = mainStage.getCamera();
    mainCamera.position.x =  player.getX() + player.getOriginX();
    // bound main camera to layout
    mainCamera.position.x = MathUtils.clamp(
        mainCamera.position.x, viewWidth/2,  mapWidth - viewWidth/2);
    mainCamera.update();

    // scroll background more slowly to create parallax effect
    tiledCamera.position.x = mainCamera.position.x/4 + mapWidth/4;
    tiledCamera.position.y = mainCamera.position.y;
```

```
    tiledCamera.update();
    tiledMapRenderer.setView(tiledCamera);
    tiledMapRenderer.render(backgroundLayer);

    tiledCamera.position.x = mainCamera.position.x;
    tiledCamera.position.y = mainCamera.position.y;
    tiledCamera.update();
    tiledMapRenderer.setView(tiledCamera);
    tiledMapRenderer.render(tileLayer);

    mainStage.draw();
    uiStage.draw();
}
```

This completes the code for Jumping Jack 2. Give the game a try, and help Jack collect all those coins!

Summary

In this chapter, you've learned how to create particle effects, tilemaps, and realistic physics using third-party tools and libraries, and you've integrated them into various projects both separately and together. These skills should increase the efficiency of your workflow as a game developer, allowing you to work on larger and more advanced game projects.

CHAPTER 8

Introduction to 3D Graphics

This chapter introduces some of the 3D graphics capabilities of LibGDX. Along the way, you'll learn about the concepts and classes necessary to describe and render a three-dimensional scene. You'll create a simple interactive demo that enables players to control both an object within the scene and the camera viewing the scene. To simplify and streamline this process, you'll adapt some old classes and write some new classes to accomplish the various tasks involved. Finally, you'll create a more sophisticated demo based on 2.5D techniques: a game that renders advanced three-dimensional graphics, while the underlying game play is restricted to a two-dimensional plane.

Exploring 3D Concepts and Classes

As it turns out, all of the previously created games in this book exist in a three-dimensional space. You may have noticed that when setting the position of a camera object, you have x, y, and z components to set. If the x axis and the y axis represent the horizontal and vertical directions on the screen, respectively, then the z axis corresponds to a straight line pointing toward the viewer, perpendicular to the *xy plane*—the plane containing the x and y axes. The camera can be thought of as positioned on the z axis, pointing straight toward the xy plane; all of the game entities have implicitly had their z coordinate set to 0. This configuration is illustrated in Figure 8-1, which shows roughly how the camera sees the Starfish Collector game from previous chapters.

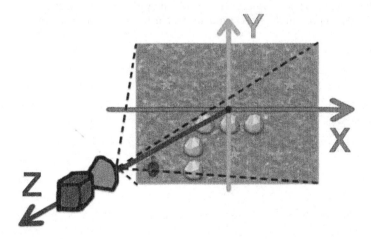

Figure 8-1. *A camera looking down the z axis at the Starfish Collector game*

Our previous projects have relied heavily on the Stage class, which manages the Camera and a Batch object (for rendering purposes). To create 3D scenes, you need the "3D versions" of these objects, provided by the PerspectiveCamera and ModelBatch classes, which are covered in detail next. However, there is no corresponding stage-like object to manage them, and so you will create your own manager class (called Stage3D) in a later section.

To render a scene, you can use one of two types of cameras: an orthographic camera or a perspective camera. (The Stage class uses an OrthographicCamera object for rendering.) The difference between these two is in how they represent, or project, a 3D scene onto a 2D surface such as a computer screen. To illustrate the difference, consider one of the simplest 3D shapes: a cube. Figure 8-2 shows an orthographic projection and a perspective projection of a cube. In an orthogonal projection, if the edges of an object have the same length, then they will be drawn as having the same length in the projection, regardless of their distance from the viewer. This is in contrast to a perspective projection, in which objects with two edges of the same length may appear different in the projection; an edge that is further away from the viewer will appear shorter. This also has the side effect that, if two edges of an object are parallel, then they remain parallel in an orthographic projection, but they appear to converge in a perspective projection. (In a perspective drawing, the point at which all such edges appear to converge is sometimes called the *vanishing point.*)

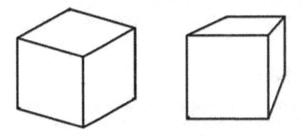

Figure 8-2. *A cube drawn using orthographic projection (left) and perspective projection (right)*

When initializing a PerspectiveCamera object, you have to define the region visible to the camera, which has the shape of a truncated pyramid, or frustum (illustrated in Figure 8-3). This is specified by five parameters: the field of view (an angle that represents how far the camera can see to either side), the width and height of the rectangle onto which the scene is being projected (determined by a Viewport object in LibGDX), and the near and far values (which represent the closest and furthest distances that the camera will include while rendering).

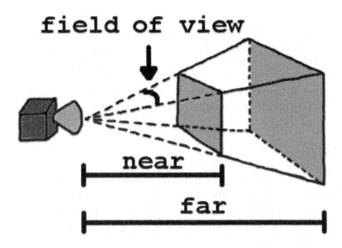

Figure 8-3. *A region visible to a perspective camera; near and far distances are indicated by shaded planes.*

The next new class is ModelBatch. Just as a SpriteBatch object can be used to render two-dimensional Texture objects, ModelBatch is used to render three-dimensional objects. The data needed to describe the appearance of a three-dimensional object is contained in a Model object, which consists of two major components: Mesh and Material. A *mesh* is a collection of vertices, edges, and triangular faces that define the shape of an object. A *material* contains color or texture data that is applied to the mesh, which defines its appearance while rendering. Figure 8-4 contains two images of a teapot: a wireframe representation of the mesh, and its appearance after applying a material. This particular teapot is a classic model called the *Utah teapot*, created by the computer scientist Martin Newell in 1975. Models can be loaded from standard 3D object file formats

Figure 8-4. *The Utah teapot, rendered in wireframe (left) and with material applied (right)*

Models can be created in two ways in LibGDX. Using the ModelLoader class, a model can be loaded from standard 3D object file formats (such as Wavefront, typically indicated by the .obj file extension), which may also contain references to image files used by the accompanying material. Alternatively, some basic shapes (such as spheres and boxes) can be generated at runtime using the ModelBuilder class. You will see examples of both of these approaches over the course of this chapter.

Finally, in order to give 3D models a realistic appearance, the effects of light sources need to be considered. In fact, if lights are not added to a scene, you will not be able to see anything at all! Lights are managed by the Environment class. The two types of lighting effects you will use are ambient light and directional light. *Ambient light* provides overall illumination, and shines equally from all directions. Typically, it is important to include ambient light in a scene so that even the sides facing away from a light source will still be somewhat visible (although this amount may vary depending on the type of location you are simulating). A *directional light* is used to simulate light shining throughout the scene in a particular direction. This helps provide a sense of depth in a scene, in particular, allowing you to distinguish between different faces when an object's material consists of just a single color.

Figure 8-5, illustrates these effects with two renderings of a cube. In the image on the left, the scene contains only ambient light, which makes it difficult to see all the edges of the cube. The image on the right has a directional light, primarily aimed toward the left (and thus the right side of the cube appears brightest).

Creating a Minimal 3D Demo

Using the previously mentioned classes, you are now ready for a minimal code example that renders a cube in LibGDX. The result is a single blue box, oriented as on the right side of Figure 8-5. You begin by creating a new project in BlueJ called Project3D. You don't need to copy any classes or assets to this project at this time. Rather than starting with the Game class as usual (which implements the ApplicationListener interface methods), you'll make this example self-contained and instead implement the interface yourself.

Figure 8-5. *A cube illuminated with ambient light only (left), and directional light added (right)*

First is the core code: import statements, variable declarations (those that are referenced in multiple methods), and the methods required by the interface. As usual, the create method is used to initialize objects, while the render method handles the game loop; the code for each of these methods is presented in detail later. (The other methods required by the interface aren't fundamental to this example, and so are not discussed later.)

```
import com.badlogic.gdx.ApplicationListener;
import com.badlogic.gdx.Gdx;
import com.badlogic.gdx.graphics.GL20;
import com.badlogic.gdx.graphics.Color;
import com.badlogic.gdx.graphics.PerspectiveCamera;
import com.badlogic.gdx.graphics.VertexAttributes.Usage;
import com.badlogic.gdx.graphics.g3d.Environment;
import com.badlogic.gdx.graphics.g3d.attributes.ColorAttribute;
import com.badlogic.gdx.graphics.g3d.environment.DirectionalLight;
import com.badlogic.gdx.graphics.g3d.utils.ModelBuilder;
import com.badlogic.gdx.graphics.g3d.Model;
import com.badlogic.gdx.graphics.g3d.ModelBatch;
import com.badlogic.gdx.graphics.g3d.ModelInstance;
import com.badlogic.gdx.graphics.g3d.Material;
import com.badlogic.gdx.math.Vector3;
```

```
public class TheTest implements ApplicationListener
{
        public Environment environment;
        public PerspectiveCamera camera;
        public ModelBatch modelBatch;
        public ModelInstance boxInstance;

        public void create() {  }

        public void render() {  }

        public void dispose() {  }

        public void resize(int width, int height) {  }

        public void pause() {  }

        public void resume() {  }
}
```

The create method begins with initializing the Environment, and adding a parameter (a subclass of the Attribute class) that defines the color of the ambient light in the scene. In general, shades of gray are used for lights (rather than, say, colors such as yellow or blue) so that your scene will not be tinted with unexpected colors. Then an instance of a DirectionalLight is created, using a brighter shade of gray, and its direction is specified (using a Vector3 object) to be primarily to the left and downward; after configuring its parameters, the light is added to the environment. A PerspectiveCamera is then initialized, with a field of view of 67 degrees, and with near and far visibility set to 0.1 and 1000, respectively (these values have been chosen to guarantee that the view area contains the object you will add to the scene). The camera's position is set, and the location it should initially be looking toward is specified via the lookAt method. Finally, a ModelBatch object is initialized, which will be used later when rendering. These steps "set the scene" and are accomplished with the following code:

```
environment = new Environment();
environment.set( new ColorAttribute(ColorAttribute.AmbientLight, 0.4f, 0.4f, 0.4f, 1f) );

DirectionalLight dLight = new DirectionalLight();
Color      lightColor = new Color(0.75f, 0.75f, 0.75f, 1);
Vector3  lightVector = new Vector3(-1.0f, -0.75f, -0.25f);
dLight.set( lightColor, lightVector );
environment.add( dLight ) ;

camera = new PerspectiveCamera(67, Gdx.graphics.getWidth(), Gdx.graphics.getHeight());
camera.near = 0.1f;
camera.far  = 1000f;
camera.position.set(10f, 10f, 10f);
camera.lookAt(0,0,0);
camera.update();

modelBatch = new ModelBatch();
```

The next task is to create instances of models to add to your scene. For the sake of simplicity in this example, you will use the createBox method of the ModelBuilder class to construct a cube. You must also create a Material to give the cube its appearance onscreen; here, a solid blue diffuse color is used. (*Diffuse* indicates the apparent color of the object when illuminated by pure white light.)

You must also determine what types of data each vertex of the model should contain: in every case, vertices should store a position, but for this example, they also store color data and a vector (called the *normal vector*) that is used to determine how light reflects off an object, thus providing shading effects. Each of these attributes has a corresponding constant value defined in the Usage class; position data corresponds to Usage.Position, color data corresponds to Usage.ColorPacked, normal vector data corresponds to Usage.Normal, and so forth. When a combination of this data is needed, a value is generated by adding together the constant values for each of the desired attributes. The resulting value is passed as a parameter to the createBox method.

You also need to decide on the dimensions of the box itself. Because of the scale used by many modeling programs, these values are often in the range from 1 to 10, and so you should use similar ranges of values when creating objects with the ModelBuilder class. After creating the Model (which you can think of as a template object), a ModelInstance is initialized. This object contains a copy of the information from the model, as well as a transformation matrix that stores position, rotation, and scaling data for this particular instance. The following code performs all these tasks:

```
ModelBuilder modelBuilder = new ModelBuilder();

Material boxMaterial = new Material();
boxMaterial.set( ColorAttribute.createDiffuse(Color.BLUE) );

int usageCode = Usage.Position + Usage.ColorPacked + Usage.Normal;

Model boxModel = modelBuilder.createBox( 5, 5, 5, boxMaterial, usageCode );
boxInstance = new ModelInstance(boxModel);
```

Finally, the render method is given, which is where all the phases of the game loop happen. In this case, the program consists of a static scene, so there is no user input to process nor updating tasks to be done—just rendering to perform. The code for this method should appear relatively familiar. One difference is that the glClear function also needs to erase the depth information generated during the previous render, since the distance from the camera to each object in the scene may change if the camera moves around, in which case the depth values will need to be recalculated. Another difference is that the ModelBatch takes the PerspectiveCamera as input in its begin method. The corresponding code is as follows:

```
Gdx.gl.glClearColor(1,1,1,1);
Gdx.gl.glViewport(0, 0, Gdx.graphics.getWidth(), Gdx.graphics.getHeight());
Gdx.gl.glClear( GL20.GL_COLOR_BUFFER_BIT | GL20.GL_DEPTH_BUFFER_BIT );

modelBatch.begin(camera);
modelBatch.render( boxInstance, environment );
modelBatch.end();
```

As usual, you'll also need a launcher-style class, as shown here:

```
import com.badlogic.gdx.backends.lwjgl.LwjglApplication;
import com.badlogic.gdx.backends.lwjgl.LwjglApplicationConfiguration;
public class Launcher1
{
    public static void main ()
    {
        LwjglApplicationConfiguration config = new LwjglApplicationConfiguration();
        config.width = 800;
        config.height = 600;
        TheTest myProgram = new TheTest();
        LwjglApplication launcher = new LwjglApplication( myProgram, config );
    }
}
```

At this point, you should try out the code. Feel free to make some modifications and rerun the code to see the effects of your changes. For example, you could alter the color of the cube, the direction of the light source, or the location of the camera.

Re-creating the Actor/Stage Framework

To facilitate and accelerate the development of future projects, in this section you'll write some classes that function similarly to the BaseActor and Stage classes, but instead store data structures and methods useful for three-dimensional graphics. For convenience, you'll continue adding code to the previously created project, which was called Project3D.

The BaseActor3D Class

To begin, recall that the Actor class stored transformation data (position, rotation, and scale) and methods to get, set, and change these values. All Actor objects contained an act method, which could be used to update their internal state, and a draw method, which the actor could use to render itself with a given Batch object. You then wrote an extension of the Actor class, called the BaseActor class, which additionally stored a Texture, a Polygon for collision detection, and related methods. Here the BaseActor3D class will be presented, which will provide similar functionality in a 3D setting.

Some of the most complicated underlying concepts in 3D graphics are the mathematical structures used to store the transformation data. I won't go into great detail here,[1] but for this example, it's important to know what the objects are and how to use their associated methods.

---

[1] For additional information, two excellent books about the mathematical details of 3D graphics are *3D Math Primer for Graphics and Game Development* by Fletcher Dunn and Ian Parberry (A K Peters/CRC Press, 2011), and *Mathematics for 3D Game Programming and Computer Graphics* by Eric Lengyel (Cengage Learning PTR, 2011).

The transformation data for a ModelInstance object is stored in its transform field as a Matrix4 object: a four-by-four grid of numbers. From this object, you can extract a Vector3 that contains the position of the object. You can also extract another Vector3 that contains the scaling factor in each direction (initialized to 1 in all directions, which results in no change in the default size). The transformation also stores the orientation of the model, which *cannot* be stored with a single number (in contrast to the rotation value of an Actor), because an object in three-dimensional space can be rotated any amount around any combination of the x, y, and z axes. For many technical reasons (such as computation, performance, and avoiding a phenomena known as *gimbal lock*[2]), an object called a Quaternion (corresponding to a mathematical object of the same name) is used to store orientation data. For convenience, rather than work with the Matrix4 directly, you'll maintain separate objects to store the position, rotation, and scale data for each BaseActor3D object, and combine them into a Matrix4 and store it in the ModelInstance when needed.

The next code listing presents the core of the BaseActor3D class: import statements, variable declarations, and the fundamental methods. This first set of methods includes the constructor; a method to set the ModelInstance for this actor; the calculateTransform method to combine the position, rotation, and scale data into a Matrix4; the act method to update the transformation data of the model instance; and the draw method to render the model instance using the supplied ModelBatch and Environment.

```
import com.badlogic.gdx.graphics.g3d.Environment;
import com.badlogic.gdx.graphics.g3d.ModelBatch;
import com.badlogic.gdx.graphics.g3d.ModelInstance;
import com.badlogic.gdx.graphics.g3d.Material;
import com.badlogic.gdx.graphics.g3d.attributes.ColorAttribute;
import com.badlogic.gdx.graphics.Color;
import com.badlogic.gdx.math.Vector3;
import com.badlogic.gdx.math.Quaternion;
import com.badlogic.gdx.math.Matrix4;

public class BaseActor3D
{
    private ModelInstance modelData;
    private final Vector3 position;
    private final Quaternion rotation;
    private final Vector3 scale;

    public BaseActor3D()
    {
        modelData = null;
        position  = new Vector3(0,0,0);
        rotation  = new Quaternion();
        scale     = new Vector3(1,1,1);
    }

    public void setModelInstance(ModelInstance m)
    {  modelData = m;  }
```

---

[2]When using three values to represent the rotations of an object around three axes, *gimbal lock* refers to the problem that occurs when an object is in one of a few particular orientations and two axes of rotation line up, making it impossible for the object to rotate in certain ways while in the given orientation.

```
public Matrix4 calculateTransform()
{  return new Matrix4(position, rotation, scale);  }

public void act(float dt)
{  modelData.transform.set( calculateTransform() );  }

public void draw(ModelBatch batch, Environment env)
{  batch.render(modelData, env);  }

}
```

Next are a variety of methods related to the position variable: get and set methods, and methods to add values to the current position coordinates. For convenience, this code includes overloaded variations of the methods that allow either a Vector3 or individual float inputs to be used.

```
public Vector3 getPosition()
{  return position;  }

public void setPosition(Vector3 v)
{  position.set(v);  }

public void setPosition(float x, float y, float z)
{  position.set(x,y,z);  }

public void addPosition(Vector3 v)
{  position.add(v);  }

public void addPosition(float x, float y, float z)
{  addPosition( new Vector3(x,y,z) );  }
```

Next, let's discuss the rotation abilities of these actors. For simplicity, you're going to limit the actor to "turning" left and right, which you can more formally define as rotating around the y-axis, which points upward in this 3D world, as illustrated in Figure 8-1.[3] We will refer to this as the *turn angle*.[4] There will be methods to get, set, and adjust this value, each of which are implemented using methods from the Quaternion class.

```
public float getTurnAngle()
{  return rotation.getAngleAround(0,-1,0);  }

public void setTurnAngle(float degrees)
{  rotation.set( new Quaternion(Vector3.Y,degrees) );  }

public void turn(float degrees)
{  rotation.mul( new Quaternion(Vector3.Y,-degrees) );  }
```

---

[3]In theory, this choice of the y axis as the "up" direction is somewhat arbitrary, as you could orient yourself in the game world so that any axis corresponds to the up direction.

[4]The amount of rotation around the upward-pointing axis is also called the *yaw* angle. Similarly, the rotation around the sideways-pointing axis (the motion from tilting your head up and down) is called the *pitch* angle, and the rotation around the forward-pointing axis (the motion from tilting your head to the left and to the right) is called the *roll* angle.

Also, methods must be written that enable an actor to move in directions relative to its current orientation. When a BaseActor3D is first initialized, it will be assumed that the forward direction is represented by the vector (0, 0, –1), since the initial position of the camera will have a positive z coordinate, and the actor will be facing away from the camera. Similarly, the initial upward direction is the vector (0, 1, 0), and the rightward direction is the vector (1, 0, 0). After the actor has been rotated, the relative forward, upward, and rightward directions can be determined by transforming these original vectors by the actor's current rotation. Then to move a given distance in one of these relative directions, you can scale the corresponding vector by the desired distance, and add the result to the current position. The methods that enable the actor to move in these ways are given here:

```
public void moveForward(float dist)
{  addPosition( rotation.transform( new Vector3(0,0,-1) ).scl( dist ) );  }

public void moveUp(float dist)
{  addPosition( rotation.transform( new Vector3(0,1,0) ).scl( dist ) );  }

public void moveRight(float dist)
{  addPosition( rotation.transform( new Vector3(1,0,0) ).scl( dist ) );  }
```

Finally, a few convenience methods will be included. First is setColor, which can be used to change the color of the material belonging to this particular model instance. In addition are copy and clone methods, to facilitate the creation of additional BaseActor3D objects from a given template instance at a later time.

```
public void setColor(Color c)
{
    for (Material m : modelData.materials)
        m.set( ColorAttribute.createDiffuse(c) );
}

public BaseActor3D clone()
{
    BaseActor3D newbie = new BaseActor3D();
    newbie.copy(this);
    return newbie;
}

public void copy(BaseActor3D orig)
{
    this.modelData = new ModelInstance(orig.modelData);
    this.position.set( orig.position );
    this.rotation.set( orig.rotation );
    this.scale.set( orig.scale );
}
```

This completes the BaseActor3D class—for now. A later section discusses collision detection, and adds the associated variables and methods. At present, let's turn our attention to writing a complementary class that can be used to manage all these actors: the Stage3D class.

The Stage3D Class

Recall that the LibGDX Stage object handles rendering tasks (using its internal Camera and Batch objects), and manages a list of Actor objects. There are also act and draw methods in the Stage class, which call the act and draw methods of all attached actors. You will create similar functionality with the Stage3D class. First, the core of the class is presented. After the import statements, the variables required for rendering are declared: Environment, PerspectiveCamera, and ModelBatch. In the constructor, you basically copy the code used to initialize these objects from the previous example. An ArrayList is declared to store the BaseActor3D objects, and is initialized in the constructor.

```java
import com.badlogic.gdx.Gdx;
import com.badlogic.gdx.graphics.Color;
import com.badlogic.gdx.math.Vector3;
import com.badlogic.gdx.graphics.PerspectiveCamera;
import com.badlogic.gdx.graphics.g3d.Environment;
import com.badlogic.gdx.graphics.g3d.ModelBatch;
import com.badlogic.gdx.graphics.g3d.attributes.ColorAttribute;
import com.badlogic.gdx.graphics.g3d.environment.DirectionalLight;
import java.util.ArrayList;

public class Stage3D
{
    private Environment environment;
    private PerspectiveCamera camera;
    private final ModelBatch modelBatch;
    private ArrayList<BaseActor3D> actorList;

    public Stage3D()
    {
        environment = new Environment();
        environment.set(new ColorAttribute(ColorAttribute.AmbientLight, 0.7f, 0.7f, 0.7f, 1));

        DirectionalLight dLight = new DirectionalLight();
        Color lightColor = new Color(0.9f, 0.9f, 0.9f, 1);
        Vector3 lightVector = new Vector3(-1.0f, -0.75f, -0.25f);
        dLight.set( lightColor, lightVector );
        environment.add( dLight ) ;

        camera = new PerspectiveCamera(67, Gdx.graphics.getWidth(), Gdx.graphics.getHeight());
        camera.position.set(10f, 10f, 10f);
        camera.lookAt(0,0,0);
        camera.near = 0.01f;
        camera.far = 1000f;
        camera.update();

        modelBatch = new ModelBatch();

        actorList = new ArrayList<BaseActor3D>();
    }
}
```

Next, are the act and draw methods, which invoke the corresponding methods on all the BaseActor3D objects contained in the ArrayList. In addition, the camera is updated in the act method.

```
public void act(float dt)
{
    camera.update();
    for (BaseActor3D ba : actorList)
        ba.act(dt);
}

public void draw()
{
    modelBatch.begin(camera);
    for (BaseActor3D ba : actorList)
        ba.draw(modelBatch, environment);
    modelBatch.end();
}
```

There are methods to add and remove actors, given by the following code:

```
public void addActor(BaseActor3D ba)
{  actorList.add( ba );  }

public void removeActor(BaseActor3D ba)
{  actorList.remove( ba );  }
```

The final part of this class is an extensive set of methods to adjust the camera. First are the methods to set the camera position, and to move the camera by a given amount; these values may be specified by either a Vector3 object or three float values:

```
public void setCameraPosition(float x, float y, float z)
{  camera.position.set(x,y,z);  }

public void setCameraPosition(Vector3 v)
{  camera.position.set(v);  }

public void moveCamera(float x, float y, float z)
{  camera.position.add(x,y,z);  }

public void moveCamera(Vector3 v)
{  camera.position.add(v);  }
```

Next, building on these methods are additional methods that move the camera relative to its current position. A Camera object stores two internal Vector3 objects: direction, which determines where the camera is currently facing, and up, which determines the direction that should be oriented toward the top of the screen. When moving the camera forward and backward in this program, the camera should maintain a constant height (even if the camera is tilted at an angle), and so the y component of the vector direction can be set to 0 in order to yield a vector that moves you forward in this way. Once the vector has been determined, it needs to be scaled by the distance you want the camera to travel, and then the vector should be added to the camera's current position via the moveCamera function. For moving to the left and right, you will similarly discard the y component of the vector; to transform the direction vector into a vector pointing to the right, interchange the x and z values and negate the z value, as illustrated by the example in Figure 8-6. In this picture, keep in mind that the values displayed refer to the change in direction represented by each of the vectors.

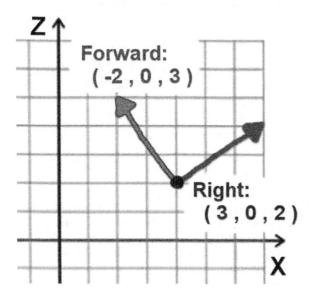

Figure 8-6. *Converting a forward-facing vector to a rightward-facing vector*

Moving the camera upward is a straightforward task. In this case, movement will always be in the direction of the y axis and *not* the camera's up vector, since when the camera is tilted, its up vector will no longer be pointing in the same orientation as the y axis. The methods for moving the camera in these ways are as follows:

```
public void moveCameraForward(float dist)
{
    Vector3 forward = new Vector3(camera.direction.x, 0, camera.direction.z).nor();
    moveCamera( forward.scl( dist ) );
}

public void moveCameraRight(float dist)
{
    Vector3 right = new Vector3(camera.direction.z, 0, -camera.direction.x).nor();
    moveCamera( right.scl( dist ) );
}

public void moveCameraUp(float dist)
{  moveCamera( 0,dist,0 );  }
```

Functionality should also be provided for rotating the camera, and once again, restricting the types of possible camera movement will make the navigation easier for the user to visualize. As with BaseActor3D objects, the camera will be able to turn to the left and right, which corresponds to rotating it around the y axis. In addition, it would be convenient to be able to tilt the camera up and down to look higher and lower. This can be done by determining the vector that points to the right, as before, and then rotating the direction vector of the camera around the vector pointing to the right. These two methods, turnCamera and tiltCamera, are given here:

```
public void turnCamera(float angle)
{   camera.rotate( Vector3.Y, -angle );  }

public void tiltCamera(float angle)
{
    Vector3 right = new Vector3(camera.direction.z, 0, -camera.direction.x);
    camera.direction.rotate(right, angle);
}
```

Finally, it is important to be able to orient the camera to look at a particular position. The is accomplished with a camera method called lookAt, but this method may have the undesired result of tilting the camera to the left or right, making the horizon no longer level, which can be disorienting to the player. So after calling the camera's lookAt method, the camera's up axis needs to be reset to the direction of the y axis to correct this problem; this method will be called setCameraDirection. As before, this method will be overloaded to take either a Vector3 or three float values as input.

```
public void setCameraDirection(Vector3 v)
{
    camera.lookAt(v);
    camera.up.set(0,1,0);
}

public void setCameraDirection(float x, float y, float z)
{   setCameraDirection( new Vector3(x,y,z) );   }
```

This is all the functionality you'll need for the Stage3D class. You're now ready to move on to using these classes to create your first interactive 3D demo.

Creating an Interactive 3D Demo

This section presents an interactive demo inspired by Figure 8-1. This demo consists of a screenshot of the Starfish Collector game on a flattened box shape, and cubes with colored crate textures to represent the origin of the scene and the directions of the x, y, and z axes. You will include a cube textured with six images that the user can turn and move in any direction. Last of all, you will enable the user to turn, tilt, and move the camera in any direction. Figure 8-7 shows this demo in action.

Figure 8-7. *An interactive 3D demo*

Continuing with the Project3D project, add the most recent versions of the BaseGame and BaseScreen classes; the BaseGame class you'll be able to use without modification, while the BaseScreen class will require a few changes to incorporate the Stage3D class in place of one of its Stage objects. You'll also need a launcher-style class, and a class extending the BaseGame class, as you've had in previous chapters; feel free to copy any of these and modify their contents as needed. In addition, copy all the files from this chapter's source code assets directory to your project's local assets directory. (Although some of these files will not be needed until the project following this one, it is convenient to copy them all over at the same time.)

Recall that in our minimal 3D rendering example at the beginning of this chapter, you created the box shape by using the ModelBuilder class. In this example, you will repeatedly need to create cubes with textures attached. To avoid writing redundant code and to simplify the process of creating materials (containing both textures and colors) and applying them to models, you'll create a utility class called ModelUtils that includes static helper functions. This is similar in spirit to the GameUtils class from previous projects, except that instead of Animation-creating methods, it will be devoted to ModelInstance-creating methods. The first part of the new ModelUtils class is provided next. The createBox method contains code similar to that used to create a box in the minimal example presented at the beginning of this chapter. The main difference is that the Material created for the model instance in this method may also contain a Texture. However, either the Texture or Color parameters may be passed in as null, in which case the corresponding attribute will not be added to the material.

```
import com.badlogic.gdx.graphics.Color;
import com.badlogic.gdx.graphics.Texture;
import com.badlogic.gdx.graphics.VertexAttributes.Usage;
import com.badlogic.gdx.graphics.g3d.Model;
import com.badlogic.gdx.graphics.g3d.ModelBatch;
import com.badlogic.gdx.graphics.g3d.ModelInstance;
```

```
import com.badlogic.gdx.graphics.g3d.attributes.ColorAttribute;
import com.badlogic.gdx.graphics.g3d.attributes.TextureAttribute;
import com.badlogic.gdx.graphics.g3d.Material;
import com.badlogic.gdx.graphics.g3d.utils.ModelBuilder;
import com.badlogic.gdx.graphics.g3d.utils.MeshBuilder;
import com.badlogic.gdx.graphics.g3d.utils.MeshPartBuilder;
import com.badlogic.gdx.graphics.GL20;
import com.badlogic.gdx.graphics.Mesh;
import com.badlogic.gdx.math.Matrix4;
import com.badlogic.gdx.math.Vector3;
import com.badlogic.gdx.math.Quaternion;

public class ModelUtils
{
    public static ModelBuilder modelBuilder = new ModelBuilder();

    public static ModelInstance createBox( float xSize, float ySize, float zSize,
            Texture t, Color c )
    {
        Material boxMaterial = new Material();
        if (t != null)
            boxMaterial.set( TextureAttribute.createDiffuse(t) );
        if (c != null)
            boxMaterial.set( ColorAttribute.createDiffuse(c) );

        int usageCode = Usage.Position + Usage.ColorPacked
                        + Usage.Normal + Usage.TextureCoordinates;

        Model boxModel = modelBuilder.createBox(xSize, ySize, zSize, boxMaterial,
        usageCode);
        Vector3 position = new Vector3(0,0,0);

        ModelInstance box = new ModelInstance(boxModel, position);
        return box;
    }
}
```

This demo also contain a unit cube that can be moved by the user. To make it simpler to see how the cube is oriented (which side is the front, which side is the back, and so forth) it would be convenient to be able to apply a different texture to each side. However, there is no method in the ModelBuilder class to automate such a construction. Writing such a method is a long and complicated process, as you need to specify coordinates for the vertices to create six separate square meshes, determine normal vectors for lighting purposes, assign a texture to each of the squares, and combine these six meshes into a single mesh for a single model. A method called createCubeTexture6 provided in the chapter's source code for the ModelUtils class accomplishes this task, but as this method is rather long, technical, and unnecessary for the functionality of this demo (it simply provides a different appearance for the cube), I will not include the code or any further discussion of this method here. When creating the user-controlled cube, you may choose whether to use the createBox or createCubeTexture6 method to generate the model instance used for this object; if you choose the latter option, you may copy this method from the source code as described previously.

The final change you need to make to this framework involves incorporating the Stage3D class into the BaseScreen class. Begin by removing all lines of code that involve the Stage object mainStage, except for the line involving the input multiplexer, from which only the mainStage parameter needs to be removed. (You can keep uiStage, because even three-dimensional games typically have two-dimensional user interfaces.) Then add a new variable declaration to the class:

```
protected Stage3D mainStage3D;
```

Next, in the constructor method, you need to initialize this variable with the following line:

```
mainStage3D = new Stage3D();
```

The greatest number of changes occur in the render method. You must insert code to call the act and draw methods of mainStage3D (just as you previously did for mainStage). In addition, the depth buffer must be cleared in the glClear method, and the rendering area for mainStage3D must be set by using the glViewport method (since a Viewport object will not be incorporated into the Stage3D object to manage this task). The final form of the render method is as follows:

```
public void render(float dt)
{
    uiStage.act(dt);

    if ( !isPaused() )
    {
        update(dt);
        mainStage3D.act(dt);
    }

    Gdx.gl.glClearColor(0.5f,0.5f,0.5f,1);
    Gdx.gl.glClear(GL20.GL_COLOR_BUFFER_BIT + GL20.GL_DEPTH_BUFFER_BIT);
    Gdx.gl.glViewport(0, 0, Gdx.graphics.getWidth(), Gdx.graphics.getHeight());

    mainStage3D.draw();
    uiStage.draw();
}
```

Finally, you're ready to write a class to run your interactive 3D demo, which you will call DemoScreen. You begin by writing the core of the class, as usual:

```
import com.badlogic.gdx.Gdx;
import com.badlogic.gdx.Input.Keys;
import com.badlogic.gdx.graphics.Texture;
import com.badlogic.gdx.graphics.Color;
import com.badlogic.gdx.graphics.Texture.TextureFilter;
import com.badlogic.gdx.graphics.g3d.ModelInstance;

public class DemoScreen extends BaseScreen
{
    BaseActor3D player;
```

```
    public DemoScreen(BaseGame g)
    {  super(g);  }

    public void create()
    {     }

    public void update(float dt)
    {     }
}
```

The player is the only object that will be accessed in both the create and update methods (other than the mainStage3D object, which was already declared by the BaseScreen class). All the other game entities will be declared and initialized within the create method. These other entities include a thin box used to display the image of the Starfish Collector game, and variously colored cubes with a crate texture applied. At the end of the create method, you also set the position of the camera. The complete code for this method is as follows:

```
BaseActor3D screen = new BaseActor3D();
Texture screenTex = new Texture(Gdx.files.internal("assets/starfish-collector.png"), true);
screenTex.setFilter( TextureFilter.Linear, TextureFilter.Linear );
ModelInstance screenInstance = ModelUtils.createBox(16, 12, 0.1f, screenTex, null);
screen.setModelInstance(screenInstance);
mainStage3D.addActor(screen);

Texture texCrate = new Texture(Gdx.files.internal("assets/crate.jpg"), true);

BaseActor3D marker0 = new BaseActor3D();
ModelInstance modCrate0 = ModelUtils.createBox(1,1,1, texCrate, Color.PURPLE);
marker0.setModelInstance(modCrate0);
marker0.setPosition(0,0,0);
mainStage3D.addActor(marker0);

BaseActor3D markerX = marker0.clone();
markerX.setColor(Color.RED);
markerX.setPosition(5,0,0);
mainStage3D.addActor(markerX);

BaseActor3D markerY = marker0.clone();
markerY.setColor(Color.GREEN);
markerY.setPosition(0,5,0);
mainStage3D.addActor(markerY);

BaseActor3D markerZ = marker0.clone();
markerZ.setColor(Color.BLUE);
markerZ.setPosition(0,0,5);
mainStage3D.addActor(markerZ);

player = new BaseActor3D();
// alternatively to using the createCubeTexture6 method,
//    you can use create a model instance for the player object using the code:
//    ModelInstance testModel = ModelUtils.createBox(1,1,1, texCrate, Color.YELLOW);
```

```
Texture[] texSides = {
        new Texture(Gdx.files.internal("assets/xneg.png")),
        new Texture(Gdx.files.internal("assets/xpos.png")),
        new Texture(Gdx.files.internal("assets/yneg.png")),
        new Texture(Gdx.files.internal("assets/ypos.png")),
        new Texture(Gdx.files.internal("assets/zneg.png")),
        new Texture(Gdx.files.internal("assets/zpos.png"))  };

ModelInstance testModel = ModelUtils.createCubeTexture6(texSides);
player.setModelInstance(testModel);
player.setPosition(0,1,8);
mainStage3D.addActor(player);

mainStage3D.setCameraPosition(3,4,10);
mainStage3D.setCameraDirection(0,0,0);
```

Finally, there is the update method to consider, which processes *lots* of potential player input. The player is controlled using the keyboard keys W/A/S/D, which correspond to moving forward/left/backward/right, a standard configuration in many computer games. To this standard, you also add the R and F keys for moving up and down (which we think of as the Rise and Fall directions). You also use the Q and E keys to turn left and right (which also seems memorable because these keys are positioned above the keys for moving left and right). The camera can be controlled in the same way, using the same keys, when the Shift key is being pressed simultaneously. The camera can also be tilted upward and downward using the T and G keys (which you can remember with the mnemonic words *Top* and *Ground*). The following is the code that accomplishes all of these tasks, which as mentioned previously, should be included in the update method:

```
float speed = 3.0f;
float rotateSpeed = 45.0f;

if ( !(Gdx.input.isKeyPressed(Keys.SHIFT_LEFT)
        || Gdx.input.isKeyPressed(Keys.SHIFT_RIGHT)) )
{
    if ( Gdx.input.isKeyPressed(Keys.W) )
        player.moveForward( speed * dt );
    if ( Gdx.input.isKeyPressed(Keys.S) )
        player.moveForward( -speed * dt );
    if ( Gdx.input.isKeyPressed(Keys.A) )
        player.moveRight( -speed * dt );
    if ( Gdx.input.isKeyPressed(Keys.D) )
        player.moveRight( speed * dt );

    if ( Gdx.input.isKeyPressed(Keys.Q) )
        player.turn( -rotateSpeed * dt );
    if ( Gdx.input.isKeyPressed(Keys.E) )
        player.turn( rotateSpeed * dt );

    if ( Gdx.input.isKeyPressed(Keys.R) )
        player.moveUp( speed * dt );
    if ( Gdx.input.isKeyPressed(Keys.F) )
        player.moveUp( -speed * dt );
}
```

```
if ( Gdx.input.isKeyPressed(Keys.SHIFT_LEFT)
     || Gdx.input.isKeyPressed(Keys.SHIFT_RIGHT) )
{
    if (Gdx.input.isKeyPressed(Keys.W))
        mainStage3D.moveCameraForward( speed * dt );
    if (Gdx.input.isKeyPressed(Keys.S))
        mainStage3D.moveCameraForward( -speed * dt );
    if (Gdx.input.isKeyPressed(Keys.A))
        mainStage3D.moveCameraRight( -speed * dt );
    if (Gdx.input.isKeyPressed(Keys.D))
        mainStage3D.moveCameraRight( speed * dt );

    if (Gdx.input.isKeyPressed(Keys.R))
        mainStage3D.moveCameraUp( speed * dt );
    if (Gdx.input.isKeyPressed(Keys.F))
        mainStage3D.moveCameraUp( -speed * dt );

    if (Gdx.input.isKeyPressed(Keys.Q))
        mainStage3D.turnCamera(-rotateSpeed * dt);
    if (Gdx.input.isKeyPressed(Keys.E))
        mainStage3D.turnCamera(rotateSpeed * dt);

    if (Gdx.input.isKeyPressed(Keys.T))
        mainStage3D.tiltCamera(rotateSpeed * dt);
    if (Gdx.input.isKeyPressed(Keys.G))
        mainStage3D.tiltCamera(-rotateSpeed * dt);
}
```

This completes the code for the update method, as well as the code for the demo. Try it out and get a feel for moving around in three-dimensional space.

Pirate Cruiser: Navigating the Sea in 3D

In this section, you'll create a more game-like demo called *Pirate Cruiser*, in which the player steers a pirate ship through the sea and navigates around various rocks. Figure 8-8 contains a screenshot of this game. Most of the difficult groundwork has been laid in the previous section. The remaining topics include loading complex models from external files, creating a skydome image that surrounds the game world, and performing simplified collision detection. As before, you will continue adding code to Project3D, as it already contains many of the classes you will need (BaseGame, the updated version of BaseScreen, BaseActor3D, Stage3D, and ModelUtils).

Figure 8-8. *The Pirate Cruiser demo*

The first task, loading a model, is relatively straightforward. To do so, you need an instance of the ModelLoader class, and then use its loadModel method, which takes a FileHandle as input and returns a Model. If the position, rotation, or scale of the Model is not what you'd like it to be, you can adjust the Mesh data if desired by applying transformations to it, which result in a permanent change to the mesh. You can then use the model to create a ModelInstance and use it in a BaseActor3D object, as before.

Second, you need to surround your game world with an image, so as to give the appearance of a sky in the background. In our previous 2D games, you created a rectangular object that simply displayed an image of the sky. Because you're in a 3D environment, here you'll create a spherical object that is significantly larger than and surrounds your game world, and apply a texture to it, such as the one shown in Figure 8-9. You may notice that the image appears slightly stretched near the top (and it would on the bottom, too, were the bottom not simply a gray color). This is because the image has been spherically distorted: while it looks strange as a rectangle, when the image is applied to a sphere, everything will appear to have the correct proportions. This the same phenomena that occurs when trying to make a flat rectangular map of the Earth, which is roughly spherical; the map will inevitably contain distorted areas corresponding to the regions near the poles.

Figure 8-9. *A spherically distorted image of the sky*

In this program, you will encounter the minor difficulty that, while the ModelBuilder class can easily create a spherical mesh, any materials applied to it are displayed only from the outside, rather than the inside (which is where your camera and game entities will be). Fortunately, you can perform a geometric trick to resolve this problem: after creating the model, you will scale the mesh by –1 in the z direction; this will cause the sphere to turn itself "inside-out," reversing the sides on which the image will be displayed. Since this process could be useful in many future projects, you'll encapsulate this process of creating and inverting a sphere in a method called createSphereInv in the ModelUtils class. Here is the code to accomplish this:

```
public static ModelInstance createSphereInv( float r, Texture t, Color c )
{
    Material sphereMaterial = new Material();
    if (t != null)
        sphereMaterial.set( TextureAttribute.createDiffuse(t) );
    if (c != null)
        sphereMaterial.set( ColorAttribute.createDiffuse(c) );
    int usageCode = Usage.Position + Usage.ColorPacked
                    + Usage.Normal + Usage.TextureCoordinates;

    Model sphereModel = modelBuilder.createSphere(r,r,r, 32,32, sphereMaterial, usageCode);

    for (Mesh m : sphereModel.meshes)
        m.scale(1,1,-1) ;

    Vector3 position = new Vector3(0,0,0);

    ModelInstance sphere = new ModelInstance(sphereModel, position);
    return sphere;
}
```

The third and final concept to discuss before moving onto the main game code is collision detection. To keep the level of complexity manageable, the motion and placement of your three-dimensional objects will be restricted to a two-dimensional plane, thus allowing this project to reuse collision code from the original BaseActor class. This technique is well-known in game development. Games that use this approach (those which have 3D graphics but restrict game play to a 2D plane and have restricted camera movement) are called *2.5D games*. Figure 8-10 illustrates how the game will appear to the player, while on the right you can see the collision polygons that will correspond to the pictured game entities (the two rocks and the pirate ship).

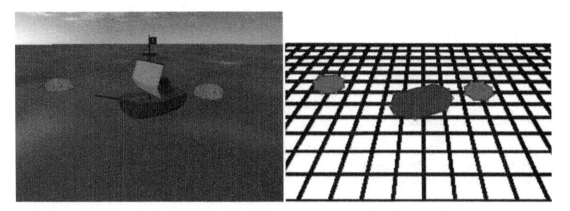

Figure 8-10. *The game world rendered in 3D, and the corresponding 2D collision polygons*

To incorporate these changes into your project, you need to make additions to the BaseActor3D class. First, add the following import statements:

```
import com.badlogic.gdx.math.collision.BoundingBox;
import com.badlogic.gdx.math.Polygon;
import com.badlogic.gdx.math.Intersector;
import com.badlogic.gdx.math.Intersector.MinimumTranslationVector;
```

Declare a Polygon variable:

```
private Polygon boundingPolygon;
```

The polygon object is initialized in the constructor as follows:

```
boundingPolygon = null;
```

Next are a pair of methods used to set the polygon to either a rectangular or approximately elliptical (eight-sided) shape. In both cases, you need to determine the dimensions of the object in the x and z dimensions; these quantities are analogous to the width and height in the two-dimensional case. These values can be determined by calculating the BoundingBox associated to the model, which is the smallest box that contains the entire model. A bounding box stores the dimensions of the model using two Vector3 objects: min and max, which store the values of the smallest and largest coordinates contained by the model, respectively. These values are used to create the array of vertices that is passed to the polygon object, as illustrated here:

```
public void setRectangleBase()
{
    BoundingBox modelBounds = modelData.calculateBoundingBox( new BoundingBox() );
    Vector3 max = modelBounds.max;
    Vector3 min = modelBounds.min;

    float[] vertices =
        {max.x, max.z, min.x, max.z, min.x, min.z, max.x, min.z};
    boundingPolygon = new Polygon(vertices);
    boundingPolygon.setOrigin(0,0);
}

public void setEllipseBase()
{
    BoundingBox modelBounds = modelData.calculateBoundingBox( new BoundingBox() );
    Vector3 max = modelBounds.max;
    Vector3 min = modelBounds.min;

    float a = 0.75f; // offset amount.
    float[] vertices =
        {max.x,0, a*max.x,a*max.z, 0,max.z, a*min.x,a*max.z,
         min.x,0, a*min.x,a*min.z, 0,min.z, a*max.x,a*min.z };
    boundingPolygon = new Polygon(vertices);
    boundingPolygon.setOrigin(0,0);
}
```

Once the polygon has been set up, you can simply copy the getBoundingPolygon and overlaps methods from the BaseActor class, with only slight modifications necessary (indicated in bold font):

```
public Polygon getBoundingPolygon()
{
    boundingPolygon.setPosition( position.x, position.z );
    boundingPolygon.setRotation( getTurnAngle() );
    return boundingPolygon;
}

public boolean overlaps(BaseActor3D other, boolean resolve)
{
    Polygon poly1 = this.getBoundingPolygon();
    Polygon poly2 = other.getBoundingPolygon();

    if ( !poly1.getBoundingRectangle().overlaps(poly2.getBoundingRectangle()) )
        return false;

    MinimumTranslationVector mtv = new MinimumTranslationVector();
    boolean polyOverlap = Intersector.overlapConvexPolygons(poly1, poly2, mtv);
    if (polyOverlap && resolve)
```

```
    {
        this.addPosition( mtv.normal.x * mtv.depth, 0,  mtv.normal.y * mtv.depth );
    }
    float significant = 0.5f;
    return (polyOverlap && (mtv.depth > significant));
}
```

In addition, you must remember to copy the bounding polygon data when copying an actor, and so the following code must be added to the copy method of the BaseActor3D class:

```
if (orig.boundingPolygon != null)
    this.boundingPolygon = new Polygon(orig.boundingPolygon.getVertices());
```

Now your improved framework is complete, and you can move on to the code for the GameScreen class. You start with import statements, variable declarations, and required methods. In this game, the interactive objects that need to be declared are the player variable, and an ArrayList to store the rock objects, which will be checked for collisions with the player during the update method.

```
import com.badlogic.gdx.Gdx;
import com.badlogic.gdx.Input.Keys;
import com.badlogic.gdx.graphics.Color;
import com.badlogic.gdx.graphics.Texture;
import com.badlogic.gdx.graphics.Texture.TextureFilter;
import com.badlogic.gdx.graphics.g3d.ModelInstance;
import com.badlogic.gdx.graphics.g3d.Model;
import com.badlogic.gdx.graphics.Mesh;
import com.badlogic.gdx.assets.loaders.ModelLoader;
import com.badlogic.gdx.graphics.g3d.loader.ObjLoader;
import com.badlogic.gdx.math.Vector3;
import com.badlogic.gdx.math.Matrix4;
import java.util.ArrayList;

public class GameScreen extends BaseScreen
{
    BaseActor3D player;
    ArrayList<BaseActor3D> rockList;

    public GameScreen(BaseGame g)
    {  super(g);  }

    public void create()
    {    }

    public void update(float dt)
    {    }
}
```

The code for the create method is presented next. It begins with initializing a thin box and applying an image of water to it to represent the sea:

```
BaseActor3D sea = new BaseActor3D();
Texture seaTex = new Texture(Gdx.files.internal("assets/water.jpg"), true);
seaTex.setFilter( TextureFilter.Linear, TextureFilter.Linear );
ModelInstance seaInstance = ModelUtils.createBox(500, 0.1f, 500, seaTex, Color.GRAY);
sea.setModelInstance(seaInstance);
mainStage3D.addActor(sea);
```

Next, the player object is created. You will use a model of a pirate ship, loaded from an external file. However, the model should first be turned by 180 degrees, so that its forward direction aligns with the negative z axis.[5] To accomplish this, the meshes of the ship model will be transformed by applying a rotation matrix:

```
player = new BaseActor3D();
player.setPosition(0,0,0);
ModelLoader loader = new ObjLoader();
Model shipModel = loader.loadModel(Gdx.files.internal("assets/ship.obj"));
for (Mesh m : shipModel.meshes)
    m.transform( new Matrix4().setToRotation(0,1,0, 180) );
ModelInstance shipInstance = new ModelInstance(shipModel);
player.setModelInstance(shipInstance);
player.setEllipseBase();
mainStage3D.addActor(player);
```

Now the skydome is initialized, using the previously described createSphereInv method from the ModelUtils class:

```
BaseActor3D skydome = new BaseActor3D();
Texture skyTex = new Texture(Gdx.files.internal("assets/sky-sphere.png"), true);
ModelInstance skyInstance = ModelUtils.createSphereInv( 500, skyTex, Color.WHITE );
skydome.setModelInstance(skyInstance);
skydome.setPosition(0,0,0);
mainStage3D.addActor(skydome);
```

The next task is to initialize the ArrayList that stores the rock objects, create a base instance of a rock, and use the clone method to create multiple rocks, repositioning them before adding them to the game world.

```
rockList = new ArrayList<BaseActor3D>();

Model rockModel = loader.loadModel(Gdx.files.internal("assets/rock.obj"));
ModelInstance rockInstance = new ModelInstance(rockModel);
BaseActor3D baseRock = new BaseActor3D();
baseRock.setModelInstance(rockInstance);
baseRock.setEllipseBase();
```

---

[5]The need for such a modification typically becomes apparent only while testing the code and visually inspecting the models. Alternatively, using a 3D modeling program such as Blender, mentioned later in this chapter, can be used to inspect and adjust a model's appearance ahead of time.

```
BaseActor3D rock1 = baseRock.clone();
rock1.setPosition(2,0,2);
mainStage3D.addActor(rock1);
rockList.add(rock1);

BaseActor3D rock2 = baseRock.clone();
rock2.setPosition(-4,0,4);
mainStage3D.addActor(rock2);
rockList.add(rock2);

BaseActor3D rock3 = baseRock.clone();
rock3.setPosition(6,0,6);
mainStage3D.addActor(rock3);
rockList.add(rock3);
```

Finally, the position of the camera is set. You won't set the look direction here, as that will be handled by the update method later.

```
mainStage3D.setCameraPosition(2,3,15);
```

This finishes the create method. The final code additions take place in the update method, and will be relatively short. The three tasks that must be accomplished include checking for collisions between the player and the rocks, processing user input (the ship will only be able to move forward and turn left and right), and setting the camera direction so that it always faces the player. These tasks are accomplished with the following code, which should be added to the update method:

```
for ( BaseActor3D rock : rockList )
    player.overlaps(rock, true);

float speed = 3.0f;
float rotateSpeed = 45.0f;

if ( Gdx.input.isKeyPressed(Keys.W) )
    player.moveForward( speed * dt );

if ( Gdx.input.isKeyPressed(Keys.Q) )
    player.turn( -rotateSpeed * dt );
if ( Gdx.input.isKeyPressed(Keys.E) )
    player.turn( rotateSpeed * dt );

mainStage3D.setCameraDirection( player.getPosition() );
```

After adding this code, you're finished with the GameScreen class. Try it out; have fun sailing your new pirate ship through the open seas, but look out for those rocks!

Next Steps

With the foundation laid in this chapter, you are now ready to try some exercises and incorporate advanced functionality in your 3D projects. This section lists some possibilities. The best place to get an overview and start reading about new features is usually the LibGDX wiki, which in addition to containing basic information, sometimes provides links to tutorials.

- Compose an interactive 3D scene containing a variety of models loaded from external files. The following are some web sites from which you can download model files (in a variety of file formats):

  - OpenGameArt: `http://opengameart.org`

  - The Models Resource: `www.models-resource.com`

  - TurboSquid: `www.turbosquid.com` (They have many free models available; this can be specified in their search options.)

- Once you have download a 3D model, before loading it into LibGDX, you can view and modify it using 3D graphics software such as Blender, which is freely available at `www.blender.org`.

- Try creating a 2.5D version of some of the earlier projects from this book.

- To implement advanced 3D physics, integrate the Bullet physics engine into your project (this process will be similar to your previous work incorporating the Box2D physics engine for realistic 2D physics).

- Add 3D particle effects to your game; LibGDX provides a 3D particle editor (called *Flame*) to help design the effects (similar to the 2D Particle Editor discussed in the previous chapter).

Summary

This chapter may have only scratched the surface of 3D game programming, but that in itself entails a lot of material. You explored the components of 3D scenes, perspective cameras, and lighting. You learned that 3D models contain meshes and materials, and instances of models store transformation data (position, rotation, and scale) using matrices. You adapted and extended your custom game development framework to include 3D versions of actors and stages, and learned the many ways you can move objects around in a three-dimensional world. Finally, you put your skills (and your code) to the test, by creating a pair of interactive demo programs. Congratulations on making it through, and good luck in your future 3D endeavors.

■ ■ ■

CHAPTER 9

The Journey Continues

This final chapter presents a variety of steps to consider as you continue on in game development. Among these, you'll explore working on additional projects, learning skills in related areas, and bringing your games to a wider audience. Along the way, the chapter presents lists of resources of all types, and general advice for many situations.

Continuing Your Developing

This section covers how to refine your current projects and start working on new projects, either on your own or as part of a game jam event. The section provides a list of online resources where you can obtain art assets to help you along the way. Finally, I'll give a healthy dose of advice for overcoming the inevitable obstacles that will arise.

Working on Projects

Hopefully, you've been working through all the project examples in this book. Many of the projects presented have concluded with a section titled "Next Steps." You should try to complete as many of these suggestions as you can! This is vital because *you learn by doing*. No matter how much sense a topic makes when you read about it, you have truly understood a topic only when you can take the next steps of designing and writing code independently. After each of the projects is functional, you should always experiment with the code and try your own variations.

Make sure that you understand each program at all levels. At the local level, you should understand the effects of each line of code, and also the purpose of each method and the design considerations that were taken into account when each was written. At the global level, you should know how all the classes fit together as a unified whole, the reasoning behind structuring the framework as it is, and the advantages and disadvantages to modifying the framework in different ways.

After you've extracted as much knowledge and experience from this book as you feel is possible, it's time to strike out on your own and start creating your own games. To start, I recommend creating simple, minimal examples that implement new game mechanics (that is, mechanics other than those featured in this book)—perhaps a shoot-'em-up style game with enemies who periodically fire lasers at *you*, or a labyrinth escape game containing many interconnected rooms that appear on different screens, or an adventure game with the main character swinging a sword to defeat the enemies, or a platformer game with a player who must also climb ladders to navigate the level. In addition to the obvious benefits of knowing how to program even more mechanics, the process of figuring out how to do so is invaluable. Only by engaging in the acts of pondering, planning, writing code, testing, debugging, and rewriting code can you build skills like inventiveness, organization, adaptability, and perseverance.

Once you become comfortable implementing game mechanics on your own, as a next step I recommend a "cloning the classics" approach for learning purposes (but certainly not for publication!). Take a classic game (particularly those from the 1980s) and attempt to re-create as many of its features as possible: implement the game mechanics, level design, artistic (graphics and audio) style, and user interface (menu screens and onscreen data displays).

In particular, I advise creating a physical list identifying and prioritizing the game-specific features within each category that you'll be working on. Furthermore, I recommend prioritizing the categories of the features themselves in the order presented in the previous paragraph. For example, if your main character is a winged archer, don't worry about the color of his belt until after the character is able to fly and shoot arrows. (In fact, it is common practice for developers to use simple colored polygon shapes during the game-mechanics phase of programming.) Don't worry if you're not an artist; many web sites exist with freely available video game graphics, and many artists in the community are looking for collaborators. Finally, once you're comfortable with your skills and abilities, it's time to develop your own game, or join a team working on a game and lend your programming skills.

Obtaining Art Resources

The typical reader of this book likely is mainly interested in the programming aspects of game development, but even so, every game still benefits from quality graphics and audio. I recommend the following web sites for obtaining artistic resources. Most of these web sites have both free and paid options, while others are driven by user donations:

- Kenney Game Assets: `http://kenney.nl/`

  Created by Kenney Vleugels, this site features over 18,000 art assets that can be useful in many genres. In this book, assets from this site were featured in Space Rocks, Plane Dodger, 52-Card Pickup, Treasure Quest, and the Jumping Jack series.

- GameArtGuppy: `www.gameartguppy.com`

  Created by Vicki Wenderlich, this site contains a collection of high-quality art crafted especially for independent game developers. In this book, the Koala character from the Jumping Jack games was obtained from this site.

- OpenGameArt: `http://opengameart.org`

  A repository for all types of media (2D and 3D graphics, as well as sound effects and music). Contributions are community driven. Licensing details and conditions are determined by the individual creators.

- The Spriters Resource: `www.spriters-resource.com`

  Features a nearly comprehensive set of game art assets from many game console systems throughout history. Due to copyright restrictions, however, these assets cannot be used in published or commercial games.

- Cool Text: `http://cooltext.com`

  A free text art graphics generator that can be useful for creating graphics for title screens as well as text and buttons for user interfaces.

- Textures.com: `http://textures.com`

  Offers images of many types of materials, both natural and constructed.

- Bfxr: `www.bfxr.net`

  Randomly generates a wide range of retro-style sound effects for use in games.

- Freesound: `www.freesound.org`

  A collaborative database of Creative Commons licensed sounds, organized into packs and also grouped by tags.

- Incompetech: `http://incompetech.com/`

  Created by Kevin MacLeod, this web site features a collection of royalty-free original music compositions that can be searched by genre, tempo, feel, or instrumentation. In this book, the background music for the game Starfish Collector (in Chapter 4), "Master of the Feast," was obtained from this collection.

Participating in Game Jams

One way to gain valuable game development experience is to participate in a game jam. A *game jam* is a gathering of game developers for the challenge of designing and creating a game in a short time span, typically about 48 hours. Participants may be programmers, artists, writers, or others with related skills. Due to the time limit, these events require rapid prototyping and development skills, and encourage participants to focus on creativity, core mechanics, and bringing a project to completion (or at least a playable state). Individuals often take part in these events for the express purpose of increasing their skills in these areas. In addition, many game jams select a theme that must be incorporated by all games developed at the event. The themes are usually announced at the start of each event, to discourage advanced planning and to encourage creativity.

Although some game jams have panels of judges and declare one or more winners, these events are typically informal and friendly, and they give participants the chance to connect with each other and provide a sense of community. Some events may be held at one or more physical locations. Some events may have no central location; developers work in areas of their own choosing (but are still held to the same time and schedule restrictions). Some notable long-running game jam events are as follows:

- Global Game Jam: `http://globalgamejam.org/`

  This is the largest game jam in the world—an international event that takes place once each year, typically at the end of January. This is *not* an online event; on-site participation is required, so there are typically hundreds of physical locations (jam sites) around the world where individuals can attend.

- Ludum Dare: `http://ludumdare.com/`

  Major events are held three times a year, and minor (mini) events are held during the months when there is no major event. Some participants attend gatherings at various sites, but most developers work from their own locations.

- One Game a Month: `www.onegameamonth.com`

  As the name indicates, these game jams are held monthly. The rules are particularly relaxed, and each jam takes place over the course of the entire month, so as to provide maximum flexibility to participants. The organizer is Christer Kaitila, who has also written a book called *The Game Jam Survival Guide* (Packt Publishing, 2012) which discusses these events in great detail and provides a plethora of advice on how to have a successful experience.

Overcoming Difficulties

On your journey as a game developer, you will stumble at times. Everyone does. Perhaps you can't figure out how to implement a particular game mechanic. Perhaps your program has an error at runtime and you're just not sure why. Perhaps your program compiles and runs, but your game entities are behaving in strange and unexpected ways. Whatever your difficulty may be, don't give up! Spend some time wrestling with the problem. Try different approaches—perhaps a different data structure, class, or algorithm is called for. Try to reduce the complexity of your code, break a problem into simpler steps or methods, or implement a simpler version first and incrementally build up to your ultimate goal. Remember that the process of overcoming difficulties is part of being, and helps you grow as, a game developer.

However, also remember that balance is key in development (just as it is in games). Yes, it is valuable to learn how to debug and correct malfunctioning code, but if any particular problem persists for a long time, take a break before you become overly frustrated or discouraged. Keep things in perspective: it probably isn't worth spending five straight hours trying to figure out why your platformer character can't walk up a ramp. Spend some time away from your computer; take a walk, think about something else, and come back to your problem later with a refreshed outlook.

After making a sincere effort to resolve any difficulties yourself, if you are still stuck, don't despair: the vibrant and active community of fellow game developers and enthusiasts out there may be of assistance. The LibGDX forums (`www.badlogicgames.com/forum`) and Stack Overflow (`www.stackoverflow.com`) are two excellent places to ask for help. Start by searching these sites to see whether someone has asked the same or a similar question. If not, the next step is to read any recommended guidelines for posting questions.

Typically, you should describe your problem or goal fully and concisely, and include details about what you have tried, what has worked, and what hasn't. Sometimes you might even find that the process of phrasing the question carefully to an external audience will help clarify the problem and inspire you with a possible solution or an alternative approach. If your post includes code, do so in moderation, but make sure that all variables are defined or explained to the reader. Most of all, be polite and patient. The people who frequent these web sites often have full-time jobs elsewhere, and voluntarily visit these forums and provide general assistance out of a sense of community. It's perfectly normal that a posted question might not generate a response for 48 hours or more. (In the meantime, be active in the community and see if anyone has posted any questions that *you* might be able to answer.)

Whenever someone responds to your question, be sure to acknowledge them; if they suggest a course of action, write a follow-up post as to whether it worked. And finally, if you turn out to be the person to resolve your own question, or decide to proceed in a completely different direction to circumvent the problem altogether, you should post that information as well, to provide future readers a sense of closure.

Broadening Your Horizons

In addition to increasing your depth of knowledge and programming proficiency, you should devote time to developing a breadth of knowledge in game-related areas, as this will have a positive impact on the quality of the games you produce. This section briefly mentions a few ways to work toward this goal.

Playing Different Games

Most game enthusiasts have a favorite genre. Some people spend most of their time playing first-person shooters, others prefer to devote their time to role-playing games, and so forth. As a game developer, you should consider playing games from as wide a range as you can: action, adventure, puzzle, strategy, role-playing, sports, simulation, storytelling, and so forth. At the same time, try games from various time periods (from classic to modern), and from different-size developers (from large professional companies to smaller studios to independent game makers and game jam competitors).

Even if you don't find a particular game or genre compelling, you will grow as a developer if you spend some time playing such games, especially when you do so with a developer's mindset. Try to understand why people like a given game. Examine each game's level progression, game play balance, narrative and character development, artistic style, and interface design. Keep an eye out for what makes each game innovative or unique. Try to mentally place yourself in the role of the original game developers who created the game and think about possible reasons that they might have made the decisions they did, and ponder whether you might have done the same, or branched out in a different direction.

Increasing Your Skill Set

While you continue to develop games, you should also consider broadening your overall skill set. A solid set of programming skills is highly desirable, but game developers (especially those working independently or in small studios) often need to be a jack-of-all-trades, especially in the areas of graphics and audio. To get started in these areas, I recommend the following software and tutorials:

- Inkscape: `http://inkscape.org/`

  Software for creating vector graphics, freely available. This web site contains a list of high-quality tutorials for all skill levels. Most relevant to our interests, however, is a set of game art tutorials written by Chris Hildenbrand, available here:

  `http://2d-game-art-tutorials.zeef.com/chris.hildenbrand`

- Spine: `http://esotericsoftware.com/`

  A 2D skeletal sprite animation tool designed specifically for game development. One of the main developers of Spine, Nathan Sweet, is also one of the main contributors to LibGDX, and thus there is a streamlined process for integrating animation files created by Spine into LibGDX projects.

- Audacity: `http://audacityteam.org/`

  A multitrack audio editor and recorder, freely available. The Audacity manual contains an extensive list of tutorials that will teach you all sorts of useful recording and editing skills.

Recommended Reading

In addition to broadening your skill set, broadening your knowledge base is also worthwhile. A variety of books are available on topics related to game development that will help you do exactly that. Of course, there are far too many to list here, and no doubt I have omitted some high-quality titles. Nonetheless, this section lists a few representative samples from across a range of fields, a cross section of topics, to give an indication of what's available out there: game design, literary aspects, history, and social impact:

- *Fundamentals of Game Design*, by Ernest Adams (New Riders, 2013)

  This book discusses a variety of topics: concept development, game-play design, core mechanics, user interfaces, storytelling, and balancing; exercises, worksheets, and case studies are also included.

- *The Ultimate Guide to Video Game Writing and Design* by Flint Dille and John Zuur Platten (Lone Eagle, 2008)

  Topics covered include integrating story elements into a game, writing a game script, creating design documentation, the creative process, team dynamics, and business considerations.

- *Vintage Games* by Bill Loguidice and Matt Barton (Focal Press, 2012)

  This book explores the history of some of the most influential video games of all time, with a particular focus on their development, critical reception, and impact on the industry.

- *Reality Is Broken: Why Games Make Us Better and How They Can Change the World* by Jane McGonigal (Penguin Books, 2011)

  In this book, the author discusses theories from psychology, cognitive science, sociology, and philosophy in the context of game playing, and explains how games can make us more productive and change the world for the better.

It is also useful to stay abreast of current news and developments in the game industry, as well as to hear the opinions, approaches, struggles, and successes of your fellow game developers. For these purposes, there is no better alternative to following blogs. The following are some particularly substantial sites featuring regular blog postings (as well as additional useful information and resources):

- Gamasutra: `www.gamasutra.com`

  A web site devoted to the art and business of making games which, among other resources, contains curated lists of blog postings that touch on all aspects of the industry.

- GameDev.net: `www.gamedev.net`

  A resource for developers of all fields and expertise, containing articles and tutorials on technical, creative, and business aspects of game development.

- HobbyGameDev: `www.hobbygamedev.com`

  Maintained by Chris DeLeon (a professional video game developer, author, and instructor), this regularly updated web site contains articles, advice, tutorials, case studies, interviews, and more.

Disseminating Your Games

Once you have designed and created some games of your own, you should consider sharing them with others—after all, games are meant to be played! This process will require you to package your work in a playable format, and find an audience of eager game enthusiasts.

Packaging for Desktop Computers

The simplest way to share your games is to create executable JAR files.

1. To do so, verify that your launcher class contains a `main` method specified as shown here (adjust the name and parameters of your method to match this if necessary):

   ```
   public static void main (String[] args)
   ```

2. Then, from the BlueJ menu bar, choose Project ä Create Jar File; a small window appears. This window indicates that the JAR file you create will be executable if the main class is specified. That is exactly what you're hoping to do! From the drop-down list, select the name of your launcher class.

3. In addition, your executable JAR file will require copies of all the LibGDX JAR files used by BlueJ when developing your game. If you have been storing these files in a +libs folder in your project directory, you may skip ahead to the next paragraph. If you have been using an alternative approach, such as storing the LibGDX JAR files in the BlueJ userlibs directory, then the section of the window labelled Include User Libraries will include a list of names of JAR files, including those containing the LibGDX classes. In this case, be sure to select the check boxes next to all of the LibGDX JAR files before continuing.

4. At this point, you can click the Continue button. A file directory appears, asking you to specify a name for the JAR file.

5. Enter the name of your game and then click the Create button. Since additional JAR files are required by your application, a directory is created in the location you specified, and in that directory you will find a file with the name of your game and the `.jar` extension; this directory should also contain all the LibGDX JAR files from your BlueJ project's +libs directory or those that you selected from the Create Jar File window. All of these JAR files must be located in the same directory in order to be able to run your game. All the contents of the other folders contained in the BlueJ project directory (such as the `assets` folder) are stored within your game's JAR file.

To run your game, all you need to do is to double-click your game's JAR file, and your game will start.[1] You can easily share your game with others, by sending them the set of files in this directory.[2] The one caveat is that in order to be able to run your game, potential users must have Java installed on their computers. For those who don't, you have two main options:

- You could inform users that they need to install Java, and direct them to the Java web site, www.java.com.

- You could use a third-party tool to convert your JAR files into native executable files for various operating systems; one such tool is called JWrapper, and is available from www.jwrapper.com.

Compiling for Other Platforms

Compiling your project for other platforms (such as Android, iOS, and web browsers via HTML5/JavaScript) is one of the main strengths of LibGDX. However, to do so effectively requires the use of an advanced integrated development environment. This section briefly covers the steps required to set up a LibGDX project for the Android Studio IDE. For further details concerning configuring the IDE setting, compiling, and exporting, you will need to consult the resources listed.

1. Android Studio[3] is an IDE based on the IntelliJ platform. After downloading and installing this software (the version bundled with the Android SDK), the installer will most likely download an updated set of packages.

2. After this process is complete, visit the LibGDX Wiki project setup site[4] and download gdx-tools.jar, which is an executable JAR file, from the link on the wiki page. Run this file, and you'll see a screen similar to Figure 9-1.

---

[1]If your project runs fine from within BlueJ but you encounter difficulties running the executable JAR file, the BlueJ web site contains various suggestions and links to helpful resources at www.bluej.org/help/ask-help.html.
[2]To ensure that no files are forgotten when sending them to others, you may want to using a program such as 7-Zip (www.7-zip.org) to create a single file (called an archive or zip file) that contains all the JAR files needed for your game.
[3]Available at: http://developer.android.com/sdk/index.html
[4]Available at: http://github.com/libgdx/libgdx/wiki/Project-Setup-Gradle

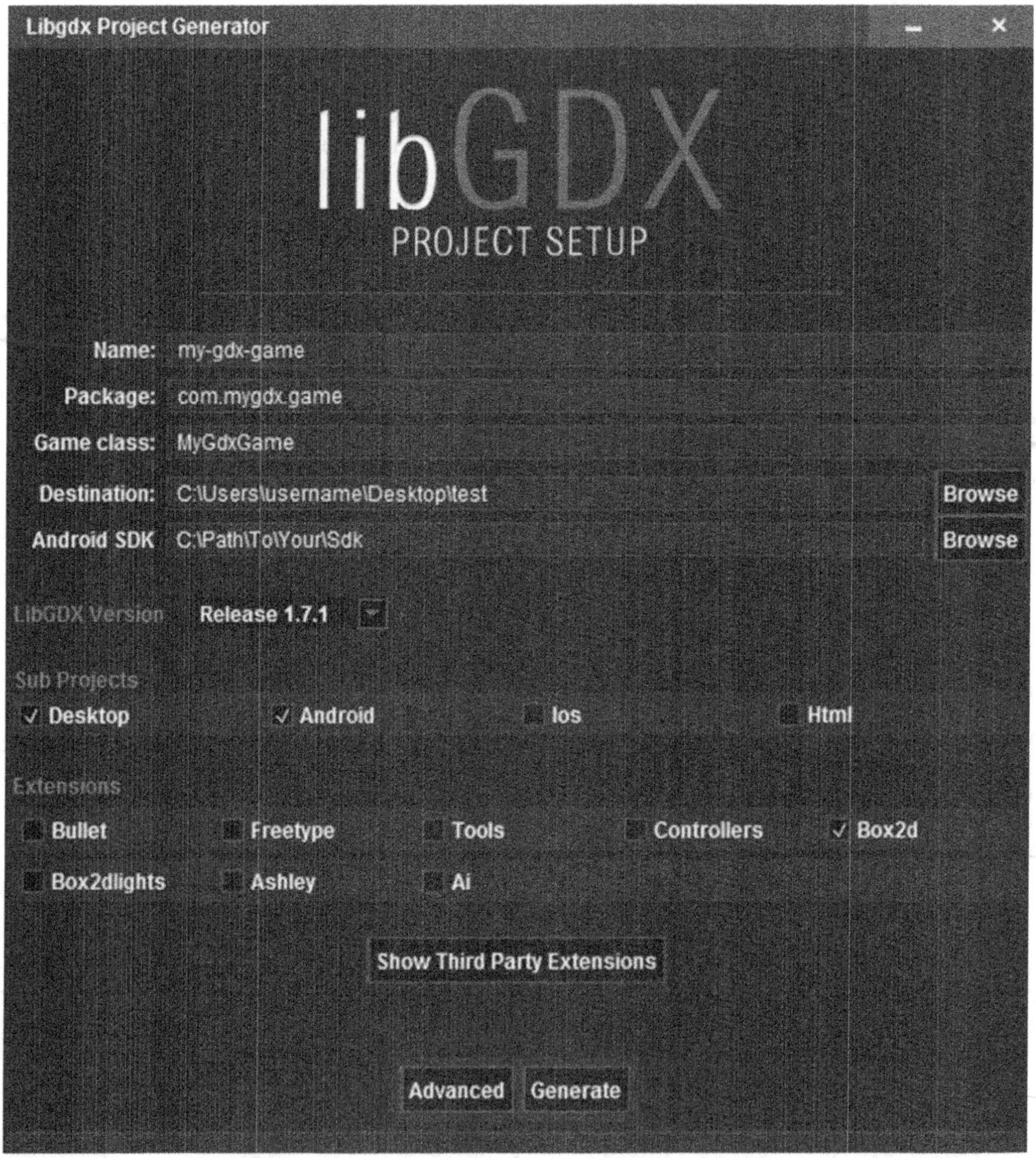

Figure 9-1. *The LibGDX project setup tool*

3. Here, you'll need to enter a name for your project, a package name (such as com.mygdx.spacerocks), the name of your Game class (or in our extended framework, the class that extends BaseGame), the directory where you'd like to store the files, and the path where the Android SDK was installed when you installed Android Studio.

4. In the next series of check boxes, you can specify which platforms you'll be developing for (for starters, I recommend selecting Android and Desktop). If your project requires any third-party libraries or extensions (such as Box2D or the game-pad controllers extension), you can specify that here.

5. Then click the Generate button, and a set of project files will be created for you in the directory you specified during setup. This process can take a while the first time a project is generated, as the setup file will download a number of dependency files.

6. When it is all finished, restart Android Studio, select the Import Project option, and choose the file named build.gradle.

When your project opens, you'll notice a directory structure has been prepared for you, including directories named *core*, *android*, and *desktop*. The latter two directories contain premade launcher files for their corresponding platforms. The *core* directory is where you should place all your other classes. There are many settings that you will need to configure for your project, such as editing the configuration to specify a working directory where game assets are located. The LibGDX wiki, referenced earlier, contains details that you will need to read through to help get your project up and running should you decide to pursue this direction further.

Finding Distribution Outlets

One of the greatest joys of being a game developer is having others play your games. Even if a project is unfinished, having people play-test your game and provide feedback can help your creations reach even greater heights and attract an even larger audience. Many web sites support independent game developers and provide forums for sharing your work with the community. Some of these web sites (such as Indie DB and Game Jolt) will even provide you with the ability to upload your games onto their servers after you register for an account.

- Indie DB: www.indiedb.com
- Game Jolt: http://gamejolt.com/
- GameDev.net: www.gamedev.net
- The Independent Games Source (TIGSource): www.tigsource.com
- Indie Gamer forums: http://forums.indiegamer.com/

If you post a game to one of these sources, while you're waiting to hear people's opinions on your work, you should strive to be an active participant in their forums. Try out a few games and provide feedback to your fellow developers. We all benefit from a vibrant game development community, so be sure to join in and be a part of it!

With that final piece of advice, we come to the end of our journey together through this book. Hopefully, however, your journey as a game developer will continue. May you have good fortune in all your future endeavors!

APPENDIX A

■ ■ ■

Review of Java Fundamentals

This appendix briefly reviews the core Java concepts that you should be familiar with to understand the material presented in this book. This is not a complete introduction to Java programming, so if any of the topics are unfamiliar, you may want to consult a textbook or tutorial series on Java[1] to learn more about the corresponding material.

Data Types and Operators

Let's begin by listing some of the basic, or *primitive*, data types available in Java:

- * int: Integers (numbers with no decimal part)
- * float: Decimal values
- * double: Decimal values, stored with twice the precision of a float
- * char: A single character (a letter, number, or symbol)
- * boolean: The value true or false

Another commonly used data type is String, which represents text: a set of characters. Technically, this is not a primitive data type, but it can be initialized in a similar way.

Java also uses the common binary *arithmetic operators*: addition, subtraction, multiplication, division (or quotient in the case of integers), and remainder, represented by the symbols +, -, *, /, and %, respectively. When used with two values of the same type, the result will also be of the same type. For example, the value of 5.0/2.0 is 2.5, whereas the value of 5/2 is 2. The results are different because in the first example the values have type double, and in the second example the values have type int.

When performing arithmetic involving two types of values, the values will be converted, or *cast*, to the more complex type. For instance, 5.0/2 yields a value of 2.5. If desired, a numeric value of one type can be manually cast to another type by prefacing it with the name of the desired type in parentheses. For example, (double)2 produces a value of 2.0, whereas (int)2.5 produces the value 2. (When casting to an int, the value is always rounded down to the nearest integer value.)

Primitive variables can be declared and initialized with a single line of code, with the following syntax:

```
variableType variableName = initialValue;
```

---

[1]The official Java tutorials, maintained by the Oracle corporation, are available online at http://docs.oracle.com/javase/tutorial/java/index.html.

Alternatively, these tasks can be carried out in separate statements:

```
variableType variableName;
variableName = initialValue;
```

In addition to using = to assign values to variables, Java provides *assignment operators* (for brevity), which modify the value of a variable by a constant amount. For example, the statement x = x + 5 can be replaced with the statement x += 5. Each of the other arithmetic operations has a corresponding assignment operator: -= , *= , /= , and %=.

Numeric values can be compared with the *conditional operators*: == for equality, != for inequality, < for less than, <= for less than or equal to, > for greater than, and >= for greater than or equal to. The result of a comparison is a Boolean value—true or false—and can be stored in a Boolean variable if desired. Boolean values can be combined with the *Boolean operators*: && for *and*, || for *or*, and ! for *not*.

An *array* is an object that contains a fixed number of values of the same type. The *length* of the array is set when the array is created. The values in an arrays can be initialized when it is created (and the size will be inferred). For example, the following creates an array that contains five characters:

```
char[] letters = { 'g' , 'a' , 'm' , 'e' , 's' } ;
```

Alternatively, an array can be created with only the length specified, shown here for an array that will contain 10 integers (and the values can be set at a later time):

```
int[] values = new int[10];
```

The items in an array are accessed by their position, or *index*, which begins with the number 0. For example, given the preceding array named letters, letters[0] produces the value g, letters[1] produces the letter a, and so forth, up to letters[4], which produces s. Note that the array has length 5, but the positions are numbered 0 through 4. (This is true in general; an array with length n will have indices numbered 0 through $n - 1$.) Note that once an array is created, its size cannot be changed; trying to store a value into an array at a nonexistent index value will result in an error when the program is running.

Control Structures

The statements within a Java program are typically run one after the other in sequence. *Control structures* can change the order of execution, either by running some statements only when certain conditions are met or by repeating a given set of statements.

Conditional Statements

An if statement is used to specify that a certain set of statements should be run only when a certain condition (or combination of conditions or a Boolean expression) evaluates to true. For example, the following code will add 100 to the variable bonus only if the value of time is greater than 60; if the value of time is not greater than 60, the code contained within the braces will not be executed.

```
if (time > 60)
{
    bonus += 100;
}
```

Any number of statements may be contained within the braces. However, if only one statement is contained within the braces, the braces may be omitted and the code will have the same results, as follows:

```java
if (time > 60)
    bonus += 100;
```

An if-else statement is used when you need to provide an alternative set of statements that will be executed when the associated condition evaluates to false. The following code builds on the previous example, adding the behavior that if the value of time is *not* greater than 60, then the value of bonus will be incremented by 50 instead.

```java
if (time > 60)
{
    bonus += 100;
}
else
{
    bonus += 50;
}
```

On occasion, you may want to test a variable for equality against a set of values, and execute a different set of statements in each case. For example, consider the following code, which prints a message depending on whether the value of itemCount is equal to 0, 1, 2, or anything else.

```java
if (itemCount == 0)
    System.out.print("You have no items.");
else if (itemCount == 1)
    System.out.print("You have a single item.");
else if (itemCount == 2)
    System.out.print("You have two items.");
else
    System.out.print("You have many items!");
```

A switch statement presents an alternative way to write this type of code (which is often easier to read). The following code features a switch statement that has exactly the same effect as the if-else statements presented previously. Each of the value comparisons in the if-else statements correspond to an occurrence of the case keyword within the switch code block, while the final else statement corresponds to the default keyword. After listing the set of statements to be executed for a given case, a break statement must be included (otherwise, the statements corresponding to the following cases will also be executed, regardless of whether the variable is equal to the value presented).

```java
switch (itemCount)
{
    case 0:
        System.out.print("You have no items.");
        break;
    case 1:
        System.out.print("You have a single item.");
        break;
```

267

```
case 2:
    System.out.print("You have two items.");
    break;
default:
    System.out.print("You have many items!");
}
```

Repetition Statements

The while statement is used to repeat a set of statements as long as a given condition is true. For example, the following code will continue to add 5 to the variable score, and subtract 1 from the value of stars, as long as the value of stars is greater than 0:

```
while (stars > 0)
{
    score += 5;
    stars -= 1;
}
```

A while statement is particularly useful when a set of statements needs to be repeated an unknown number of times. You must be careful when using a while statement, because if the associated condition always remains true, then the statements will continue to execute forever!

The for statement is used to repeat a set of statements a fixed number of times. In typical usage, a variable is set to an initial value, and as long as a condition involving the variable is true, a set of statements is executed. Afterward, the value of the variable is changed by a given amount, the condition is checked again, and so forth, until the given condition evaluates to false. The following example initially sets a variable n to 1, and as long as n is less than 10, adds 3 to points; the value of n is increased by 1 with each iteration of the loop:

```
for (int n = 1; n < 10; n++)
{
    points += 3;
}
```

for loops are particularly useful in tasks involving arrays. As an example, the following code initializes an array named numbers to store five integers, and the for loop stores the value 10*n at each position n in the array. Note that the loop variable is initialized to 0 (as this is the first index in an array), and the condition is that the variable is less than the length of the array. (You must use the *less than* comparison in the condition, since the largest index in an array is always equal to the length of the array minus 1.)

```
int[] numbers = new int[5];
For (int n = 0; n < numbers.length(); n++)
{
        numbers[n] = 10 * n;
}
```

A variation on the syntax of the for statement, called the *enhanced* for statement, is convenient for accessing the values of an array. As a motivating example, consider the following code, which takes each of the values from an array called grades, and adds them all to a variable called total:

```
for (int n = 0; n < grades.length(); n++)
{
    int num = grades[n];
    total += num;
}
```

The exact same result can be achieved more efficiently with the following code, which automatically extracts the elements of an array (in order), and stores them into a variable before proceeding to the statements contained within the loop:

```
for (int num : grades)
{
    total += num;
}
```

Methods

A *method* is a set of statements, grouped together, that can be called upon repeatedly to perform a task. Every method has an associated name, can take zero or more values as input, and may or may not return a value. Each method is contained within a structure called a *class*, which is covered in further detail later. The syntax for a method is presented here, and the various components are summarized immediately afterward.

```
modifer returnType methodName ( variableType variableName , ... )
{
      // statements
}
```

- modifier is a keyword (such as public or private) that indicates where this method can be used in the program.

- returnType indicates the type of data being returned, and can be set to void if no data is returned by the method.

- methodName is the name of the method.

- Within the parentheses, for each input that is to be provided, you must list the type of input (indicated by variableType) and the name by which it will be referred to in the statements that follow (indicated by variableName).

For example, the following public-access method called average takes two float values as input, calculates their average (which is also a float), and returns this value:

```
public float average(float x, float y)
{
    return (x + y) / 2;
}
```

Methods can be called upon in two ways, depending on how they are written. Some methods may be called from the class that contains them. For example, the Math class contains a method named sqrt that calculates the square root of a number; to use this method to calculate the square root of 4, you would write

`Math.sqrt(4)`. Alternatively, some methods are called from a variable. As an example, every `String` variable contains a method named `charAt` that returns the character at a given position in the string. If you create a `String` named word that contains the text games, then `word.charAt(2)` returns the character m.

Objects and Classes

An *object* is a collection of related data and methods that operate on that data. A *class* is a set of code that is used as a prototype or a blueprint from which objects can be created. Some classes are automatically available in Java (such as the `String`, `Math`, and `System` classes). To use other classes in your program, you must indicate which of the many available classes should be loaded by using an `import` statement. For example, to be able to use the `Random` class in your program, which is part of the `java.util` package,[2] at the beginning of your program you must include this line:

```
import java.util.Random;
```

To create an object from this class (also called an *instance* of the class), you use the new operator, followed by a special method of the class called the *constructor*. The name of the constructor method will always be identical to the name of the corresponding class, and it may require input values to initialize the data that belongs to the class. For example, to create an instance of the `Random` class, you would use the following code:

```
Random rand = new Random();
```

Following this, you could then use the methods of the variable rand, such as `nextInt` (which returns a randomly generated integer) as follows:

```
int secret = rand.nextInt();
```

The previously mentioned `String` class is special, in that it may be initialized in the same way as a primitive type variable (like `int` or `float`), but it may also be initialized using the new operator (which requires the text to be stored in as input):

```
String name = new String("Lee");
```

One of the most powerful features of Java (or any object-oriented programming language) is the ability to define your own classes. As an in-depth example, the following class, called `Fraction`, stores the data used in a fractional number: a numerator and a denominator (both integers). There is a constructor to set these values, a method to create a `String` representation of the fraction, and a method to convert the fraction to a `float` value (by calculating the quotient).

```
class Fraction
{
    // numerator
    int n;
    // denominator
    int d;
```

---

[2]To find out the package that contains a particular class, you can consult the Java documentation or the documentation for the particular library you are using.

```
    // constructor
    Fraction(int a, int b)
    {
        n = a;
        d = b;
    }

    // creates a String representation
    public String toString()
    {
        return (n + "/" + d);
    }

    // convert to a float value
    public float convertToFloat()
    {
        return (float)n / d;
    }
}
```

Next is a sample class that uses the Fraction class as defined previously. In particular, it creates and initializes a Fraction object, and then uses its methods and prints their results to the screen. (A technical aside: you must declare the main method as static in order to be able to run the method directly from the class rather than from an instance of the class.)

```
class Sample
{
    public static void main()
    {
        Fraction frac = new Fraction(3,4);
        String fracString = frac.toString();
        float   fracValue  = frac.convertToFloat();
        System.out.println( "The value of " + fracString + " is " + fracValue );
    }
}
```

Sometimes when you write a class, you'll want to control access to data, either to restrict the possible set of values that can be assigned, or to prevent another part of the program from accidentally changing the data (possibly due to a mistake in the code). *Access modifiers* are used in such situations; they can be included to specify whether other classes can use a particular field or method. The two most common modifiers are public, which indicates that any class can access the corresponding variable or method, and private, which indicates that it may be accessed only within the class in which it is defined. There is a less frequently used modifier, protected, which allows access within the defining class and any subclasses (that is, those that extend) the defining class.

As a practical example of when access modifiers are useful, let's return to our custom Fraction class. The denominator of a fraction should never be set equal to zero (because division by zero leads to contradictory mathematical results). You prevent this unwanted behavior by setting the class fields to private, and rewriting the constructor (or any other relevant methods) to take action in this case, as demonstrated here:

```java
class Fraction
{
    // numerator
    private int n;
    // denominator
    private int d;

    // constructor
    Fraction(int a, int b)
    {
        n = a;
        if (b == 0)
        {
            System.err.println("Invalid denominator; changing value to 1.");
            d = 1;
        }
        else
        {
            d = b;
        }
    }

    // other methods remain the same as before
}
```

Summary

These topics—data types, operators, control structures, methods, and classes—are the foundations from which you will create your own programs. In real applications, your code will typically be much longer than the examples presented; your classes will no doubt contain multiple import statements, declare many variables of various types, and have an assortment of methods, each of which contains a significant number of statements. When working on your own projects, in addition to writing your own classes, your programs will probably use many predefined classes as well. For this reason, it is good to spend some time becoming familiar with the style and type of information that is presented in the Java documentation format, whether it be the official Java language reference[3] or the documentation for any Java libraries you include in your projects.

---

[3]http://docs.oracle.com/javase/8/docs/api/

Index

Get the eBook for only $5!

Why limit yourself?

Now you can take the weightless companion with you wherever you go and access your content on your PC, phone, tablet, or reader.

Since you've purchased this print book, we're happy to offer you the eBook in all 3 formats for just $5.

Convenient and fully searchable, the PDF version enables you to easily find and copy code—or perform examples by quickly toggling between instructions and applications. The MOBI format is ideal for your Kindle, while the ePUB can be utilized on a variety of mobile devices.

To learn more, go to www.apress.com/companion or contact support@apress.com.

CPSIA information can be obtained
at www.ICGtesting.com
Printed in the USA
LVOW03s1605040216

473704LV00003B/3/P